Praise for

THE GOSPEL OF TREES

"In this finely crafted memoir . . . a series of tense, detailed vignettes capture the complexity of the time and place . . . Irving moves seamlessly between the wide-eyed perspective of the child and the critical gaze of the adult, creating a tale as beautiful as it is discomfiting. The question that haunts her also haunts her book: 'Should we have kept trying, even if we were doomed to fail?' "

—*The New Yorker*

"The daughter of a dedicated missionary, Irving grew up in Haiti, where she learned both the power and the risks of working to improve the world—and the toll it can take on a family. An eye-opening memoir."

—*People*

"Powerful . . . grapples with the ethical uncertainties of aid work."

—*Wall Street Journal*

"Lush, emotional debut . . . A beautiful memoir that shows how a family altered by its own ambitious philanthropy might ultimately find hope in their faith and love for each other, and for Haiti."

—*Publishers Weekly*

"A timely and often insightful perspective on modern-day Haiti."

—*Kirkus Reviews*

"With insight and admirable even-handedness, Irving shows the complex forces at play in both the story of Haiti's cycle of poverty and the more personal dynamics at play in her family as they struggle mightily to do God's work."

—*Booklist*

"Provide[s] a useful view of the inherent ethical and moral ambiguities of well-meaning but sometimes ineffective charitable interventions in Haiti."

—*Library Journal*

"Apricot Irving's honest memoir highlights the good, the bad, and the ugly of missionary life, challenging traditional 'white savior' narratives."

—*Paste Magazine*

"Irving's commitment to dwelling on the complicated makes her beautifully written memoir a compelling, absorbing read . . . beautifully written."

—*The Christian Century*

"If a memoir's worth lies in the truths it's willing to tell, then *The Gospel of Trees* is the most worthwhile of memoirs, an unflinching and gorgeously written account of a young girl's coming of age in a difficult family, in one of the world's most difficult places . . . [Irving's] story hits hard, and sticks, as only the very best stories do."

—Ben Fountain, *New York Times* bestselling author
of *Billy Lynn's Long Halftime Walk*

"Neither sugar-coated nor cynical, Apricot Irving has mastered the most difficult aspect of this kind of memoir: the just-right tone of compassion and hard-earned hope . . . A family memoir, a coming of age story, an exploration of a country greatly loved and little understood. A cautionary tale for all those setting out to do good, may this gospel be read as the good news it is—a moral compass and a must-read for all of us who struggle with how to create a better world."

—Julia Alvarez, author of numerous novels including
How the García Girls Lost Their Accents, In the Time of the Butterflies,
and *Saving the World,* as well as the memoir *A Wedding in Haiti*

"A beautiful exploration of hope and hubris. Irving shows us the many entanglements among our relationships with the land, other cultures, and the mysteries of our own families."

—David George Haskell, author of *The Songs of Trees*
and Pulitzer Prize finalist *The Forest Unseen*

"*The Gospel of Trees* is rich with such passionate insights; also, it's a rare thing to find an insider account of missionary life not blunted by conventional piety. Very particularly sensitive to Haiti, this book is an object lesson for anyone wanting to do good in the world: forget about moving that mountain of sand with your tweezers; you will (as the old Vodou song has it) be carrying water with a spoon. This book reminded me of *The Poisonwood Bible,* except it rings more true."

—Madison Smartt Bell, award-winning author
of *All Souls' Rising*

THE
GOSPEL
OF TREES

a memoir

APRICOT A. IRVING

Simon & Schuster Paperbacks
New York   London   Toronto   Sydney   New Delhi

Simon & Schuster Paperbacks
An Imprint of Simon & Schuster, Inc.
1230 Avenue of the Americas
New York, NY 10020

Some names and identifying characteristics have been changed.

First Simon & Schuster trade paperback edition March 2019

SIMON & SCHUSTER PAPERBACKS and colophon are registered trademarks of
Simon & Schuster, Inc.

For information about special discounts for bulk purchases, please contact
Simon & Schuster Special Sales at 1-866-506-1949
or business@simonandschuster.com.

The Simon & Schuster Speakers Bureau can bring authors to your live event. For
more information or to book an event, contact the Simon & Schuster Speakers
Bureau at 1-866-248-3049 or visit our website at www.simonspeakers.com.

Interior design by Carly Loman

Manufactured in the United States of America

1   3   5   7   9   10   8   6   4   2

Library of Congress Cataloging-in-Publication Data is available.

ISBN 978-1-4516-9045-3
ISBN 978-1-4516-9046-0 (pbk)
ISBN 978-1-4516-9047-7 (ebook)

to Suzette
and to my parents
for your courage

BOOK ONE

No human eye has ever beheld a more beautiful land;
nowhere is nature so immeasurably lush,
so green, so untouched.

COLUMBUS, 1492 SHIP'S LOG

Far from comic or absurd . . . the missionary
is a breath of fresh air
in a world of swirling cultural conflicts.

DR. WILLIAM H. HODGES,
APRIL 1985 NEWSLETTER:
"IN DEFENSE OF MISSIONARIES"

BOOK ONE

Prelude

Oregon, 2001

I WAS SIX years old, a freckle-nosed girl with long red braids that whapped against my elbows, when my parents moved to the north of Haiti to be missionaries—not far from where Columbus sank the *Santa María*.

By the time I was in my twenties, a recovering missionary's daughter, most of the stories I had read about missionaries seemed to fall into one of two categories: hagiography or exposé; the Sunday school version or *Lord of the Flies*.

When we don't know what to make of a situation, we grope for a familiar pattern, a path worn into the grass. The danger, of course, is that by imposing our own expectations, we fail to see anything clearly. I am as guilty of this as anyone.

Stories, like archaeology, are fragmentary, composed of scraps and nuances, and—depending on what is left out—most narratives can be constructed so as to end in either glory or ruin. But the missionaries I had grown up with were neither marauders nor saints; Haiti was neither savage nor noble. The truth was far more complicated.

My father, a missionary agronomist, is a man of the earth, his fingernails perpetually stained with berries and dirt. His first language is trees, and he can still recite the genus and species of every tree that grew outside every house we ever lived in. He shimmied up willows and Chinese elms, black walnuts and canyon live oaks, to tie rope swings for my sisters and me to play.

Leave every place better than you found it, he taught us—a mantra from his forest ranger days. He pruned and fertilized a neglected apricot tree across the street from a crack house in Los Angeles county. He rescued an apple tree imprisoned by blackberries in Oregon. In Haiti, he planted avocados and mangoes, and twenty years after the seeds had been buried in the soil, he could still carve a path through an overgrown garden to a cedar so wide that his outstretched arms could not span its trunk.

Yet his anger, too, left its mark. He longed to make the world a better place, but by taking on the sorrows of others, he buried his own until that thwarted grief exploded into rage: a dinner table upended, a window shattered as a Bible hurtled through the air, a daughter slammed against a wall.

I have seen my parents venerated, in church circles, as heroes of the faith. We were *the sent ones*—for that is the root of the word "missionary"—sent by the Holy Spirit; sent by the churches who paid for our plane tickets and salary, who expected glory stories. A redemptive theme was expected in each and every newsletter and slide show. If my parents couldn't deliver, then the funding would be redirected to more eloquent storytellers.

My father's fear and anger was a story we didn't know how to tell; a story that, for long years, the church didn't seem to want to hear.

I was fifteen when my parents hosted their last slide show in a church fellowship hall, having left the mission field, this time, for good.

The slide shows, a fixture of my childhood, began with metaphor: a sunrise tilting in white heat over the edge of a mountain; light filling the darkness. But by the time my father had clicked to images of eroded Haitian hillsides so steep and desolate that farmers would, on occasion, be carried into the missionary hospital with broken limbs after having fallen from their gardens, his voice would have dropped into a bitter cadence. The anecdotes grew only more discouraging as the slide show wore on.

My father's vision of utopia was agrarian: trees on every hillside, vegetables in every garden, water in every dry streambed. Seeds were small, but they could change the world. Roots to hold the soil in place, to allow the rain to drip slowly through a thicket of green leaves, to fall soft into loamy soil, replenishing the groundwater. It was through trees that the earth breathed. And the soil of Haiti was rich—a twelve-month growing season, without cold nights to slow down the pace. Stick a cutting in the ground and out fluttered roots and buds, all on their own. But so little of his missionary vision had unfolded as planned.

One photograph from the slide show, taken during a year of drought, showed a Haitian farmer, his wife, and their five children standing in front of their mud-walled home. At their feet lay a withered pile of corn no bigger than a Thanksgiving turkey: their entire harvest for that year.

In the face of such poverty, further deforestation seemed all but inevitable. Trees could at least be cut and smoldered into charcoal, light enough to transport down the twisting mountain paths on a donkey's back or a motorcycle to pay a debt in a moment of crisis: a child's school fees, a doctor visit, a funeral.

The following year, with fewer trees to hold the soil in place, the gardens would be even sparser, the rainfall more sporadic. There were ways around this, for the patient. But patience was a luxury of those who had enough food to eat, whose children were not dying. Patience was what the poor could not afford.

To keep the slide show from being a complete downer, my mother would usually pipe up at this point with anecdotes of our family adventures—rafting trips, crocodile sightings, a haphazard expedition on an overcrowded fishing boat to a remote island off the coast of Haiti. She also mentioned our few small, notable successes: the rabbit projects, the seedling trees, the green beans that grew as long as my little sister's arm. Sufficient to thrill the supporters, but for my father, it was never enough.

We did not describe, during church slide shows, the time we were evacuated for fear of riots, or the man we watched burned alive inside a rubber tire.

No matter how volatile Haiti became, devastated by drought and military coups, my father rooted himself all the more stubbornly in its eroded soil, so that by the time we finally left, resentment had grown between us like a hedge of *rakèt* cactus, barbed and impenetrable.

For more than a decade after we left, my family seldom spoke of Haiti. It wasn't until I was in my mid-twenties that I asked my parents if they had kept any of our missionary newsletters.

My mother, who seemed reluctant to even talk about Haiti, said she didn't know why we would have kept them. My father pulled on his rain boots and told me to follow him out to the barn.

It was a bright, cold Oregon afternoon in early November, and the air was sharp with decaying leaves and the mumbled whir of the food dehydrator. My father pulled out a stack of Chiquita banana boxes sticky with tractor grease, hidden under baseball gloves and loose bales of hay.

I pried open the lids and found cobwebs stretched across church bulletins and toys dank with must. Western Barbie, my prized eight-year-old birthday present flown in on the missionary plane, was trapped under a doll bed carved from Haitian mahogany. Her left eye was snapped shut in a permanent blue-lidded wink.

My mother kicked at a box with her muck boot and asked: Why did we even keep this junk?

We both knew it was my father who had guarded the relics.

I waited until I was alone to sort through the detritus. Though I doubted that the cassettes we'd sent to the grandparents would still work, the wheels strained, then slowly spun. The delicate ribbons unraveled tinny, otherworldly stories of near-accidents on the highway to Port-au-Prince, torrential rainstorms, roosters that crowed all night, and peripheral arguments between my sisters and me about who got to play with the coveted blond Barbie. To listen to our childish voices was to reenter a lost world. It was more joyful, and bewildering, than I had remembered.

Buried beneath one stack of papers was a black spiral notebook whose cover bloomed with blue-gray mold. As I cracked open the stiff pages, I realized that the day planner had been used as a journal.

I sat back on my heels and slowly turned the pages. It was no small feat to decipher my father's cramped left-handed scrawl, each day's synopsis limned into a single calendar entry the size of a postage stamp.

Came home tired from Garde Conjac, he had written shortly after we returned to Haiti for the last time. *Think it was all the suffering I saw.*

My eyes burned with the strain, and after a few pages I had to set the journal down and stare out the window. My own journals from those years—in bubbly adolescent penmanship, the "i"s dotted with hearts—were full of passionate meditations on the most recent boy I'd happened to fall in love with, alongside diatribes about my boring, goody-two-shoes father. I had resented him for as long as I could remember—hurt that his agricultural projects always seemed to come first, that the needs of others appeared to matter so much more than our own. Now, for the first time, I saw Haiti through his eyes.

Beautiful sunset coming down the mountain, he had written after hiking miles in the damp heat.

A short while later, he observed: *Girls forlorn tonight.*

I put my hand over my mouth and choked back a sob. I hadn't realized that he noticed.

My father is not an easy man to keep up with. My father the missionary will gladly walk for hours under a searing tropical sky with only a few sips of water and a handful of dried fruit to deliver tree seeds to subsistence farmers to keep the soil from slipping down eroded hillsides. My father the forest ranger can traverse miles of unmarked wilderness without a map. My father has never known how to be gentle with those who do not live up to his expectations.

I inherited my father's anger and his perfectionism. Haiti was a wound, an unhealed scab that I was afraid to pick open. But I knew that unless I faced that broken history, my own buried grief, like my father's, would explode in ways I couldn't predict.

Even as a child, I had understood that the missionary compound was a place I would have to one day untangle with words.

I sat down at my empty desk and wrote:

> *Here's to home, wherever that is, and whatever it takes to find it. Here's to taking risks and not running away anymore. Here's to failing, probably, at everything that I am setting out to do. But here's to trying anyway.*
>
> *Here's to my sisters, and my mother, and to the farm in Oregon; here's to my father (God bless his emotionally atrophied, demanding, workaholic soul). Here's to the missionary compound that broke us all. And to Haiti: a country that I have never understood, and have always resented (and have always wanted to belong to).*

When I found a map of Haiti among my parents' letters, I hung it on the wall above my desk—a reminder of the place that I had tried for so long to forget. The illusion of order felt comforting, as if so much jagged history could be made small enough to carry in the mind and make sense of.

On the map, the sea was pale blue, and the names of the bays and rivers were written in French in bold dark letters: *Océan Atlantique, Mer des Antilles, Baie de l'Acul*. Limbé was no bigger than a citron seed, in a green valley at the base of a yellow sweep of mountains. Three thousand miles from where I sat, pen in hand, trying to find my way through a story that I was still afraid to tell.

When I closed my eyes, I could hear the jangle of bicycles over hard-packed dirt and the sudden insistent clatter of rain as it hammered across tin roofs, the swell of voices running ahead of the storm: *lapli tonbe, lapli tonbe*—the rain is falling, the rain is coming.

In the Beginning

Oregon, 2002

THE BOXES THAT my father unearthed from the barn marked the first of many excavations, of many conversations. Eventually, though it took her almost a decade, my mother gave me her journals, too, to read—along with her blessing—and consented to innumerable interviews. Thick manila envelopes arrived from Limbé, full of newsletters and blurry family photographs, and I flew thousands of miles to track down fellow students from the missionary school and volunteers from the hospital.

I buried myself in words—everything I could find on Haitian history and missions, from Columbus laying claim to the island for the king and Christendom in 1492 to the bitter legacy of colonization that was still playing out five centuries later, a tired reenactment.

One rain-sodden afternoon, stumbling across a Carib origin myth, I read how the first inhabitants of the Caribbean (so like the missionaries who followed) arrived in the islands and sealed their fate. It seemed to explain so much—perhaps because it had been translated from oral history into verse by a missionary himself, one W. H. Brett by name, though I have taken some liberties with his Victorian-era verse.

In the beginning the Caribs, the first people, lived above the sky.

As they gazed across the heavens, one lone planet caught their pity, for it neither sparkled like the stars nor shone like a moon. The Carib people murmured among themselves—it was not right for the earth to remain barren; they must cleanse the land and free it from its curse.

And so it was that they left the heavens, their first home, and descended on cloud chariots to transform the desolate earth into a garden that they might gaze upon with more pleasure.

The land was shrouded in darkness when they arrived, but as they set to their task, colors began to emerge through the gloom: the red bark of mahogany, bristles of gray-green pine, spiky yellow pineapples, and papayas that deepened to orange. Parrots appeared, chattering in the treetops, the flash of their plumage red and blue against the canopy. Iguanas crawled out to bask in the sun, and shy hutia retreated into the shadows.

Twilight ebbed from the hills as the steep mountainsides flamed orange and gold. Moonlight glimmered on rivers. The pale scent of orchids wafted on the breeze. No more would this be known as the accursed planet. Surely their god would be pleased.

The Carib children, released from their labor, scattered into the forest to find the cloud chariots on which they had descended, but while their attention had been fixed elsewhere, the clouds had lifted—they were trapped on the very island they had come to save.

The elders, worried, commanded their people to pray, and for a day and a night their voices echoed through the trees. But the heavens remained deaf to their pleading.

Weak with hunger, they wandered into the forest to search for food. The realization dawned slowly: There would be no return to that lost homeland. They had intended only to leave their mark, then retreat to admire their work; they had not imagined that their lives and the fate of the broken planet would become entwined.

———————

There are, of course, other versions of the Carib origin myth, but the one penned by W. H. Brett offers a cautionary moral, like a warning label on the back of a religious tract:

From on high mankind descended . . .
They to cleanse this world intended.
. . . Thus mankind remained below,
In a world of toil and woe.

Its missionary author, like so many others who tried to leave their mark on the Caribbean (Columbus and my father among them) seemed to have learned the hard way that loss was inevitable.

Ayiti, the land of mountains beyond mountains, does not submit easily to external control; it acquiesces and then resists, plays along but then turns feral.

Even in suffering, the island remains defiant. The mountains struggle against the sky like a woman straining against a heavy load, her backbone arched, her sharply angled shoulder blades slipping out of her dress. The rivers run dry, the mountains are nearly stripped of trees, and each year more soil erodes from the barren hills like flesh slipping from bones.

Yet it is still possible to imagine the land as it was before it was defiled, for even in desolation it remains beautiful—steeply carved mountain ranges, wide green river valleys, shimmering white sand beaches.

Envision, if you will, your feet pressed against that warm sand—privy to Columbus's luck but plagued by none of his shortsightedness. What would you enact, given the power to redeem this Pearl of the Antilles?

Free education, roads, medical care? Reliable electricity, reforestation, Sunday school? If your head grows cloudy imagining the possibilities, perhaps you, too, have felt the tug of that siren song—the song that captivated my father, and the mythical Caribs, and the ten thousand nongovernmental aid organizations that were registered in Haiti at the time of the earthquake—the song that whispers: *Perhaps you can be the one to make a difference in Haiti.*

This is how the story always begins.

Talking to Trees

California, 1973

M Y PARENTS WERE not yet missionaries in the making when they met, high in the sugar pines of the San Jacinto Wilderness in Southern California. In 1973, the only church they could claim had a roof made of sky.

My father, Lee Jonathan Anderson III, had been born at the foot of the San Jacinto Mountains, the son and grandson of Coachella Valley date farmers. The only conversion that he has never doubted took place on a hike in that wilderness when he was eleven years old. Born a desert rat, wiry and strong, he had never seen so much unirrigated green. Squirrels leapt and chattered overhead. Branches swayed. Then he saw it: a battered trail-building tool hidden beneath a prickly chinquapin bush—the metal teeth dented, the wooden handle worn smooth with use. It must have been stashed there by a ranger. The boy who would grow up to be my father knew at once that he had found his calling: to protect God's green earth.

At age eighteen, he walked into the California state park office in mile-high Idyllwild to ask for a job in the San Jacinto Mountains. His only qualification was that he was a farm boy, unafraid of hard work. He walked out with a crisp beige button-up shirt with a grizzly bear stitched in gold.

Three summers later, my mother, Flip Divine, a skateboard city girl with curls that bounced against her backpack, waltzed into his life without a permit (or so he claimed). My mother had iron calves and a winsome smile. Having just returned from a fifty-mile hike in the Sierra Nevadas, she was barely winded after an eight-mile climb over thirty-two hundred vertical feet, and felt strong enough to drop her pack and stroll back down the switchbacks to help a friend's dad carry his gear the last few miles.

My father, though impressed, did not fail to reprimand her later that evening when she whirled across the meadow with her girlfriends in an impromptu hora: She was in danger of trampling the wildflowers and delicate native grasses.

Family legend has it that she simply grabbed his hand and made him dance with her. I would like to believe that this is true, although it would have been out of character for him. He isn't usually one for dancing.

It wasn't an easy courtship. Not specializing in romance, my father once boxed up a roadkill turtle to send to a girl who had expressed a fondness for tortoises, never suspecting that the gesture might be misconstrued.

When they discovered that they would both be attending Cal Poly Pomona agriculture school that fall—where she had enrolled for the sole purpose of marrying a farmer—she was on the lookout. But when she finally spotted him, two and a half weeks later, in front of the cafeteria, she blurted out: Why, Ranger Jon, I didn't know you were so short! (She is not one to hide her disappointment.) He was five-five sans uniform and hiking boots. She would have loomed over him if she had worn heels instead of Birkenstocks.

Eventually, they won each other over. She wooed him with homemade bread; he brought her radishes and carrots that he had grown in boxes on the roof of his apartment (the manager mistakenly assumed that he was growing weed). After botany class, the twenty-one-year-old farm boy who could hike his friends into the ground lingered to point out wildflowers to a girl.

The first time she visited the Anderson family date ranch in the desert, several hours away, he took her on a hooting-like-screech-owls joyride in the moonlight. The headlights picked up the scared wide eyes of jackrabbits in the dust. He howled, then grinned.

He wasn't yet ready to relinquish his bachelorhood when she ran out of money to finish college, so she moved a thousand miles to Oregon to prove her independence. She woke at five a.m. to ride her bike in the rain to the strawberry fields and answered his letters with whimsical watercolor sketches. A fox flicked his tail in the woods; musician friends kept her up all night to sing in the dawn.

He drove up to see her in a green Toyota pickup, and they hoed the mint fields side by side while she quoted lines from Romeo and Juliet.

—*But soft, what light from yonder window breaks? It is the East, and Juliet is the sun!*

—Don't stop working to talk, he chided. —The farmer is watching.

Her hair and hands smelled of spearmint.

They were married a few months later, on a cloudless January day in 1975, under a palo verde tree in the California desert. The homespun wedding, planned in four weeks, went off without a hitch (aside from the neighbors' dogs running off with a few of the wedding gifts to chew to shreds under the pomegranate trees). My father's only regret was that the Thermal Thrift Store didn't offer a wedding registry.

My mother wore a hand-stitched cotton dress in olive, tangerine, and ochre, with a ruffled yoke and high neckline; she thought she might wear it again for potluck suppers. The great-grandmothers, not quite sure what to make of this new generation, perched on hay bales and exchanged stiff pleasantries. One gray-haired rancher's wife noted that Flip Divine had done well to marry the Prince of Coachella Valley; Grandma Tyrone, not to be outdone, said that Jon Anderson was lucky indeed to have won the Queen of Long Beach.

For two future missionaries, the religious overtones of the ceremony were notably muted. Under the bright blue of a desert sky, a friend read lines from the Sufi mystic Kahlil Gibran: *Sing and dance together and be joyous, but let each one of you be alone, Even as the strings of a lute are alone though they quiver with the same music.* My father's former Baptist youth pastor offered a blessing, and the Divine siblings warbled a Presbyterian hymn in four-part harmony.

My parents' faith, such as it was, had grafted on to the stolid root-stock of the Protestant work ethic the generous ecumenicalism of the Jesus movement, where peace and love trumped religious obligation. For my mother, religion was a loose-fitting dress that allowed her to whirl around and drink in the beauty: God loved her; God loved the earth; it was all so beautiful. In more desperate moments, when she felt pinned under the weight of a darkness that she could not shake off, she discovered that if she spoke the name of Jesus out loud, the heaviness vanished. But sin was not an agony that she lost sleep over.

My father, more rule-abiding by instinct, had been shaped by the date ranch, where hard work and self-restraint were defining virtues—even though his shaggy beard and overalls no longer fit the crew-cut profile of a Future Farmer of America.

If Grandma Lois had any reservations about her eldest son's back-to-the-earth spirituality, she was too polite to mention them. He studied his Bible from time to time but reserved his deepest allegiance for the nature mysticism of John Muir. Alone in the mountains, he threw his arms around eight-hundred-year-old limber pines. He needed no greater miracle than the unfolding of a seed in the dark earth to anchor his faith in a Creator God.

As the newlyweds drove off into the sunset to begin their honeymoon, barefoot kids cavorted on the trampoline. My mother was at the wheel—an incidental detail that the more conservative uncles never let her forget.

Not wanting to be trapped inside a motel, they pulled over beside the highway and camped at an overlook just inside of Yosemite—technically illegal, but my ranger father had a good instinct for which roads would go unpatrolled on a winter night in the off-season. They fell asleep to the moonlit summit of Half-Dome, silver above the snow. A lifetime of unplanned adventure had begun.

My mountain-man father and his high school buddies were founding members of the Guadalupe Martinez Society (it mostly involved camping out under the stars with cans of beans and bed rolls, having sworn to protect the wilderness), so for their honeymoon hike the newlyweds followed the faint traces of Cahuilla Indian trails across the exposed dry ridges that loomed over the Coachella Valley floor.

The desert was wild with spring: red tongues of ocotillo licked the sky as jackrabbits bolted through yellow poppies and pale white ghost flowers. Hiking one afternoon in only his boxer shorts, my father was stung by a honeybee where it hurt. My mother laughed so hard she had to sit down on a rock to breathe.

They had packed just enough water to get them to Agua Alta Spring, where he assured her they'd be able to drink their fill, but when they arrived, they found only a dark circle of moist sand. It was near dusk, too dark to hike any farther—they were still days from civilization—so they dug with bare hands until their fingernails jammed against a stiff obstruction: the rib cage of a dead horse. Buried beneath the bones was a slow seep of water. With this, they refilled their canteens. Contamination might have been a concern, had they been prone to alarm. But they didn't like to dwell on worst-case scenarios—a sign of things to come. They camped there two nights. The wildflowers were beautiful.

They settled into a love shack at the edge of a citrus grove, a mile from the family date ranch, and when his buddies warned the young bride that her husband would never leave the desert, she got up from the kitchen table and circled a date on the calendar.

—*This,* she announced, —is when we're moving to Oregon.

She hadn't stopped dreaming about the mint fields and apple orchards.

Three months later, they loaded the green pickup with cardboard boxes and drove the long way, via Nebraska, to stay with her relatives in the heartland—the ones whose Jell-O salads and ten-course breakfasts for the farmhands had convinced her that the life of a farmer was the life for her. The plan was for both of my parents to finish ag school in Oregon.

As a summer hailstorm roared across the plains, they pointed the pickup northwest. My father let out an admiring whoop when they detoured through Yellowstone to see the white furious surge of

Old Faithful. A month later, just before classes were due to start, my mother called her mother to complain of a strange sickness that left her nauseated—but only in the mornings. My grandmother laughed and congratulated her.

I was her first feminist dilemma. Neither of her sisters nor her parents had graduated from college, though her older brother was about to. There was no one to insist that she earn a degree. She joked that she had already acquired the one credential she'd gone to ag school to find—she was a bona fide farmer's wife. (The regret over this lost opportunity wouldn't kick in for a few more years.)

They moved three times in nine months and spent the last trimester scrambling like field mice to hoard a nest of savings. She drove a school bus with wooden blocks bolted to the pedals so that she could reach the brakes around her lumbering belly. He shoveled manure from the university chicken barns into an empty gravel lot and harvested sweet corn and fat, round squash from soil that a skeptical neighbor had assured them would never yield a crop.

He even dusted china and raked leaves for an imperious professor's wife who paid a stingy two dollars an hour, hinting that the landed son of a date baron must already have a vast inheritance tucked away. He cut and hauled Christmas trees in the rain. But the worst by far was the cannery, where he donned a hairnet and stood in a clanging assembly line to stuff three ears of corn into a tin. When a coworker told him he'd never find another job that paid so well, he felt the noose tighten around his neck. Work that bruised the spirit wasn't worth the paycheck. He quit.

I arrived two weeks before their first anniversary and made the front page of the local paper as the first baby of the United States of America's bicentennial year, born at home in a green chair (the joke was that they should have named me Liberty Sparkle).

In a faded newspaper clipping tucked into the family photo album, my mother smiles wearily up at the photographer. Her curls spill over her ears like a spunky halo as she holds a squalling baby in her arms, caught like an unwitting Madonna in the glare of the flash. My father, bearded and grizzly, leans protectively over us in the plaid shirt that she had sewn for their first Christmas together.

When strangers at the park complimented my parents on their front-page act of defiance (even in hippie-friendly Oregon in the 1970s, midwives were still a scandal), they laughed and tried to change the subject. They were happy to jettison the status quo for the sake of idealism, but they hadn't planned on the unwanted publicity.

In the evenings, they propped me in a baby walker by the chicken coop so I could watch the hens while they weeded the garden. We had moved yet again, this time to a field outside of town where musician friends had parked a mobile home.

All we can say is thanks a lot, my father sang, his scratchy voice soft as he rocked me to sleep, *for Jon and Flip and Apricot.*

Not until his graduation from ag school did my father begin to grapple with his destiny. My mother argued for land in Oregon, where they could start a new life together, but my father was adamant: it was time to shed the prodigal lifestyle and return to the family date ranch (as well as the desert mountains). Duty trumped impulsiveness, and the hard-earned diploma was tucked into the back of the pickup alongside the stuffed green chair.

My mother, once again in the driver's seat, pulled onto the side of the road just before we crossed the California border to stretch her tired shoulders. *Will I ever come back?* she wondered as she gazed back across the forests of Douglas fir and incense cedar.

Oregon disappeared behind us in the tilted rearview mirror.

For three months that summer, until the date harvest herded us down the mountain, we shared a six-by-ten cabin in the San Jacinto Wilderness—the very same valley where my parents had met four years earlier. After a day on the trails, my ranger father told stories around the campfire and sang lines of poetry from John Muir while she strummed her autoharp: *Climb the mountains, and get their good tidings. Nature's peace*

will flow into you, like sunshine flows through the trees. And the storms will
blow their energies into you, while cares fall off like autumn leaves.

My mother washed my cloth diapers in a basin of cold creek water
and sewed me a pint-size ranger outfit by lamplight, one painstaking
stitch at a time. Once, in an attempt to stave off loneliness, she picked a
thousand tiny gooseberries for a pie. My father swore he'd never in his
life tasted anything so delicious.

I tottered along the trail in tiny leather boots that had cost a full
day's wages. My mother had tied bells to the laces so she could hear me
if I wandered off. The creek sang and the branches swayed overhead, a
curtain of green through which I could see the sky. I tipped back my
head and babbled my first words to the trees.

Saved

Thermal, 1978

WHEN WINTER SNOWSTORMS buried the tent cabin in the mountains, my parents towed an eight-foot-wide aluminum trailer to the edge of a mesquite grove on my grandparents' ranch in the desert, surrounded by eighty acres of dates, pecans, and citrus.

In the California desert, only tenacious plants survive without human interference. The spindly ocotillo plays dead at the first sign of drought, dropping its gray-green leaves like a showgirl stepping out of her sequins. The barrel-chested cactus shrivels to a shadow of its former self. But when raindrops spatter the flood-carved arroyos, watch out, world: Here come the glitterati. Flame-red blossoms burst from the withered ocotillo. The barrel cactus, swollen with hoarded rain, plumps out bright globes of fruit. Palo verde trees glow under neon yellow blossoms, buzzing with hummingbirds.

It is a landscape of excess—showbiz or bankruptcy; a landscape that breeds either loyalty or despair.

On nights when I squirmed with heat rash, my father plopped me down on the bench seat of the green pickup and took me on aimless drives through the desert, where the bumpy rhythm of the ruts and windblown hillocks of sand lulled me drowsily to sleep, my sweaty face imprinted with the seat fabric. His rough hands were gentle when he carried me back inside.

He disappeared early, before the sun's glare rendered him useless, to cut firewood or work the date ranch with his brothers. The ten-acre plot of organic vegetables that he and my mother planted in an unused corner of the ranch, called Palm Shadow Produce, was their first entrepreneurial adventure, a quixotic attempt to get out of the shadow of the family business; my mother had deduced in short order that there were too many great-aunts, siblings, and second cousins waiting to divide a limited inheritance.

As my parents walked the long rows of vegetables in the evenings, bending over to uproot weeds and check germination, I understood that the jackrabbits were our enemies, creeping out of the shadows to tear off tender leaves. My father and the uncles kept them at bay with twenty-two-caliber rifles fired from the back of the Jeep. I sat between my mother's legs in the passenger seat and screamed encouragement. Search lights glared from the roll bar as the Anderson brothers hooted war cries and clouds of dust kicked up, white in the headlights. Ranch dogs ran alongside, ears flapping. I couldn't wait until I was old enough for a gun of my own. I was disappointed when another pregnancy put an end to that wild jostling, the crack of the rifles fading into the night as my mother washed my feet and, despite my protests, put me to bed.

After my first little sister arrived—Laura Meadow, yet another girl with an unexpected blaze of red hair—my mother had even less energy than before. Left to myself, I figured out how to shimmy up the veneer walls of the trailer while my mother clattered in the kitchen. I wedged one sweaty footprint onto each side of the hallway until I could touch the ceiling: a child's momentary conquest, the illusion of perspective.

Sent outside to play while the baby napped, I ordered my invisible friend Bango Bongo around the cardboard playhouse. I was careful to avoid the thin patch of grass that bloomed into green only in the two-foot radius of the dripping faucet, where the bees swarmed and stung.

On slow afternoons, I hiked up the sand dune to Grandma and Grandpa's trailer. Sometimes Grandma Lois filled the corn tank with water so I could splash in aimless circles, then flop on the trampoline in wet underpants. Or I'd sit at the kitchen table and scribble with broken crayons while she typed up church bulletins.

—Oh, that's just wonderful, Grandma would say, glancing up and readjusting her glasses before turning back to the typewriter as the dryer tumbled yet another load of frayed cotton T-shirts.

I lived for the days when the Nishimoto cousins drove down to the desert to visit and we sat cross-legged under the damp wheeze of the swamp cooler with a stack of Uncle Linden's comic books. In the hallway, a row of framed high school pictures smiled fixedly at the opposite wall: the six Anderson siblings. My father was the eldest.

I saw Grandpa Lee only in passing, when he tramped out the door in his irrigating boots, a plastic mug of iced Pepsi in his hand. Sometimes I tagged along out of boredom or curiosity. If he caught a gopher, he'd let me help feed it to the cats.

At four years old, I already knew how to walk carefully through the tall grasses, laying the blades flat with my feet so that I never stepped on a rattlesnake unaware. My father explained this trick when he swung me onto his shoulders in the evenings to get me out of my mother's hair. He crouched beside me to point out the tracks of roadrunners in the dust and told me to quit talking so we could hear the bullfrogs sing. He told stories of my great-grandfather, who had cleared the desert with a mule, and of men who scaled ladders fifty-six feet high to harvest the clustered dates.

My father, as I understood it, wasn't afraid of anything—not even scorpions and rattlesnakes, as long as he saw them first. When he was four years old, there hadn't been room on the single foldout bed in his parents' trailer for four children, so he, as the eldest son, and his younger brother had slept in a separate outbuilding. He'd learned early how to fend for himself; he wasn't a sissy city kid.

I memorized the warning.

My mother, on the other hand, didn't bother to hide her terror of the desert. Rattlesnakes, tongues flickering, wound through the dust under our trailer, across the strip of yellow carpet where I had set up my dollhouse, and into the verdant allure of my mother's kitchen garden, in search of rabbits and small fat mice. Their narrow heads slipped easily through the fence, but when they realized, too late, that their swollen bellies—taut from an earlier feast—were unable to slip through, they thrashed wildly, their scales caught on the flimsy chicken wire.

So proud, those rattlesnakes, they never suspected that their desires could lead them astray. Or perhaps they couldn't smell the danger. We must have seemed such simple fools, so easily taken advantage of: a disarray of children, one harried mother trying to keep up with the laundry and meals in the desert heat.

If Grandpa Lee was in shouting distance, death came quickly. His hand, holding the shovel, seemed to me as firm and unforgiving as that of the angel who forbade entrance to the Garden of Eden in the illustrated children's Bible that Grandma Lois had given us for Christmas. Grandpa's jaw tightened—I could never tell if it was in concentration or pleasure—as the blade descended and the bones of the snake's twisting neck cracked and split.

If my father came to the rescue, he'd ignore my mother's frantic pleas to *Kill it, please, Jon!* As far as he was concerned, the rattlesnakes were free pest control; they kept the field mice out of the vegetable seeds.

He trapped them in empty garbage cans, then released the snakes into the canyon where they could hunt in peace. But if the deed was done, well, my father was not a man to pass up an opportunity.

I watched, spellbound, my sweaty toes curled around the legs of the orange vinyl chair in the kitchen as he gutted and lowered the pale headless rope into the Crock-Pot. Unzipped of its scales, bereft of its venom, the muscles still craved movement, even after the brain had been severed. Tiny synapses leapt and shivered in the sinewed flesh as it thrashed and uncurled. Drops of water flicked onto my bare arms and I jumped, unnerved, as the dead snake danced.

We ate rattlesnake tacos for dinner that night.

My mother could never understand my father's fealty to such a hostile landscape. A withered extrovert, confined to a trailer the size of her sister's garage in the suburbs, she resented that her husband disappeared just after dawn. He'd return intermittently throughout the day, but it wasn't until evening, caked with sweat and dust, that he'd kick off his boots and rejoin the family. Lush, neighborly Oregon with its potlucks and house concerts had faded to a mirage.

My father couldn't explain his allegiance. He simply put his shoulder to the plow and didn't look back. He expected his wife to do her part, just as his mother had. It hadn't occurred to him that she would be unhappy.

The night he found a pile of dead Christmas trees dumped by the side of the road and burst in the front door, euphoric, to phone his parents, my mother had just sat down in the rocking chair to nurse baby Meadow. He reached over her shoulder without even looking at her.

—We hit the jackpot! he crowed into the phone.

Baby Meadow startled and let go, spurting milk onto Mom's dress. My mother's body crackled with anger. He missed the warning.

—We can run the dead trees through the chipper and they'll make great mulch for the date trees!

—Oh, Jonny, that's *wonderful!* Grandma Lois's voice trilled from the other end of the line.

I sat very quiet at the kitchen table, pretending that I was invisible.

My mother sucked in her breath, her cheeks as red as rooster combs. My father, still grinning, hung up the phone and ambled down the hallway to take a shower.

—I hate you! *I hate you!* she screamed after him. Meadow stopped nursing and wailed. My mother slung the baby over her shoulder and patted with hard, rhythmic thumps. My father sighed and ran callused fingers through his dusty hair.

—What did I do this time? he asked, befuddled by the incoherent emotions of females.

She plotted her escape when she was alone at the clothesline, stabbing wooden pegs onto my father's ragged T-shirts, onto the cloth diapers and stained dresses, onto the heavy canvas pants worn as protection against rattlesnakes and date thorns.

For months there had been no running water in their tiny bath-room, so they had to hike up the sand dune to his parents' trailer to take showers. Every time she turned the door handle, she worried that she'd find her father-in-law squatting on the john.

Why had she stayed with this man, she asked herself at the clothes-line. The only prospects in sight were more children and another season to endure. The joke was on her for having ever wanted to be a farmer's wife. She was a rattlesnake snagged on chicken wire: cut off before she could even enter the garden.

She wondered what it would feel like to begin again, alone. She told herself that she'd just gotten off to a bad start: an emotionless husband, his insular family, the cramped trailer—but there was nothing to pre-vent her from walking away.

Baby Meadow fussed from inside the trailer, and my mother grabbed for the wash basket. Easing into the rocking chair as she unbuttoned her blouse, she reached for a cookbook only to realize—after the baby had latched on hungrily to feed—that she'd instead picked up the prim pa-perback devotional that her mother-in-law had given her for Christmas.

My mother was suspicious but bored. She skimmed the first few pages. The intro to *God Calling* explained that two ordinary women who preferred to remain anonymous had waited in front of a blank piece of paper until they heard the voice of God.

Mildly curious but braced for exasperation, my mother read the first few entries.

> *Never think things overwhelming. How can you be overwhelmed when I am with you?*

The tone surprised her. It had been so long since anyone had spo-ken to her that gently. She turned the page.

> *You must be as one who runs a race, stumbles and falls, rises and presses on to the goal. Be calm, no matter what may befall you. Rest in me.*

Closing her eyes and leaning in to the words, she climbed up into that offered stillness. It was as if Christ Himself had jumped down from the cross and knelt before my mother's rocking chair: the rebuke mixed with sorrow, the authority of pain, the hidden gentleness. Here was a God who understood loneliness. A God who promised that He would not leave her. She lifted the baby and leaned her face against Meadow's damp hair. Her limbic reflexes—the thrashing reptilian brain, clamoring for flight or fight—quieted.

She knew that she faced a crossroads. If she submitted to that still, small voice, nothing in her circumstances would change. She would be stuck growing vegetables in the dust with a husband who no longer seemed to notice her. But she would no longer feel alone.

And so it was that, on the very first Sunday after my mother's encounter with God in the rocking chair, she dressed me in my frilliest skirt and blouse, put shoes on my feet, and off we went to the first church she could find while my father, left at home with the baby, raised his eyebrows and let her go. Which was how my mother came to be a member of the Coachella Valley Christian Church on Jackson Street; if she was going to devote her life to this Jesus, then she might as well learn what He had to say.

My father came with us a few weeks later, curious to understand the change in her. He bounced Meadow on his hip while he made small talk with retirees. I knocked back a Dixie cup of Kool-Aid and buzzed around on a sugar high.

Recruited to direct the children's choir, my mother took to belting out musical numbers while she cooked dinner. I couldn't believe my good fortune. The mother whom I'd been afraid might walk out on us had revved to life again.

As the months went by, the habit coalesced into identity: We became a churchgoing family. My mother had sworn allegiance to the Christ who had captured her, and my father and the rest of us were along for the ride.

Which is not, by any means, to suggest that we had stumbled onto a primrose path. She was still married to a man who would rather work all day than talk to his wife, and they were not above the odd shouting match in the kitchen. (She perfected a snappy, sardonic quip to get a laugh at church potlucks: Opposites attract—is that some kind of a cosmic joke?)

But there were also the afternoons when we played whiffle ball with a whole herd of uncles, great-grandparents, and second cousins, and nights that we camped out under the stars. Plus, my parents were able to borrow from the extended family just enough for a cash down payment on a one-room cabin in the Idyllwild mountains—a haven that we could escape to when the heat became unbearable.

Even after a third daughter arrived (unplanned, as usual), the fragile balance held. I took a deep breath. We had been saved.

The Bear Went Over the Mountain

Idyllwild, 1981

THE CALL TO the mission field arrived on an otherwise ordinary afternoon, the mustard yellow phone jangling from the wall of the Idyllwild cabin. Grandma Lois was on the other end of the line, her voice trembling with excitement—she'd just learned that a forty-acre Baptist agricultural center in the north of Haiti needed a caretaker for a year. My parents held the phone between them. My father shrugged, curious.

—Where's Haiti? my mother wanted to know.

Friends at church had already told my parents that they would make good missionaries, as they had the requisite pioneer spirit, but as far as my mother could tell, being a missionary just meant framed family photos in the church lobby and monthly updates in the bulletin. Too much pressure. No, thanks. Not to mention being unable to speak the language. Or make friends. It sounded lonely.

My father liked the idea of using his expertise to help others, and had briefly contemplated joining the Peace Corps in college—until the recruiting officer found out that my mother was already pregnant and explained that developing countries were considered too high-risk for children. My parents agreed to at least pray about it, a newly acquired habit, but it seemed unlikely that anything would come of it.

It was Grandma Lois who had always dreamed of being a missionary, before six children and a family date business cut her adrift from that destiny. My mother was far from convinced that the best way to serve God was to move to another country.

—Why not just find ways to help others here? she asked my father, loath to lose momentum on her latest plan: to get rid of the trailer in the desert and construct a real house up the canyon, a respectable distance from the family date ranch.

As far as I was concerned, my parents had only just hammered out a seasonal compromise that suited all five of us: summers in Idyllwild; winters in the desert. The Idyllwild cabin wasn't much bigger than our trailer in the desert—one twelve-by-sixteen-foot room with a woodstove and a pit toilet out back—but it was just down the ridgeline from the San Jacinto Wilderness. We woke to the tinkling music of a stream overhung by mint and azaleas. My parents slept in the loft, Meadow and I on a fold-down bunk bed that doubled as a couch, and baby Rose Ember (born while my father was fighting forest fires) got a foam pad on the floor. There was no insulation, and there were cracks in the walls through which we could watch the sunlight flicker on the manzanita, so when the temperatures dropped, we packed up and moved back down to the desert. Winter was the time to plant seeds, anyway; summers in the desert were brutal on vegetables (and wives).

I, for one, wished that summers in Idyllwild could last forever. My mother lugged grocery bags of books home from the library, and Meadow and I spent hours on the hand-me-down couch that my father had dragged onto the porch. Twice a week we gathered a fistful of change to take showers at the state park campground. My ranger father hauled us up on his shoulders when we met him on the trail, and my mother strummed her autoharp and sang Little Rabbit Foo Foo songs around the campfire. We ate dinner at the picnic table, where a tame scrub jay swooped down from the live oak to steal peanuts from our outstretched hands.

Only when my father roared and smashed supposedly unbreakable plates on the deck, or when full bladders forced us to slip bare feet into worn tennis shoes and brave the pit toilet, did I regret our mountain solitude. Meadow and I hated to go alone, so we'd shake each other awake and carry a candle between us, glancing furtively over our shoulders in the dark. There were two holes—one labeled *Bucks* and the other *Does*—and we'd pee in tandem, squinting sleepily at yellowed Sears & Roebuck ads for woodstoves and rifles. The worst part was creaking the door back open. The stench helped, as did the queasy feeling in our guts when we turned for one last irresistible look at what we had accomplished. Still, it took forever to race back across the porch and slam the door behind us so we could dive back under the covers, safe from whatever had stalked us in the rustling darkness.

After the initial phone call from Grandma Lois about a possible job in Haiti, nothing more persuasive emerged to sway my parents, so my mother proceeded as planned with the dreamed-of house in the desert. She picked out double-paned windows and filed permits with the county. Relatives in Nebraska had even offered a loan—that is, until the U.S. boycotted the Moscow Summer Olympics because they'd invaded Afghanistan and, in retaliation, the Soviet Union stopped buying American grain, which caused the market to plummet. At which point, serendipitously, Grandma Lois received a second phone call, this time from a high-spirited missionary matriarch named Ivah Heneise, who had just flown in from Cap-Haïtien with drums, bamboo pipes, conch shells, and a traveling band called the King's Messengers, all crammed into a fifteen-passenger van for their first U.S. tour.

Ivah, as my parents were soon to learn, was not easy to refuse. She had thinning burgundy hair and bright eyes that blinked excitedly behind her glasses. She and her now legally blind husband, Harold, had moved to a thatched-roof house in Haiti in 1947, well before electricity or running water had reached the Limbé Valley, and after evicting the snakes from the rafters, she'd given birth to four children on Haitian soil, plus incubated a theological seminary, several Baptist churches, a Haiti Handicraft enterprise that sold brightly colored embroidered skirts and blouses, an ag center, and a missionary hospital.

The Baptist Centre Agricole, Ivah explained cheerfully, was managed by her son, Ken, and was just fifteen minutes outside of Cap-Haïtien, where cruise ships pulled up to the wharf in the summer months; it was also only twenty miles from the Baptist hospital in Limbé, if we needed medical treatment. The Heneises, at the Baptist seminary, and the Hodges family, at the Good Samaritan Hospital, had both lived in Haiti for decades—and they had a dozen grandchildren between them, most still living in the north of Haiti. We would be in good hands.

As for the language barrier, Ivah assured my mother that she need not to worry—you didn't learn to speak a language; you learned to *sing* a language.

My parents, dazzled into curiosity, consented to an interview with the American Baptist Foreign Mission Society, who explained that if my father served for a year as a volunteer missionary, he would oversee the chicken and rabbit projects, teach horticulture seminars, and manage the Haitian staff and the greenhouses. The salary would be seventeen thousand dollars for the yearlong assignment. (By contrast, Palm Shadow Produce, their organic vegetable business, had brought in only fifteen thousand in its first year of operation—and that was before taxes, fuel, irrigation water, fertilizer, and labor.)

My parents did a few quick mental calculations. After a year in Haiti, they'd come home with money in the bank; I could be homeschooled for kindergarten.

The Divine grandparents (unlike Grandma Lois) were initially hesitant—having spent the war years, respectively, in the South Pacific and as a nurse in a military hospital, where they'd been given ample opportunities to visualize worst-case scenarios—but even they eventually conceded that the adventure seemed like the perfect fit for my parents: concern for God's creation, plus a fair dose of the impulsive. My father would be able to share his knowledge of plants, and my mother would be able to extend hospitality to strangers.

He is no fool who gives up that which he cannot keep to gain that which he cannot lose, my mother doodled on a piece of notebook paper, twirling the pen nib between her fingers as she stared out at the trees.

The American Baptist Foreign Mission Society, to ensure that my parents were qualified for their roles as missionary volunteers, asked the pastor of our church, Mike Noizumi, to fill out a four-page evaluation, wherein he was asked whether or not my parents were:

- *Impatient, intolerant, argumentative, domineering, "cocky," or critical of others.*
- *Frequently worried, anxious, nervous or tense; given to moods.*
- *Prejudiced toward groups, races, or nationalities.*
- *Given to exclusive and absorbing friendships, i.e., to "crushes."*
- *Lacking in humor, or in the ability to take a joke.*

The ability to take a joke seemed at first an odd prerequisite, for we did not yet understand how essential it would be to be able to laugh at our shortcomings. In the category of physical condition, the pastor rated them both as rugged, though my father earned the additional commendation: *I have hiked with him once and I know he is vigorous. He is a healthy, handsome and courteous young man.*

In his summary paragraph, Pastor Noizumi maintained that he had no reservations about my parents' decision to enter missionary life, nor were there any indications that their decision was significantly influenced by:

1. *a desire for travel, adventure or cultural development*
2. *a desire to exercise power or control over less privileged people, or*
3. *a desire to escape a difficult personal, family or vocational situation*

This was perhaps not entirely accurate—adventure was certainly a motivating factor, although to my parents' credit, they had no conscious intention of exerting control over less privileged people. It is, however, no small task to screen would-be altruists for signs of incipient imperialism. For who among us can know how we will respond when the dynamics of power and privilege suddenly shift without warning?

I was at Grandma Lois's trailer when my father called to announce that we'd be moving to Haiti. The rest of the family was still in Idyllwild. My father had promised that he would drive me down to the desert for my first day of kindergarten, but it was forest-fire season, and he had a mountain to protect. He had been on duty at a wilderness lookout tower when a lightning storm blew in, and his eagle eyes spotted wisps of smoke that no one else had seen. Given the chance to keep working on his day off, he proudly answered the call of duty, which meant that the Forest Service dispatcher was given the unenviable job of calling my mother to inform her that it was now her responsibility to round up her three daughters so that she could drop me off at Grandma Lois's trailer for the month (no one else in my family being willing to leave the Idyllwild cabin).

At five years old, alone at the date ranch, I felt my tangled hair whip my elbows as I spun flips on the trampoline. I missed my sisters and hated the long walk home from the bus stop, so I wasn't overly worried at the news that we'd be moving again; we already packed up twice a year to go from one house to the other. The coiled springs rebounded and hurled me so high against the sky that I felt I could almost brush my fingers against the woven baskets of the hot-air balloons as they wafted over the date trees. I hung suspended as the earth slowly tilted on its axis. Gravity had not yet taken hold. I could land anywhere.

By Christmas 1981, we had shiny blank passports and visas stamped with palm trees and official signatures from the Haitian government. Our shoulders ached from last-minute immunizations. Battered suitcases from the Salvation Army flopped open on the floor of the trailer like books with broken spines, half-filled with silverware, toys, swimsuits, and sheets. The missionaries we were due to replace had instructed us, via a typed letter, to pack multivitamins (to compensate for the nutrient-depleted soil) and a cassette player, along with an apologetic disclaimer that we might find it difficult to adjust to life without a television. My parents scoffed at this; they'd never owned one. We were also warned to watch the Haitian customs officials closely when they searched our suitcases, lest any of our valuables disappear, but apart from this one confusing directive, we set off more or less unencumbered by cross-cultural training.

My parents knew next to nothing about the history of colonialism, the lingering imbalance of power, resentment against white rule, nor any other significant details from the nearly two hundred years of Haitian independence. Nor were the church members who applauded our commissioning service any more politically savvy. A few assumed that we were moving to Tahiti. At least one mistook Haiti for Hades.

Everyone, of course, had heard of zombies and voodoo, which was enough to get my mother backed against the wall by a livid octogenarian who accused her of being an unfit mother for dragging her three precious little girls into such a dark, heathen nation. My mother offered a strained smile and tried to placate: Thank you for praying, I'm sure God will take care of us!

It took me years to understand this fear disguised as pity. Haiti, as the first Free Black Nation to shake off the yoke of slavery—more than half a century before the country whose founding document had declared that all men were created equal—seemed to be prefaced always by its tagline: the Poorest Country in the Western Hemisphere. It was a quick, dismissive epithet. A way to denigrate what could not otherwise be understood. Poverty provided a reliable excuse for self-congratulatory concern; a salve to our imagined superiority.

A few days before we were to begin our career as missionaries, my father asked my mother to cut his hair extra-short, even though she protested that it made his ears stick out. He hauled an orange vinyl chair out of the trailer and stripped off his T-shirt. She stood behind him, snipping wisps of coarse brown hair. His exposed back glared white and pale beneath his sunburned neck, a farmer's tan.

Three-year-old Meadow stood on the seat of the tricycle in her underpants, her arms held out like a circus acrobat's. I hollered at Rosie to quit ringing the school bell on the dollhouse because it was shaking my classroom full of plastic Little People. My father twisted his head around to intervene, and my mother grimaced and took the comb out of her teeth. —Hold still! she complained, positioning his head back in place. Rosie shook her head sulkily, an armless Fisher-Price figure in her mouth.

There was no reason to assume that we knew what we were doing. Like the proverbial bear tromping over the mountain to see what he could see, we had set our course for altruism or adventure—as missionaries, as explorers, for the hell of it. It was a chance to pick up a new language, to help out however we could. How hard could it be?

It was our first airplane ride, the first time my sisters and I had ever seen the Los Angeles basin from the air. I shimmied my seat belt down around my knees to press my nose against the glass. The lights disappeared behind us. The horizon twinkled like a miniature engineering set, the kind you could take apart and put back together on a whim.

As the flight attendant made his way down the aisle to hand out orange juice and headsets, I reminded Meadow to sit still. This was uncharted territory, and we needed to be on our best behavior. We wiggled plastic headphones into place and poked at the buttons. I pulled a strand of hair into my mouth and chewed as I listened to the story of the Little Match Girl. Shivering in the streets of London, she struck her last match and died, the flame flickering in her cupped palms. I shivered with her.

My father reached over us to pull down the window shade. California was already behind us, the lights of Los Angeles fading into the dark.

One row behind us, Rosie woke my parents several times, hollering like a banshee as my mother lifted her blouse to nurse, but Meadow and I slept deeply, our arms and legs intertwined, chests rising and falling as we twitched and nestled against the seats. My mother had to reach over and untangle our hair from the headphones while we dreamed, the tinny murmur of *the bare necessities, the simple bare necessities* still schmaltzing in the background.

At three-thirty a.m., California time, my father shook my mother awake: Flip, look!

She pushed up the shade as sunlight flamed across the clouds. Beneath us was Florida. Beyond that, the Caribbean.

My father propped Meadow and I groggily upright for the descent, and a businessman across the aisle glanced over and smiled indulgently. He asked if we were on our way to Orlando to visit Disney World.

My mother flashed him a winning smile: We're going to be missionaries to *Haiti*!

If They Tried to Warn Him,
He Didn't Listen

The Caribbean, 1492

THE ISLAND OF Ayiti, rechristened Hispaniola by Columbus—the western half of which was later renamed Saint-Domingue by the French, and Haiti by the freed slaves—erupted during the Cretaceous era as volcanic fissures forced granite batholiths upward through the crashing waves, and the submerged mountains, encrusted with sandstone and lime, met the sky.

Slowly, over several millennia, airborne seeds took root and forests rose from the red clay. The wide, upturned leaves released moisture into the air, forming high cumulus clouds. Rain fell in torrents, careening down through the dense canopy, seeping into the earth, slowly filling the water table.

Storms swept across from the mainland, with animals caught in the branches of uprooted trees. Beds of kelp hid shy, lumbering manatee (which Columbus later mistook for mermaids).

This New World was discovered in approximately 4000 BC, when the first humans paddled east across the narrow strait from the Yucatán Peninsula and settled along the coast of what is now Cuba, moving slowly into the Bahamian islands and Ayiti. The Casimiroid peoples gathered fruit and guáyiga roots and hunted to extinction the slow-moving sloths.

Two thousand years later, yet another wave of humans, Ortoiroid settlers, arrived from the tip of Venezuela and moved north. They looked primarily to the sea for their food, hunting crocodiles, turtles, and shellfish, as well as the occasional whale. Ayiti, with its densely forested mountains and wide alluvial plains, marked the contentious border region between the two competing migrations.

It was an age of confrontations. In Europe, the Romans were pushing the empire into Gaul, and the Gauls were resisting. In Palestine, a relatively unknown Jewish man whose gospel would come to have such unanticipated consequences in the Caribbean was setting off a religious upheaval in the Judean desert. On Ayiti, a new civilization was emerging.

The Taínos—the good or noble people, as they called themselves— were, like their forebears, equally at home in the forest and at sea. Raised beds carved out of the jungle yielded corn and cassava; traders skimmed across to neighboring islands in sleek dugout canoes that could hold a hundred and fifty warriors. Poets composed ballads in Arawak for the great feasts. Artisans carved elaborate ritual figures of zemis on amulets and stone outcroppings—the spirits who hid in the trees and rivers and whispered mysterious counsel.

The Taínos did not yet know that they would have a scant millennium to enjoy their tenure in the Caribbean before Columbus arrived and laid claim to it.

On that first voyage, sailing into the unknown, Columbus studied in his gently rocking ship's cabin a fifteenth-century map marked with the islands described in Marco Polo's *Travels*. He calculated where he thought they should touch land: somewhere near Cipango (Japan). Marco Polo's tales were already two centuries out of date, but few books about the Far East had been translated into the languages of Europe; Columbus marked his with careful notes in the margins.

He never did discover Polo's streets paved with gold or the men with tails, but he did find the mermaids. They were a disappointment. He wrote:

> *Yesterday when I was going up the Río del Oro, I saw three sirens that came up very high out of the sea. They are not as beautiful as they are painted, since in some ways they have a face of a man.*

Columbus had defied the odds and found land—by sheer luck, his mathematical calculations having grossly underestimated the distance to the Far East—but to the end of his life, he refused to believe that he had stumbled onto a new continent, and remained firmly convinced that he was just off the coast of China.

He handed out tiny tinkling hawk's bells and Venetian glass beads, which the inhabitants of the islands repaid with hand-spun cotton thread and *a kind of dry leaf* that Columbus, not yet initiated into the virtues of tobacco, found puzzling. In his ship log, he recorded the shocked observation that the natives were *as naked as their mothers bore them.* In his letter home to the king and queen of Spain, however, he described them as a well-mannered and gentle people, useful as servants.

Columbus understood from their gestures that they believed he had come down from heaven, and was flattered. He did not understand that, according to their own origin stories, they, too, had descended from the sky. Perhaps as they pointed and gestured, they urged him to escape while he still could.

If they tried to warn him, he didn't listen.

Baptized

Haiti, 1982

WE WERE BAPTIZED into missionary life on a muggy January afternoon in 1982. I had turned six a few days before, and the hot, wet air made my dress cling to my back as I clanged down the metal steps of the airplane onto the tarmac. In the sweltering Duvalier terminal, my mother let go of my hand to protect the slumped head of baby Rosie, which left me free to take it all in. The clickety-clack whir of ceiling fans, the gold-plated jewelry on soft wrists, the jumble of armpits ripe with sweat and perfume.

My parents hovered watchfully during the customs inspection, but nothing went missing. Ken Heneise, Ivah's son, recognized us from the photos we'd mailed ahead and waved. He was tall and gangly, with dark sunglasses and an impressive mustache. My mother pushed back her damp curls and beamed with flustered charm. My father extended a firm handshake. When uniformed airport attendants grabbed for our bags, Ken brushed them aside with a confident flick of his wrist.

Emerging into the tin-can glare of Port-au-Prince felt like an explosion of noise and light. Overloaded buses honked and veered around kids in gingham school uniforms, donkeys piled high with woven baskets and plastic jugs, a wheelbarrow filled with sugarcane. The rules were inscrutable—clearly, no one was restricted to just one side of the road—but there was a swaying, animated rhythm, as if everyone but me were following the steps to some complicated dance.

Ken shouted over the wind that whipped through the open windows as he drove down the dry central coast road, hemmed in by mountains. He had been born in Haiti in the 1940s, a few months after his parents moved into a grass-roofed house on a former rubber plantation. He was six when Hurricane Hazel hit, nine when Papa Doc Duvalier declared himself dictator for life. Those had been terrifying years, but politics had settled down a bit, he assured us, once the son, Baby Doc, took power. Haiti still had plenty of corruption, and police checkpoints, but there was far more stability than there used to be.

When Ken was a teenager, his missionary father's eyesight started to fade. Ken taught himself to fix vehicles by leaning over the engines while Harold gave instructions by memory. Ken left the Limbé Valley to spend a few unhappy years at a boarding school in the States, followed by college at Cal Poly Pomona (the very same ag school, they all realized, that my own parents had attended—though Ken had graduated before they arrived). Still, he insisted, Haiti was his motherland.

At a serene white-sand beach near Montrouis, he pulled over so we could dip our toes in the Caribbean Sea for the first time.

—It's warm! I shouted as Meadow and I raced to collect the pink-lipped conch shells that dotted the sand. I pouted, disappointed, when I realized that every single one had a gaping hole knocked into the otherwise perfect crown. Ken explained that the rubbery *lanbi* meat was harvested for food, but I wanted an unblemished souvenir; surely it was my right as an explorer.

(I had so much to learn.)

On the four-hour drive to our new home, I stared out the window at kids my age who bathed in a river beneath a bridge, tossing water over their bare shoulders. In the green, flat Artibonite Valley, men on skeletal donkeys picked their way along the shoulder. Women with head scarves lifted and tossed rice in woven baskets, the wind scattering the dry husks like confetti. At roadside markets, hands thrust sugarcane candy and tiny yellow bananas through the open windows. Schoolchildren in checkered uniforms shouted: *Blan! Blan!* as we drove past.

—What are they saying? my mother asked. Ken explained. Even

though he'd been born in Haiti, he was still considered a *blan,* like us. *Blan* meant white but was the pejorative used for any foreigner. We were a novelty; we didn't belong here.

I dangled my fingers out the window and breathed in the sharp tang of salt air. Brightly painted buses roared past on blind corners, horns blaring, as chickens and goats scattered. Ken slowed to inch around a recently tipped-over *kamyon,* bald tires belly-up. There were no policemen with whistles to direct traffic, no ambulances or fire trucks. We thumped over torn burlap sacks and squashed mangoes. Dark red stains on the highway buzzed with flies.

My father let out his breath with a low whistle. Later, in a postcard to Grandma Lois that would be displayed proudly on the church bulletin board, he'd confess: *The thought that I will soon be driving these roads is frankly terrifying.*

The engine groaned as we climbed the mountains above Gonaïves. Blood-red blossoms of *flanbwayan* trees trembled in a rainstorm, and rivulets of topsoil washed across the highway. My father asked if erosion was much of a problem. Ken laughed. Trees took years to grow, he explained, but it didn't take long to cut down an entire forest for charcoal. And few Haitian farmers seemed interested in replanting what they harvested, he added—which was why the agricultural center was so important, to teach farmers a better way to manage their land.

By the time we descended into the Limbé Valley, the sun had just begun to slip behind the mountains. Ken pointed out a collection of whitewashed houses on the other side of a low cactus fence: Hôpital le Bon Samaritain, the Baptist hospital run by the Hodges family.

Dr. Hodges, Ken explained, was a Renaissance man—not only a medical doctor but a self-taught archaeologist as well. The Hodges and Heneise kids had grown up together, all eight of them crowded around Ivah's dining room table for school or off on expeditions to Indian caves or pirate ruins with Dr. Hodges on Saturday afternoons when the clinic was closed.

In fact, the Doctor was even now in the process of opening an archaeological museum—we should plan a visit. We craned our necks as the Musée de Guahaba disappeared behind us, just visible through the trees.

A few miles up the valley, Ken pointed out the dirt road that led to the Baptist seminary in Haut-Limbé—Upper Limbé—where he and his siblings had grown up. In the gathering dark, shadowy figures lined the streets, backlit by flickering kerosene lamps. Ken's sister, Laurie, had married a Haitian pastor named Jules Casséus, and the couple had just moved into Ivah and Harold's old house because Casso (as everyone called him) had been promoted to president of the Baptist seminary. We'd meet them soon, Ken promised—Laurie taught piano and her son, Tony, was the same age as Meadow.

It was so much to take in all at once. As we drove the final stretch, over the mountains and through ramshackle Cap-Haïtien to the quiet ag center, Ken pointed out the moonlit edge of the Baie de L'Acul, the very same stretch of water where Columbus himself put down anchor in 1492. My little sisters commemorated the journey by getting carsick on both of our parents' laps.

As soon as we opened the car doors, in Quartier-Morin, we were surrounded by black Labradors that licked at our hands, and the shrill noise of night insects. Sour with kid vomit, my parents listened distractedly as Ken gave a brief tour of our temporary accommodations. For the first month, until he and his family left on furlough, we would be sleeping in a dormitory built to house Haitian students during agricultural seminars, though no students were currently in residence. The walls smelled of damp concrete, and my sisters and I, sponged clean, curled up on thin mattresses and fell immediately to sleep. Mosquitoes thrashed against a bare lightbulb as my parents sat up to record their first impressions.

Hello HAITI—The temperature is absolutely delightful with a feel of humidity, my mother inscribed in a gilt-edged journal, a Christmas gift. A flock of ruffed grouse graced the cover, above the delicately scripted title: *The Happy Family.*

In the family journal, my mother's penmanship is looped and even, aside from my father's jagged corrections. Where she recorded that the plane had landed in Port-au-Prince exactly on schedule, at 1:51 p.m., he had crossed this out and written: *2:41 p.m.*

They still can't tell a story without interrupting each other.

At six a.m., when we rubbed our eyes and squinted at the ceiling, the world that we had stumbled into was already wide awake and throbbing. Roosters crowed, donkeys brayed, and voices called out in a language so emphatic and musical that I couldn't tell where one word ended and the next began.

We followed the straight and narrow sidewalk to breakfast that first morning at the missionary residence—oatmeal and sardines, an unhappy surprise. Ken's wife, Debbie, had apple-blossom cheeks and soft brown hair pulled back in a headband. She wore long sleeves and hats to protect her flawless skin from the harsh tropical sun. Our wild commotion at breakfast seemed to unsettle her, though I was in awe when I learned that she and her horse had thundered across racetracks and leaped over hurdles before she became a missionary wife.

Rosie cried and Meadow picked at her oatmeal, but I scarfed mine in record time so I could get the lay of the land from the Heneises' son, Ryan, the five-year-old commander of the tree house in the mango tree. Adeline, a soft-voiced Haitian woman, cleared our empty plates to the kitchen as Ken inducted my father into a pastime that would become an irresistible obsession: speculation on Haitian politics. The radio that morning had announced that a failed assassination attempt had been made on Jean-Claude Duvalier, and the price of diesel had jumped twenty-five cents a gallon. The menfolk mused that a major coup was perhaps in the making. At any moment, everything could change. Ken pushed back from the table. It was time for a crash course in Ag Center management.

Ken demonstrated with no small amount of pride how a missionary property should be maintained. In the shed, every tool was hung neatly on its hook and outlined so that if anything were out of place it would be immediately obvious. In the three long greenhouses, the pungent smell of cucumbers and tomatoes hit us like a wall of perfumed green. Rabbits nudged their water bottles in long, orderly wire cages. Laying hens clucked. My mother took particular note of the hundreds of fluffy, shrill five-week-old chicks, bred for the tropics, and grabbed my father's arm. *Raising chickens in the back yard is a far cry from having 1,200 in cages and figuring out what diseases they have!*, she admitted in a postcard dashed off to the grandparents.

Under Debbie's watchful eye, my mother jotted down the time and location of the weekly English-speaking women's Bible study (sample lesson: "The Virtuous Woman") as well as a list of Kreyòl phrases and instructions on how to manage the household help. A cassette tape sent to the grandparents recorded the exact tone of my mother's voice as she repeated: *Adeline, koupe sa. Adeline, cut this.* And what precise and oblivious condescension was contained in that earnest mimicry.

That first evening at the Ag Center, after the Heneises had retreated behind closed doors to pack for furlough (that strained, strange, once-every-four-years holiday from the mission field that never quite became one, jammed instead with fund-raising slide shows in church basements and missionary conferences, all of which were designed to keep the mission afloat), my mother grabbed a whiffle ball and whipped up an improvised game on an open patch of grass. Meadow and I took turns whacking wildly at the ball, then racing around an invisible baseline. Before long, a crowd of Haitian children had gathered to watch, until someone kicked a soccer ball onto the infield, and then it was our turn to stare, amazed, as lean, strong legs darted in to score a goal.

The flashing feet moved almost as quickly as the language itself. After a few breathless minutes on the sidelines, I threw caution aside and dove in, my hair slipping loose from my braids, my feet fumbling with the unfamiliar steps, happy to be lost in the dance.

Vacation Land

Quartier-Morin, 1982

THE INITIAL EUPHORIA swept us along like bath toys bumped and spinning in a rain-clogged ditch for a good few weeks before we realized that we were stranded. We knew nothing of the four stages of cultural adaptation and had no clue how brief the honeymoon stage would be—that golden age of astonishment during which each new discovery would be greeted with effervescent eagerness—nor that this would be followed by frustration, an awkward period of adjustment, and (if we were lucky) acceptance.

Kreyòl language lessons, which we badly needed, started on day two and consisted of a few words repeated onto a battery-powered tape recorder, which we were sent out on the road to parrot.

—*Bonjou, mwen memn se Agwonòm Jon. M'ap aprann pale Kreyòl. Se sa sèlman mwen kapab di.* Hello, my name is Farmer Jon. I'm learning to speak Kreyòl. That's all I can say.

If people paused to talk with us, we smiled miserably. The most important phrase, the one we repeated most often, was: *Pale dousman, souple.* Speak slowly, please. Usually, people just talked louder.

We learned quickly that when the sun fell into the sea, darkness abruptly followed. Without flashlights or streetlamps, we stumbled on loose rocks and slowly picked our way home. Bicycles raced without headlights over the hard-packed dirt, a jangling noise the only warning of their approach. My mother grabbed our arms and pulled us into her skirt, terrified that she'd lose one of us under the spinning spokes. Her sharp inhalation sent a shiver down my spine.

On cassette tapes mailed home to the grandparents, we recorded our amazement: giant hummingbirds whirred along the hibiscus hedges and glow bugs sparkled in the grass. When it rained, wide green banana leaves were held overhead instead of umbrellas.

Exactly two weeks after we arrived, just after we'd taken our places around the dining room table, a high-pitched scream broke through the buzzing roar of the cicadas.

My father pushed back his chair to have a look.

—Jon! my mother called after him as the screen door slammed shut, vibrating convulsively on a rusty spring: thrumming, thrumming, then a rattle like a fading drum roll.

—Come outside and see! he called from under the mango tree. Meadow and I ran out after him. Rosie put up her arms to be held.

—What is it? we asked, staring up into the dense, dark canopy.

There above us, half hidden in the leaves, was a frog clenched in the jaws of a small green snake. Our mouths slacked open with awe as it unhitched its jawbone and begun to suck that slippery, green, very alive tree frog slithering and screeching into its gullet.

We did not move until the last writhing finger pads had disappeared and the high-pitched, nails-on-a-chalkboard death spasm had ended. Behind the gleaming yellow eyes of the now rather satisfied snake was an untidy bulge, no longer writhing.

We stared at each other, eyes dilated. My father grinned and asked, —Wow, how's that for a natural history lesson?

I was starting to realize that anything could happen in this brightly colored country. Naked boys raced tin-can toy cars down the middle of the streets, and no one stopped them or made them put on clothes. *Kamyon* drivers blared carnival-music horns and barreled down on unsuspecting bicyclists like an orchestra gone insane. Even the mud houses were the color of bubblegum ice cream. Haiti, it seemed to me, was a cacophony of joy.

Flagging down a crowded *tap tap* to visit the open-air market in Cap-Haïtien was an adventure in itself. My mother was careful not to let her hair touch the scuzzy painted-on curtains of the improvised bus: two benches wedged into the back of a sagging pickup, baskets jammed against knees, a chicken or a goat dangling upside down from the roof. Market women heaved Meadow and me onto their knees with powerful arms, and I'd burrow against the damp body heat, jostled by the rhythm of the worn-out shocks and the thumping stereo. When we tapped the side of the *tap tap* to clamber out, we lifted our sandals to avoid the gray-green refuse that floated down the gutters to the sea.

Sweet potatoes, grapefruit, and pineapple were stacked like jewels on squares of plastic. Barefoot children reached for Rosie's blond curls. (Meadow and I got more wary attention; red hair, we'd been told, meant *kwashiorkor*—protein deficiency—an emblem of shame in Haiti.)

The market women insisted that my mother distribute her purchases equally: ten oranges from one *machann*; ten from the next vendor. Marmites of rice were sold just like the gospel parables—a good measure pressed down, shaken together, and running over the sides of a clean-scoured coffee can. If I tried to haggle over a mango or a scrap of lace, the market women laughed and egged me on, their hips spread uncomfortably over low chairs, the smoke from their pipes drifting into a loose halo as they translated my butchered Kreyòl into music.

Everything in me wanted to holler a resounding yes to this new world and dive headfirst into the quicksilver flourishes of the language, but when I watched the grown-ups out of the corner of my eye—the ones who looked like me; the other missionaries—I saw that something in them seemed to hesitate and hold back.

On my mother's twenty-ninth birthday, we drove into Cap-Haïtien so we could call the grandparents collect from a hotel pay phone, but the operator spent an hour trying to establish a crackling, erratic connection, and a stray dog kept jumping up on Rosie. Afterward, my mother was disillusioned when she tried to walk along the Cap-Haïtien seawall. The reek of the clogged gutters was impossible to ignore, and faded plastic bobbed in the surf.

Longing for serenity, she led me down the dirt road in front of the Ag Center on the bony back of the Centre Agricole donkey. Old women squatted in front of charcoal fires, and boys called out across a cactus fence. They told us we should give them the donkey, plus the pants that my mother was wearing. I was confused and annoyed. My mother didn't know how to respond. The staggering inequity between their lives and ours demanded an explanation.

And yet poverty was more or less what we had expected to find. Conversations around the missionary dinner table made it seem obvious that Haiti was a country in need of our help. This was, after all, why we had come.

What caught us off guard was the sharp divide between those who had so little and those whose luxuries far outstripped our own.

It didn't take my mother long to give up on homeschooling. A small English-speaking school run by missionaries catered to expats as well as to local business owners, and within weeks, we had been inducted into a community of well-traveled Dominicans and Haitians who could lean back casually by their private pools to discuss politics and art in either French or English, then switch to Kreyòl to give orders to the servants.

At a birthday party perched on the palatial slopes of Bel Air, high above Cap-Haïtien, one elegant Dominicana confided to my mother that when she had moved to the U.S. for grad school, she was surprised to discover that she was expected to wash her own dishes. My mother laughed, at a loss for what to say. We felt like backwoods yokels.

Beyond the lights and music of the birthday party, my parents could just make out over the slums and the sugarcane fields the Baptist Ag Center, whose lights twinkled religiously until the generator shut off promptly at nine p.m. A man with dark sunglasses explained dryly that electricity had not yet been granted to the common folk; it was not one of the priorities of the dictatorship.

My sisters and I paid little attention to this monotonous grown-up conversation, for we were wedged onto a leather couch between twin four-year-old girls with gold jewelry, our eyes glued to a television as big as our dining room table. We stared, slack-jawed, as the indomitable Mighty Mouse performed yet another feat of derring-do, rescuing his hapless victims with unruffled aplomb. The heroic narrative was hard to resist. (We had certainly succumbed.)

I felt like a diplomat instead of a hick missionary! my mother confessed afterward to the grandparents, a bit stupefied at this sudden ascendancy to a life of privilege.

As farm stock, we were unaccustomed to being treated like dignitaries. My parents knew how to plant their feet on the earth and work, hard. They valued self-reliance and stubbornness. They looked up to no one. Nor did they expect anyone to look up to them.

And yet there was an undeniable deference shown to us as missionaries. The Haitian pastors who visited the Ag Center, from working-class families, came only as far as the gate, where they waited and did not enter without permission. Was there some unspoken rule we didn't know about? Were they afraid of the dogs? I couldn't imagine anyone being scared of the black Labradors that licked our ears and noses—so much friendlier than the farm dogs under Grandma Lois's porch. But the Haitians tapped and waited until someone emerged from the missionary domain.

At first it felt uncomfortable. Then it began to feel routine. We had become the *blan*—the wealthy foreigners—even if, in our own country, all that we owned was an eight-foot-wide trailer and a cabin with a pit toilet. For even that small hoard, meager though it might be, so far outstripped the earnings of subsistence farmers, fishermen, pastors, and market women that in truth we had been privileged all along, and we hadn't even realized it.

To make matters even more complicated, we had servants for the first time in our lives. At the insistence of the outgoing missionaries, my parents paid a cook, Adeline, as well as a woman named Ma Homer to wash the evening dishes—lest the two women lose their livelihoods while the Heneises were on furlough—and my father supervised a staff of ag technicians and gardeners, but it wasn't the life that my parents had imagined servants of God to lead.

Adeline, who spent hours stirring cornmeal mush in an aluminum pot over a charcoal stove while her three-year-old son, Nosben, played beside her, never complained. Adeline's husband worked in the U.S. and sent back money, but he didn't have a green card and couldn't legally bring the rest of the family over to join him.

It did not escape my mother's attention that while someone else cooked our dinner, her daughters leaned over her arm and narrated whimsical stories to inscribe in graceful calligraphy; our job was to illustrate these and other fantasies. While Adeline hunched over a plastic tub in the yard to scrub our clothes into a sudsy lather, my mother had time to teach us to sew on a treadle machine set up under the mango tree. We pumped furiously, our feet propped against the foot pedals, amazed as the round wheel spun and sang. With our mother's fingers to guide it, the needle bobbed and pierced the clean-cut fabric, leaving ribbons of thread in its wake. When she stomped her foot down firmly to force the rocking pedal into submission, from under her fingers emerged a dress with a bright ruffled hem.

One afternoon when it rained more than five inches in a single day, my sisters and I played in the yard in our bathing suits. I can still remember the throbbing, tingling pleasure of standing under the gutter with my eyes squinted shut, the water coursing over my bare head as I squeezed the sweet, dark mud between my toes.

My parents later found out that houses had collapsed in Cap-Haïtien because there were not enough trees on the surrounding hillsides to slow the force of the pounding rain.

How miserable for the Haitians with leaking roofs and mud everywhere, my mother wrote in the family journal. *Where do they sleep at night? Where do they lay their mats? How can I ever complain about small houses?*

Hearing about a local Baptist women's group that sewed clothes for the poor, my mother herded the three of us girls along to see if we could help. The *Dames Dorcas,* as they called themselves, were already hard at work when we arrived. Thirty women hovered around two treadle sewing machines. Those with scissors knelt on the dirt courtyard to snip, without patterns, around the outline of finished dresses. The unpinned fabric was then handed to the women at the sewing machines, who turned over the finishing work to assistants on the periphery, needles flashing as they mended hand-me-down children's clothes and frayed pants.

As soon as we arrived, the fluid movement eddied to a halt. Bustling, officious women swiped the chairs from the ladies at the sewing machines and lifted them over the heads of the others so that we could sit down.

My mother tried to refuse, but the leaders waved away her protestations. We were their guests. My mother submitted, uncomfortably queenlike, and perched on a woven grass chair. Meadow and I were lifted and plunked down beside her. The leaders nodded approval. The old pattern of colonialism, however distasteful, was a well-worn rut.

Worse yet, our arrival signaled the beginning of a Bible study. A woman with a commanding voice broke into a dramatic opening prayer as lace handkerchiefs were adjusted atop tight braids. I waited until my mother wasn't looking, then slid down to scrape at a trapped stone with my fingernails. Meadow followed suit, and before the prayer was finished, we were squabbling over who had commandeered whose territory. Rosie went after the chickens. They squawked noisily as she gave chase, fluttering irresistibly toward a steaming *chodyè* of rice and beans on a bed of hot coals. Motionless Haitian children watched our antics from a small square of fabric, presumably having been warned not to move.

As soon as the Bible study ended, my mother whisked us away, stammering apologies. On the slow, sweaty walk home, she felt surprised at her sharp envy of the women in the dirt courtyard. She tried to explain it to the grandparents on a cassette tape: The *Dames Dorcas* had one another. And they had found ways to care for their community using the little resources they had.

Despite my mother's misgivings, she didn't give up trying to help. She donated money and bought fabric at the open-air market, and brought along her autoharp when the *Dames Dorcas* prayed and sang for the sick. The women seemed delighted that she, a *blan*, wanted to join their group. But it was clear to my mother that they didn't need her.

What am I doing here in Haiti? she asked the family journal. *Has God brought me to Haiti to enjoy the luxurious lifestyle? I don't think so. Aren't we servants of Christ? I'm not serving anybody. They're all serving me. I need to have a long talk with God and get my assignment straight.*

We had left the honeymoon stage. The frustrations had begun to accumulate. I developed heat rash, Meadow vomited in her bed, my mother discovered cockroaches in the silverware drawer, and Rosie learned—by mimicry—to yank open the silverware drawers and scream.

When my mother plugged in the iron in the kitchen, it turned on the light in the bedroom. —Who's the electrician around here? she complained loudly to no one in particular.

Feel like I'll never speak Kreyòl or take control of this place, my father confided in the journal after a dispiriting morning of cleaning the cobwebs off the chicken coops while the Haitian ag workers pelted him with questions he couldn't begin to understand.

Just before the real missionaries left on furlough, there had been a tense conversation about leadership, after which my mother jotted down, surprised: *They thought it was fortunate we didn't speak Kreyòl well so we wouldn't create friendships that would undermine our effectiveness at being boss.*

Perhaps she had misunderstood—by then there were already a host of miscommunications between the two families—but my mother didn't feel free to ignore the unsettling advice: We were, after all, novices.

Never before had we lived in a world so adept at throwing us off balance.

The solitary Centre Agricole loomed above a plain of half-harvested sugarcane like a billboard for idealism. Farmers in the adjoining fields worked long hours in the heat, pulling rough wooden plows behind bony oxen, as if struggling to escape the cycle of poverty. My father tried unsuccessfully to recruit them to his agriculture extension seminars on vegetable cultivation, but the only people who seemed to sign up were young men in tailored slacks and button-up shirts who took copious notes but had no intention, as my father saw it, of muddying their hands with fieldwork.

What my parents did not yet understand was that these educated sons of church elders, whose parents had scrimped and sacrificed to give their children the possibility of a better life, aspired to a world with more opportunities. Agronomy classes were a door behind which lay knowledge and, quite possibly, if they were lucky, business connections. For the young men had observed an economic corollary that the missionaries had failed to anticipate—which was that no Haitian farmer, no matter how innovative, could hope to equal the salary of a foreign agronomist who was paid in U.S. dollars and provided, free of charge, with housing and a vehicle. The American God appeared to be very affluent indeed, and the young aspirants seemed to have fallen sway to a logical, if unreliable, conclusion: If they threw in their lot with the missionaries, opportunities should follow.

My father grumbled that they just wanted desk jobs, preferably with a fan. He would have much rather saved his insights for the subsistence farmers who had no choice but to throw in their lot with the land, but none came to his seminars. Perhaps because the farmers with holes in their shirts and broken sandals couldn't afford to leave their fields (or were skeptical of a sales pitch from foreign do-gooders, who seldom stayed long enough to find out if their ideas made any difference).

We had come, or so we told ourselves, to improve Haiti: noblesse oblige. But there were unanticipated consequences to this new role. If, for example, the son of a missionary commanded the son of one of the Haitian agricultural technicians to get off the tricycle, my sisters and I noted with surprise that he obeyed.

Three-year-old Meadow decided to give this new technique a try.

—*Desann!* she commanded in a high, squeaky voice. —Get off!

A Haitian boy named FanFan, several years older than my sister, studied her pale outstretched arm and the timid look on her face. He paused, then obeyed.

My mother, watching through the screen windows, ran outside, horrified.

—Meadow! You can't do that! she explained in a strangled voice. —He's a person! He's a kid, too.

Meadow's face crumpled into guilt. My mother insisted that FanFan climb back on. His alert face appeared to be calculating this new shift in power.

My mother combed Meadow's hair out of her eyes, feeling confused and overwhelmed. The children of the Ag Center technicians didn't have bikes of their own, and the tricycle in question didn't technically belong to us. As my mother understood it, FanFan had been taught by his Haitian parents to respect the *blan*. If she let him play with her girls as an equal, she would upset the delicate balance.

She had imagined, before we left the U.S., that in no time at all we'd make Haitian friends and learn to speak Kreyòl, but navigating the minefield of power and privilege required skills she didn't possess. Perhaps, she concluded, it would be easier not to let her daughters play with the local children. It wasn't what she'd hoped for, but a wealthy Dominican family had already insisted on weekly play dates to help their children learn English—a far easier compromise than figuring out how to create harmony in an unjust world.

She shooed us inside to play with Barbies and listen to a children's Bible hour in English while she helped Adeline finish dinner. The screen door banged shut behind us. FanFan was left alone on the tricycle, his emotions no doubt as conflicted as our own.

It was one split-second decision; our first betrayal of the missionary ideal: *Love your neighbor as yourself.*

In our inaugural newsletter home from the mission field, two months after we arrived, my mother included a paragraph titled "Vacation Land!?," in which she confessed her embarrassment over living the life of a rich woman. She explained why we had come—to oversee the weekly sale of 280 dozen eggs, to promote chickens and rabbits as affordable sources of protein, and to offer reforestation seminars to farmers whose lands were stripped of trees—then added: *Our only reassurance is this, if God brought us here, He must know what He is doing!*

Our first family portrait in Haiti, despite our mounting doubts, was the very picture of earnest idealism (how easy it was to slip into the expected role). Sun-bonneted and smiling, I clasped my hands primly and posed in front of the Centre Agricole sign. Rosie sat on our father's shoulders and played with his hair as he squinted, sunburned and blond, into the camera. Meadow stared down at her sandals, her cheeks still round with baby fat. My mother's face was shadowed under her new straw hat, but she, too, was smiling. We were only a few months into the missionary venture. A farmer, his wife, and their three daughters, all lined up for the benefit of faraway church members who didn't understand any more than we did what it meant to try to save the world.

We didn't realize that the cloud chariots had already begun to dissipate. We had only just begun to be humbled by disappointed ideals.

Rabbit Banquet

Quartier-Morin, 1982

WHEN MY FATHER bent over the Ag Center account books in the evenings with a calculator and a half-bitten pencil, the rabbit project and the caged chickens were his biggest headaches. My mother rubbed his shoulders, pointing out new gray hairs over his ears that she'd never noticed before. The rabbit project, it seemed, lost more money than it brought in. My father had already canceled the food pellets flown in on the missionary plane—the rabbits adjusted just fine to a diet of wild green kudzu—and he was determined to replace the prohibitively expensive tin-roofed cages with thatch. It irritated him that the rabbits had better roofs than the local farmers.

The chicken project was even more vexing. The imported hens in wire cages produced significantly more eggs than the half-wild Haitian breed that ran loose through dirt courtyards, but there was little demand in the rural north for such volume (plus, like true foodies, the locals preferred the quality of the free-range egg).

To make the numbers work, my father had to load the egg cartons into the back of the Ag Center pickup each week and drive the length of the country across the harrowing roads to sell to the hotels in Port-au-Prince. No Haitian, he had been warned, could be entrusted with the task.

Late one night, when my father was supposed to be on his way home from the capital, my mother shook me awake. I didn't know that she was still waiting for the sound of the truck on the gravel driveway.

Without a phone, there was no way for him to tell us that he was safe in the capital, staying with missionary friends. She was left to imagine the worst: a military checkpoint gone sour, the truck tipped over; stranded with three small girls in a country where she barely spoke the language. Her voice was tense when she nudged me awake.

—Apricot! she whispered.

I groaned and rubbed my eyes.

—Come and see!

I stumbled down the hallway, through the kitchen, into a dark corridor where the charcoal stove was kept. While she'd been awake worrying about Dad, the female Labrador had gone into labor. The exhausted mother panted and whined on a pile of torn sheets as one slick wet sac, then another, slid from between her legs. I stared, mesmerized by her snapping teeth as she gnawed at the glistening purplish cords.

When the dog had tongued the last of her babies clean and a squirming litter of blind puppies mewled against her teats, I crawled back into bed and fell into a dreamless sleep. Mom stayed up to make sure that the new mother, in her nervous anxiety, didn't kill any of her offspring by mistake.

Slept very bad all night with puppies and no Jon, she wrote in the *Happy Family* journal. *Woke up in morning sick as could be—just like I was pregnant, sick to my stomach and tired.*

Although my mother remained ambivalent about Haiti, by six months into that first year as missionaries, it was obvious to nearly everyone that my father was hooked. He collected new vocabulary like seeds, storing away the words for "crops," "weather," and "dirt." Coworkers encouraged his fumbling Kreyòl and laughed at his corny jokes. And while he was certainly guilty of complaining at a moment's notice about how the Ag Center was managed, he didn't seem to mind the jaw-rattling roads or the strangers who dropped by without warning. The improvisational nature of agricultural development work—everything dependent on the weather and politics—suited him just fine. As a farmer, he understood that life was unpredictable.

The heavy clay soil of the Ag Center was cracked and arid in the dry season and impassably muddy in the rainy season, and the American-bought tractor was forever in need of unavailable replacement parts. My father slammed doors and yelled when he discovered that the rabbit and chicken manure was being burned as waste—but this, at least, was something he knew how to fix. He taught the technicians how to mix the weeds that they pulled from the vegetable plots with chicken manure, so that it decomposed into rich, dark humus to spread on the gardens. Within weeks, the broccoli florets were as wide as his out-stretched hand.

And if the vehicles were left untended and the manicured grounds fell into disarray, well, so be it. The only progress that mattered, as far as he was concerned, was work that satisfied, food for the hungry, the slow but relentless transformation of shit into gold.

It didn't hurt that Haiti was well equipped with adventure, a defining virtue in our family. On weekends, having crested the ridgeline behind Cap-Haïtien, white-sand beaches disappeared into lapping waves. Hearing rumors of pirate ruins, we stuffed snorkels and towels into a picnic basket and paid someone to watch the car for us when the road dead-ended at a fishing village. Fishermen with thick, knotted arms rowed us across pristine Labadie Bay for a pittance. Our snorkels wheezed as we lifted wet tennis shoes over the sharp spikes of sea urchins. Bright fish darted through the coral. We bought fresh-caught lobster to roast over a fire of twigs, cracked open the shells, drizzled the meat with lime, and took our first bite of the good life, a crumbling pirate fortress at our backs.

The coral and fish and undersea gardens here are like what you see in National Geographic, my mother updated the grandparents. *(Maybe I should be a travel agent instead of a missionary!)*

The relative ease with which we had adjusted to life in Haiti did not go unnoticed when my parents rubbed shoulders with the other missionaries at the Sunday-evening English church (my mother, naturally, had been asked to help with the music), and when we received a coveted lunch invitation to the home of Dr. Bill and Joanna Hodges, who ran the Baptist hospital, my parents were bona fide starstruck.

In Limbé, cooks cleared away the lunch dishes from a fantastically long dining room table—built to feed the Hodges clan, plus a dozen or more medical volunteers at Hôpital le Bon Samaritain—after which the Doctor cleared his throat with ponderous dignity and led us into his study for a private exhibit of archaeological treasures. In his weathered palm he held a tarnished five-hundred-year-old coin, then demonstrated how he used electrolysis to remove the rust and dirt, revealing, as if from behind a veil, the fading image of King Ferdinand and Queen Isabella of Spain.

Joanna's curly gray hair tumbled over her shoulders when she got started on a good story.

—Sometimes you go into a missionary's home, and they're all down on their knees praying! But when you go into Doc Hodges's home and they're all down on their knees, they're looking at a map and they're saying: Well, how do you get here?

She had a movie-star smile and a laugh that sounded like a donkey braying. She handed out mimeographed stacks of the Doctor's more famous newsletters, including several on Columbus.

Proudly surveying her realm—which included half a dozen homes, a playground, a tree nursery, and an on-site missionary school—Joanna dropped the hint that if my parents wanted to return to Limbé after our term at the Ag Center was complete, my father could manage the hospital tree nursery.

My father raised his eyebrows hopefully. My mother looked dismayed. As soon as my sisters and I were given permission, we raced off to play with Joanna's half-a-dozen adopted children and grandchildren on the swing set under a towering green almond tree—the very epicenter of paradise, as far as I could tell.

That night, back at the Ag Center, my parents tucked us girls into bed and sat up late to confer. When the generator switched off, the trappings of modernity—lights, fans, cassette player—shuddered to a stop. (At the hospital, Joanna had informed them, the generators ran all night long.) My mother lit a wobbling kerosene flame and slapped away a mosquito. Outside, cicadas chirped.

My parents understood, better than they used to, what they had been offered. Hôpital le Bon Samaritain was one of the most coveted missionary appointments in the north of Haiti. If we were to move to Limbé, we would no longer be relegated to an isolated agricultural outpost. There would be other missionary kids to play with right outside our front door, and my father would finally be able to focus on reforestation, which he'd been hankering to do ever since he laid eyes on the stripped-bare mountains.

But my mother, despite her allegiance to Jesus, hadn't set her sights on missionary life. She was already counting down the days until we could break ground on our new house in the desert, and was looking forward to summer in Idyllwild. Another two-year stint in Haiti wasn't at all what she had in mind.

Until, that is, she snapped awake after a lucid dream in which a voice, which sounded very much like the voice of God, asked whether she wanted to be a bright light shining out across the water or a stagnant, going-nowhere stream, eddying and foamy.

She confided to my father that the Lord had shown her a vision. Maybe they were supposed to stay in Haiti.

The rabbit banquet may have helped sway her vote.

The problems with the floundering rabbit project were manifold. Though it was designed to supplement the perceived paucity of the Haitian diet with a cheap source of protein, rumors had nevertheless gotten out that ingesting rabbit meat would lead to raised boils on the skin. It seemed that the entire venture was just another missionary blunder—it looked great on paper but faltered as soon as it hit the ground.

To this day, my father claims that the rabbit banquet was his idea, but I suspect the credit belongs to my mother. Feeding guests is her gift and her calling. And she is usually able to talk my father into her schemes.

If a feast was to be served, they would need to cull the herd. They could also use the unsold rice from the Ag Center fields. For one night, at least, all the employees would eat well. And to pique the interest of the guests, my father offered a prize for anyone brave enough to taste the unfamiliar meat: a live rabbit to take home and raise.

He talked up the scheme during his morning Bible study with the ag technicians, and the men spent an entire afternoon separating the soft downy pelts from the lean, tender meat.

On the night of the feast, my father hoisted Rosie onto his shoulders and Meadow hugged our mother's shins as we made our way into the echoing cafeteria, transformed for a night into a banquet hall. The cooks set out steaming cauldrons of rice and beans followed by spoonfuls of warm, rich rabbit—fried in hot oil, then slow-cooked over charcoal with shallots and tomatoes until the meat shuddered loose from the bone, everything glistening under a golden glaze of fat.

The first in line for the bounty was skinny Mueller Jean-Jacques, a twenty-year-old Ag Center employee with big hair and an even bigger grin. I liked Mueller. He always stopped to chat if he found me wandering around the farm, and he cheered on my clunky, half-baked Kreyòl. My father complimented Mueller's two enormous plates of food as he took his seat at the table, for not a single grain could have been added to his perfectly mounded portion of rice and beans, after which came yet another plate heaped high with rabbit.

It was a feast to be remembered, a banquet to set the mouth aquiver with juices. Farmers, even when famished, seldom spent their money on food (a luxury of the shortsighted) but on this night, every stomach, including mine, was taut and swollen with the sacrificial rabbit. Meadow leaned against Mom, taking it all in. Rosie was already asleep, her blond curls draped over Dad's shoulder, her round belly leaving a stain of sweat on his chest.

As the men leaned back in their wooden chairs and sighed, their tongues loosened. They clapped each other's backs and shouted encouragement when one from among them stood to regale the others with a joke.

My parents, who spoke just enough perfunctory Kreyòl to have issued the instructions to prepare the meal, watched with dumbfounded pleasure as the evening unfolded. Guests at their own banquet, they strained for familiar words, studied the faces of the others for clues, and leaned down over our nodding heads as we tried to follow the words that flew through the air around us. The concrete walls resounded.

Mueller, no longer reduced to patiently pantomiming words for foreigners, was masterful. His raspy voice swelled, soared, and thundered, then dropped abruptly to a whisper. When he dove in for the punch line, it was with the confidence of a tightrope walker, the pride of an unchallenged king.

The room exploded with laughter as he sat down and another stood to take his place—to tell the unfinished story, to sing the unbroken song of Haiti.

A song of defiance and survival, which could never be adequately translated into the broken half-language of foreigners.

A master parable of persistence against all odds.

A riddle of resistance.

Annou leve kampe. Rise with me and we will take our stand.

My parents left the banquet hall that night—as did all of the guests— with a rabbit cage in hand, complete with a nose-twitching, leg- thumping bunny.

Ours lived under the mango tree in the front yard until our year of missionary service was complete. My sisters and I took it upon ourselves to see what rabbits might be willing to eat, given the opportunity (plenty, we discovered: plantain peels, mango skins, hibiscus leaves, petals). The rabbits, in return, peppered the decorative gravel with untidy round brown droppings that the real missionaries were left to clean up—horrified to discover that their carefully manicured front yard had become a compost heap, presided over by a cage of unsightly rabbits, which they relegated to the animal sheds where they belonged.

When Ken tried to lecture my father about the chaos we'd left behind, my father gave him a thin smile and shook his head, stubborn as a mule and just as unrepentant. Plus, we'd already promised Joanna that we'd be in Limbé by August, which was where his real work was to begin—to reforest woefully eroded Haiti, one scrawny tree at a time.

Front-Row Seats

Coachella Valley, 1983

A FTER OUR YEAR at the Ag Center was completed, we touched down in California for six short months. We had left the Coachella Valley as nobodies; we returned as homegrown celebrities. A low-budget regional paper, the *Press Enterprise*, devoted a sensationalized paragraph to us in the local gossip column, as explorers with firsthand accounts of distant lands. The write-up was as glib and condescending as anything that ever popped out of a missionary's mouth (and at least we knew better than to use words like "primitive" or "the natives," having acquired the bare minimum of sophistication after a year abroad):

> *Giant rats, mosquitoes, and malnutrition among children are facts of life in Haiti, but helping the natives learn to support themselves is very rewarding, reported Jon and Flip Anderson on their recent return to Coachella from that primitive land. The Andersons will go back to Haiti for another two-year stint of agricultural missionary work in August. Meanwhile, their three daughters, Apricot, 7, Meadow, 4, and Rose, 2, are learning about life here.*

What had we forgotten in one year's time? The buzzing drone of Grandpa Lee's baseball games on the radio, the damp whir of the swamp cooler. My mother went back to hanging up our wet clothes on the line. My father planted a crop of organic spaghetti squash that no one would buy—in our absence, the price had dropped from eighteen dollars a box to three dollars. It disgusted him that just on the other side of the ocean, farmers in Haiti didn't have enough to feed their families, whereas in the U.S., he had to disc a perfectly good crop into the dirt.

Joanna had offered to put us on the payroll at the missionary hospital, but only if we raised our own support—a savvy fund-raising strategy. I rather liked getting dolled up in my bright red Haiti Handicraft sundress, as if, by tying the straps over my thin shoulders, I could now claim to be a Haitian girl (the dresses, embroidered by Haitian artisans and promoted by Ivah, were worn almost exclusively by tourists and missionaries). I yelped when Mom held my chin firmly and stuck bobby pins into my braids to keep the tiny woven baskets from slipping off my head. I was annoyed that I needed the help; on trips to the beach, I had seen plenty of Haitian girls my age balance forty-pound loads down a steep mountain trail without once losing their footing.

Sometimes, all five of us took the stage like the Von Trapp family to sing hymns in Kreyòl, which the little old ladies loved. But to really wow the church audience, we'd grab the bony ankles of the chickens that we'd brought along as props and flip them upside down, wings fluttering, until they stopped squawking and we could proceed into the sanctuary, the carpet tickling our bare feet, the baskets on our heads tipping precariously as we turned to face the delighted applause. In church circles (albeit not in the wider world), being a missionary was almost as good as being a movie star.

My parents wrote endless thank-you notes for the crumpled five-dollar and twenty-dollar bills that filled the velvet donation bags at the end of each presentation, not to mention the more substantial pledges of fifteen dollars a month, but I began to feel like a jackrabbit in the Palm Shadow Produce vegetable patch: trapped in the glare of the spotlight. I squirmed away from the too-soft hands of church ladies who patted our shoulders and assured us that they were praying. The audience was too gullible, too easily charmed by our showmanship. Our stage act was a parody of the splendid, cacophonous world we had left behind.

I couldn't begin to explain all the things that I missed about Haiti— the lizards that puffed green throats against the ceiling, the crack of thunder and the roar of rain on tin, snorkeling in bathtub-warm beach water, the buzzing cicadas, *tap taps* bouncing over potholes with music blaring—but it seemed like the only stories our church supporters wanted to hear were about how sad and poor everyone must be in Haiti, and about how much good we must have done, bringing God's light into such a dark place. I gave up trying. They didn't get it.

Joanna, at least, knew exactly what stories to tell, and sent a personalized form letter from Limbé for the donations our church in Coachella had collected for orphans in Haiti, complete with a poem:

> *Dear Children of Daily Vacation Bible School*
>
> *This month to you we send our thanks,*
> *Your gift has done the trick*
> *It's helped to buy so many things*
> *To provide succor for the sick*
>
> *Each day the lines grow longer*
> *As they mill about the yard*
> *The sick ones sprawl and moan and groan*
> *"Which one?" to choose is hard*
>
> *But each day many seek health here*
> *So the Doctors thump and probe*
> *The lab pricks fingers for their blood*
> *To diagnose by a small microbe*
>
> *They stand in line to get their pills*
> *And holler at a needle*
> *But they fuss the most whene'er they learn*
> *Their health is back and there's no return!*
>
> *Greetings from Limbe, Haiti and the Hôpital le Bon Samaritain. We are more than thankful for your most recent* **check** *gift of* **$115.00** *which we will use* **to help buy milk for our**

orphaned children—the babies in the maternity nursery whose mothers died when they were born. Thank you so very much—they will grow big and strong with all this good milk.

Thank you so much.

Most gratefully,
Joanna & Bill Hodges

Grandma Lois had already photocopied and passed around to relatives and supporters a stack of Dr. Hodges's newsletters (sample titles: "Of God, the Tropics and Wood," "The Cultural Significance of Christian Medical Care," and "*Charité*—Do the Haitians Have Gratitude?"), leaving my parents with an additional responsibility: to explain how a missionary doctor in rural Limbé had time to publish such insightful essays about Haitian culture and history.

Nor was his reputation limited to church circles. When the president of Senegal, Léopold Senghor, visited Cap-Haïtien, no less a person than the president of Haiti, Jean-Claude Duvalier, had requested Dr. Hodges's presence at an exhibition of historical articles.

But it was the Doctor's most recent accomplishment that was the clincher. Joanna broke the good news via newsletter: a team from the University of Florida had arrived to excavate the site that Dr. Hodges believed was Columbus's first settlement in the New World—an archaeological puzzle that had haunted historians for five centuries. My father grinned whenever he let this detail slip. We would have front-row seats on history.

La Navidad

Ayiti, 1492

I T HAD STARTED off so well—Columbus, kneeling on a beach on the north coast of Ayiti, to claim the island for the crown and Christendom. The curious Taínos who gathered to watch. The hawks' bells and glass beads; the hammered thin fragments of gold they pressed into his hands.

Later that afternoon, rocking at anchor in the blue, quiet Baie de L'Acul, Columbus rhapsodized that in twenty-three years at sea he had never seen a harbor so protected and vast that it could contain, he wrote, *all the ships of Christendom.*

As he set down his quill, more than a hundred canoes closed in around the *Niña,* the *Pinta,* and the *Santa María.* According to Columbus's records, over the next several days more than a thousand Taínos arrived to pay their respects to the visiting Spaniards, holding gifts above their heads: cotton cloth, parrots, cassava bread and fish, earthenware jars of water infused with aromatic seeds, and gold. Some, he claimed, swam the distance, though he estimated that the ships were anchored several miles from shore.

For two days and one night—perhaps longer; the dates in the ship's log grow confused—the Spaniards did not sleep. In the log, Columbus made particular note of the Taíno women, who, he explained, were quite beautiful.

Exhausted, just before sunrise on Christmas Eve, Columbus gave the command to weigh anchor. A chieftain named Guacanagarí, from a vil-

lage nine miles distant, was said to have summoned representatives from
all of the Taíno kingdoms, and a gathering was to be convened—or so
Columbus understood from the men he had kidnapped earlier in his
travels and kept as translators. Envoys were already said to be en route
from the interior, where there were rumored to be gold mines.

When the wind rose, the three ships crept up the coast toward what
is now Cap-Haïtien. For days the air had been too stagnant to fill the
sails, and Columbus was eager to make up for lost time.

Just before midnight, when the first watch ended, Columbus took
to his cabin with a splitting headache. Soon thereafter, the sailor he had
left in charge, who also had a headache, gave the wheel to the ship's
boy—a lapse in judgment that had been expressly prohibited, but the
sea was calm, and the captain was sleeping.

When the vessel ran aground some hours later, it happened so gently that the jolt felt like a caress. Only as the rudder dug into the sand
and the waves began to push the ship broadside did the boy cry out and
the crew realize their fate.

Columbus tried in vain to save her. The men hung lanterns over the
side to gauge the depth of the water and shouted warnings in the dark.
By the dim light of unfamiliar stars, Columbus gave the order that the
ship's mast be cut to lighten her.

But it was too late; the water was too shallow. The boat seams strained
with the force of the waves. The great burgeoning *Santa María,* named
for the Virgin who had given birth on this night, heaved and swayed,
swollen with unplanned cargo. The waters broke. The hull opened. The
flagship was lost.

By dawn on Christmas Day, Columbus and his men stood on the
deck of the much smaller *Niña,* which had sailed back, somewhat reluctantly, to assist with the rescue. Columbus sent a rowboat to beg the
cacique Guacanagarí for help.

By noon, Taíno canoes had rescued every single flask and barrel
from the broken ship, every flake of gold and woven basket of spices.
Columbus concluded that not a single treasure had been lost. Moreover,
the great chief had emptied several of his own houses and provided

guards to stand watch over his guests' possessions. Columbus was moved as Guacanagarí wept openly at the Spaniards' loss.

When it came time to summarize this seeming catastrophe for the benefit of the king and queen of Spain, Columbus castigated not only his men, who had against orders left a mere boy at the helm, but also the people of Palos, Spain, who had provided him with such a faulty and cumbersome vessel, so ill suited to the work of discovery.

Guacanagarí and the Taínos received nothing but praise:

> *They are an affectionate people, free from avarice and agreeable to everything. I certify to Your Highness that in all the world I do not believe there is a better people or a better country. They love their neighbors as themselves, and they have the softest and gentlest voices in the world and are always smiling. They may go naked, but Your Highnesses may be assured that they have very good customs among themselves, and their cacique maintains a most marvelous state, where everything takes place in an appropriate and well-ordered manner.*

He concluded piously, having chosen thirty-nine men to leave behind:

> *I recognized that Our Lord had caused me to run aground at this place so that I might establish a settlement here . . . All this was the will of God: the ship's running aground so easily that it could not be felt, with neither wind nor wave; the cowardice of the ship's master and some of the crew . . . ; the discovery of this country.*

Columbus understood the importance of putting a good spin on the narrative for the sake of the donors. The first European settlement in the New World had been conceived in desperation, but it was christened in triumph: La Villa de la Navidad.

By the will of God, victory had been snatched from the wreckage. The fortress, built to protect the thirty-nine men he was obliged to leave behind, would be constructed with wood salvaged from the wrecked *Santa María*. The additional precaution of a tower and a moat would protect the Spaniards from an (as yet inconceivable) attack. Columbus fully anticipated that when he returned, he would find barrels of gold awaiting collection, the first payment of tribute from the mines. He had laid claim to Hispaniola, and its people had showered him with gifts.

All this Columbus recorded in his logbook as his two remaining ships set sail, heavily laden with the spoils of conquest: gold and parrots, tobacco, a few slaves taken at gunpoint from smaller islands.

For a brief moment—before anyone challenged his version of the truth—he would be the most celebrated man alive.

In Defense of Missionaries

Limbé, 1950–1983

Hôpital le Bon Samaritain, before the missionaries intervened, had begun as a much humbler enterprise: a Haitian pastor dispensing donated medicine from under a mango tree in his front yard. But it was not long before the missionary influence was felt.

In 1950 Pastor Ludovic St. Phard joined forces with fiery Ivah Heneise, who lived four miles away at the Baptist seminary. Ivah had a certain gift for persuasion (my parents were among the many who eventually fell under her spell) and a seemingly inexhaustible supply of energy. With two infant sons to cuddle and a seminary to run, she and her husband parted company on Sundays so that tall, soft-spoken Harold could drive the Jeep to a church on the other side of a mountain, while Ivah left the children with a cook and rode her bicycle four miles to the Baptist church in Limbé to teach Sunday school.

Ivah, too, opened a small outdoor clinic near her home, and though the two small clinics, in Limbé and Haut-Limbé, could do little more than offer quinine for malaria and pills for worms and dysentery, they were quickly overwhelmed by patients who walked or were carried down the steep mountain trails. Their collective medical expertise was negligible, but the needs were impossible to ignore.

Pastor St. Phard used his influence in Limbé to form a Haitian Baptist committee to purchase a *karo* of land—slightly more than three acres—for a future hospital. Ivah's job was to squirrel away the meager

Sunday school offerings until the small pile of gourdes and centimes began to take on the promise of materiality.

Three years later, land was purchased, and parishioners from the Limbé Baptist church heaved smooth round river rocks on their heads, the foundation stones falling with a thud onto the dusty building site that would one day become the Hospital of the Good Samaritan.

The red ribbon was cut in 1954 by none other than the president of Haiti, Paul Magloire. Ivah baked a giant homemade cake in a dishpan (whose inelegant proportions she concealed under thick swirls of patriotic blue and red frosting), and Magloire sipped four glasses of good Baptist grape juice—served in lieu of the explicitly requested presidential champagne. Hôpital le Bon Samaritain was open for business.

Finding a trained doctor who was willing to administrate the tin-roofed Baptist hospital was an entirely different challenge.

Haitian politics did not aid the cause. President Magloire, accused of misappropriation of funds in the aftermath of Hurricane Hazel, lost the support of his military generals. When a coup d'état seemed imminent, he left Haiti in the capable, merciless hands of Papa Doc Duvalier.

Duvalier's secret police, the Tonton Macoutes, paid midnight visits to enemies of the state. *Time* magazine christened Haiti *the snake pit of the Caribbean*. Pastor St. Phard, unlike the Heneises, did not have the safeguard of American citizenship to protect his family. He weighed his options and emigrated. It was an age of exodus.

If Ivah felt momentarily daunted by this rapid-fire reversal of fortunes, she didn't mention it in her letters home to her mother, later published as a slim paperback: *By the Light of My Kerosene Lamp*. She and Harold simply packed up their family, now grown to four children, and set off for a year of furlough at a Baptist seminary to reassess. It was there, in the tinder-dry foothills of California, that Ivah's gift of persuasion met its highest match.

The dour young William Herman Hodges and his pink-cheeked wife, Joanna, still awaiting a missionary assignment from the American Baptists, were not, at first glance, the most likely candidates to administrate a barely-on-its-feet Baptist hospital in rural Haiti. The doctor, like Columbus, had his sights set on the Far East, not the Caribbean. Having served during World War II as a meteorologist in Japan—which he deemed a very clean and civilized country—he and his family had joined a Japanese Baptist church in Los Angeles while he completed his medical residency. He and Joanna even went so far as to give their four children culturally appropriate middle names: Reiko, Kikuye, Kazuo, and Takeo.

The only unforeseen obstacle was that the American Baptists didn't own a missionary hospital in Japan and didn't intend to open one. Missionary posts to the Philippines and Burma likewise fell through. Which is right about when Ivah Heneise spun into Bill and Joanna's orbit.

The four Hodges children, roughly the same ages as the four Heneise children, sized each other up in the hallways of the Baptist seminary, recognizing allies. Ivah thrilled at the thought that she might have found, at long last, her dreamed-of administrator for the Limbé hospital: a bona fide missionary doctor—as yet without an assigned post.

It wasn't an easy sell.

Joanna remembers grumbling after Ivah's preliminary sales pitch. —Who wants to go to Haiti? If you're a missionary, you want to get on a boat and *go* somewhere. Haiti's practically in Florida's backyard, that's not going anywhere!

But Ivah knew how to bait the trap.

It was no secret that the doctor happened to be a history buff, so Ivah casually let it slip that in almost five hundred years, no archaeologist had ever been able to find the ruins of Columbus's first fortress in the New World, La Navidad.

It was a well-aimed lure. Columbus was one of Dr. Hodges's childhood heroes. Without telling Ivah, he dropped by the public library and returned with a heavy stack of books. The children peered over their father's shoulder at pictures of donkeys loaded with green cooking bananas and women who balanced wicker baskets on their heads. He was the kind of man to read gross domestic product statistics aloud to his children, and Haiti's numbers were depressing, even for the post–World

War II era—a mere $236 per person per year. There was also the grue-some history of slavery, revolutions, dictators, and poverty to consider. But it was the 1950s. Optimism was in.

After a week of deliberating, Dr. Hodges closed the history books and announced to the excitable Joanna (or at least this is how she re-members the conversation): *I think we'll go to Haiti. We're going to find Christopher Columbus's fort.*

If he had second thoughts, Joanna never faltered. As the daughter of an itinerant pastor, missionaries had been the heroes of her childhood. At eight years old, she had stood up in front of her father's church and announced that she wanted to share God's love in some dark corner of the world.

Two decades later, she radiated confidence at her commissioning ceremony. Dark hair framed high cheekbones as the camera bulbs flashed and the room broke into applause.

In the photograph taken just before they left, Joanna smiled broadly, her hand resting lightly on the head of her youngest son. Paul was three, barely old enough to remember the country he was about to leave behind. Beside them were trunks packed with crinoline skirts, medical textbooks, and unbreakable dishes meant to last a lifetime. Barbara, a timid eight-year-old, buried her hands in her pockets and rocked on the edges of her feet. Susan, one year older, faced forward with her feet firmly planted and grinned. Only seven-year-old David held luggage in his hands—his mother's purse, lest it be left behind in the excitement.

Joanna remembered fondly the white camellia tucked into the but-tonhole of her red Christmas coat; she loved how it whirled around her when she walked into a room. The Doctor jammed his hands into his pockets and leaned on the edge of one foot. He looked distinctly uncomfortable at the center of so much attention.

Dr. Hodges's first night in Haiti was a hard one. Ivah met them at the airport, but after six hours on substandard roads, the young doctor dis-covered that the much advertised hospital was little more than a few concrete rooms with bare lightbulbs dangling from the ceiling. The squalor and noise seemed almost unbearable. Bedded down on army cots in Ivah's living room, Dr. Hodges worried that he had ruined his life and the lives of his children. His heavy sighs distracted Joanna, who was happily counting fireflies.

And yet despite his misgivings, he wasn't a quitter. Within weeks, he had evicted the wriggling tadpoles from the hospital water tank and repaired the broken generator. He dutifully waded into his first day at the new clinic with a French-English dictionary under his arm—his new Bible, as it were. The laboriously memorized Japanese kanji with which he had prepared himself for missionary service were now as useless as outgrown crutches.

Strangers in the Limbé marketplace lifted up his daughters' skirts to see their crinoline undergarments, and his children came home crying after other kids rubbed their skin to see if the white would come off. Joanna was usually able to cheer him up again.

—Well, he would concede, —we'll give the Lord two more weeks.

He called himself an optimistic pessimist.

When it was Joanna's turn to feel overwhelmed, he would pour her a cup of coffee, listen to her litany of complaints, and then advise her to go wash her face and do something nice for somebody (she liked to bake cookies).

Joanna and Ivah patched together an improvised school for the children, with biology labs at the hospital and archaeological forays on the weekends. The missionary school also included a family who had fled genocide to begin a new life in Haiti. Uncle S____, as he was known among the missionary children, was an exceedingly charming man who would dangle upside down from the branches of trees when they went on outings to the beach, and was always up for a long prayer session or a chat over coffee with the missionary wives. It wasn't until years later that his other, hidden legacy was disclosed. Such things were not discussed among the missionary families.

On weekends, Dr. Hodges scoured the coast for Columbus relics and found Taíno petroglyphs and the remains of a pirate settlement along the Limbé River. He gained a reputation as a man who valued the detritus of history, and patients at the clinic brought him pre-Columbian pottery and Spanish coins they'd unearthed from their fields, as well as buccaneer swords and decaying colonial diaries.

In the evenings, after he had pushed his chair back from the dinner table, cleared his throat, and excused himself, he settled into a chair in his study and taught himself to read colonial French and Spanish with a dictionary at his elbow, reverently turning the pages of leather-bound tomes by Bartolomé de las Casas, Abbé Raynal, and Cristóbal Colón.

Over the years, his amateur field research earned him commendations from the preeminent Caribbean archaeologist at Yale, Irving Rouse, and he began to correspond with the luminaries of the Haitian intellectual community: the novelist Jacques Roumain; the philosopher Jean Price-Mars; the sculptor Albert Mangonès.

From his beloved history books, he discovered that the property of Hôpital le Bon Samaritain had once been a slave plantation—one of the first to be burned to the ground during the slave rebellions of the eighteenth century. Limbé, he noted with interest, had been a hotbed for insurrection.

The Hodges family, after five years in Haiti, were no strangers to upheaval, having arrived a year after Papa Doc Duvalier seized power. Rural Limbé was somewhat sheltered from the brutality of the capital, and missionaries were more protected than ordinary citizens, but even the Hodges had witnessed the violence firsthand. A patient in the missionary hospital who had been savagely beaten was dragged from his bed by Duvalier's rural militia. When the Doctor protested, the militia turned their guns on him.

Shielded by their American citizenship, Bill and Joanna had felt relatively safe from harm, but in May 1963, as tensions escalated between Duvalier and the Dominican Republic, the Hodges family huddled around a crackling Voice of America radio broadcast as the announcer warned all American citizens in Haiti to stand by for evacuation.

A night of terror followed. In the streets of Limbé, suspects were dragged from their houses and shot. Hospital staff members, shaken and terrified when they reported for work the next morning, described relatives murdered and houses ransacked. The Hodges children ranged in age from eight to thirteen years and pleaded that they didn't want to leave their home and their friends behind. But Bill and Joanna weren't willing to take unnecessary chances. Theirs was a rare freedom: They could leave if they chose.

At three-thirty a.m., having loaded the family station wagon, they braved the long, hazardous route to the capital. The countryside was eerily quiet, aside from the military checkpoints, and there were few other vehicles on the road. There were no streetlights. The moon had already set. There were only the faint outlines of the mountains against the stars and their own small headlights fading into the dark.

When morning found them safely in Port-au-Prince, Bill and Joanna tried, exhausted, to secure an exit visa and seats on the next plane, but ran into a quagmire of bureaucracy. A politely evasive Haitian official folded his hands on his desk and explained that the evacuation was merely a political ploy; if the Hodges family were to leave, the people of Haiti would not forget. There would be no return.

The Doctor cleared his throat and explained that in five years' time, he and his family had not once taken a vacation. The official pursed his lips and slammed the necessary exit visa onto the paper.

No more planes would be leaving that night. Having hardly slept in the past thirty-six hours, Dr. Hodges drove to the mountains above Port-au-Prince to stay with missionary friends. The Turnbulls, veterans of seventeen years, assured them that it was indeed a political power-play—the U.S. government just didn't want Duvalier to stay in power (a suspicion that would be confirmed decades later by declassified information from the embassy).

The Doctor, not knowing what to believe, went straight to bed after supper. As Joanna tells the story, she shook her husband awake early the next morning, feeling strongly that the Lord wasn't ready for them to leave.

—Besides, she reminded him, —what are we going to say to our supporters back home? We told all the young people in Sunday school that we were going to the ends of the earth!

Their spirits fortified by having reread the Great Commission in their Bibles—*surely I am with you always, to the very end of the age*—they drove back to Limbé later that afternoon. The roads were empty aside from vehicles racing south to the airport. One expatriate warned Dr. Hodges that he was surely going back to his death.

By the time they reached Plaisance, perched on the spine of the northern mountains, still over an hour's drive from Limbé, bystanders began to recognize the missionary station wagon.

—*Woy! Woy!* Dr. Hodges! He came back! former patients shouted as they ran alongside. In Limbé, a pro-Duvalier/anti-American rally turned into an impromptu parade. A crowd accompanied the Hodges family into the hospital yard, clapping and singing: *Port-au-Prince is not the only one to have a Papa Doc, we've got a Papa Doc right here!*

Local dignitaries hurried over to declare: Dr. Hodges, you have voted with the people. Everyone shook hands.

As Joanna told the story in subsequent newsletters—for it was to become a defining moment, told and retold—the Hodges family had shown solidarity with the Haitian people. Willing to sacrifice personal safety for the good of the community, they had won the trust of those whose lives they had come to save.

The only detail that Joanna was expressly forbidden from mentioning in print was the Papa Doc song; François Duvalier, like Dr. Hodges, had started out as a simple country doctor, but Dr. Hodges found the comparison odious. Joanna kept her promise—loosely. No newsletter ever contained the lyrics, though she was fond of regaling visitors with the tale.

In 1969, six years after the Hodges family's triumphant return to Limbé—in spite of Duvalier's threats—*Christianity Today* published an article that described missionary hospitals as underfunded and poorly administrated, and asserted that the era of the "White Father" was over; it was time for missionary doctors to seek new roles.

Dr. Hodges typed an indignant rebuttal from Limbé: "A Bruised World still seeks Good Samaritans." Rural Haiti, he argued, was poor, and disease was rampant. Illiteracy was widespread. Well-educated families too often left for better opportunities elsewhere, and the vast majority of physicians—Haitian as well as foreign—aspired to social diversions unattainable so far from an urban center. *This condition keeps away all but the most determined idealists . . . The world is crying for men and women who are so motivated and are willing to pay the cost.*

In his letter to the editor, Dr. Hodges did not explicitly address the underlying critique of missionary paternalism—a complaint that, in the post–civil rights era, was being raised not only by *Christianity Today* but also, increasingly, by local Haitian pastors.

Ivah took detailed notes on the strained conversations between the newly formed Haitian Baptist Convention and the missionaries, during which Haitian Baptist leaders voiced their dismay at the seeming reluctance of missionaries to recognize the competency of national leadership, or to delegate authority, and pointed to a subtle but pervasive spirit of paternalism. Missionaries who had devoted their lives, as they saw it, to serving the Haitian people found the accusations painful. The American Baptist Foreign Mission Society weighed in from afar to recommend a gradual transition of authority from the missionaries to national leaders. The Hodges family, among others, argued that a rapid transfer of authority could be disastrous; putting Haitian pastors without medical training in charge of the hospital budget would leave fragile patients at risk.

No one disputed that the foundation of Hôpital le Bon Samaritain had been laid by parishioners of the Limbé Baptist church, ordinary Haitian citizens who had purchased the land, slowly and methodically, through their own labor. But onto that foundation other stones had been laid. The rudimentary clinic had grown to include a maternity ward, a pediatrics wing, a laboratory with X-ray and sterilization equipment, and a pharmacy—and all this progress rested squarely on the capable shoulders of the Hodges family. Furthermore, Dr. Hodges had just begun an ambitious hydroelectric project on the Limbé River, funded by a German not-for-profit organization, to provide electricity and clean drinking water to the town. Barren hillsides were in the process of being replanted through an experimental forestry program administered by the missionaries. The four Hodges children, who had left for boarding school in Port-au-Prince or college in the States, were slowly returning to help manage the hydroelectric dam, the pharmacy, and the growing facilities.

By the time my family moved to the compound, it had been a solid quarter century since the Hodges family had first touched their feet to Haitian soil, sighed, and committed themselves to backwater Limbé.

Every morning, Dr. Hodges walked over to the hospital to deliver babies, combat virulent tropical diseases, and dispense prohibitively expensive pharmaceuticals for less than the price of a marmite of rice (he kept his rounds brief on Sundays so that he could teach Sunday school). Joanna presided over the office, tapping out cheery newsletters to raise yet more money for the missionary enterprise. The hospital's nominal fees were heavily subsidized by churches in the U.S.: the price to give birth in the safety of the hospital, attended by trained nurses with sterilized equipment, was only one dollar; it was free for those who couldn't afford that. A twenty-four-hour generator ensured that doctors would not have to probe a dehydrated child's flattened veins by headlamp, or deliver a baby by the flickering light of kerosene lamp. A pump and a well provided up to eighty thousand gallons of clean water per day, and also supplied the five public fountains in Limbé, which prevented the spread of waterborne viruses and intestinal parasites.

From time to time, the American Baptist Foreign Mission Society advocated for a gradual transition to Haitian Baptist leadership, but its board members seemed to have accepted that such things took time.

The history of the hospital was known. The future remained unclear.

Life in Paradise

Limbé, 1983

M Y SISTERS AND I, after six boring months in the U.S., were already bouncing in our seats as the plane began its descent into Port-au-Prince. Haiti, as far as I was concerned, contained every good thing in the world, cousins and grandparents excepted (though lizards and snorkeling went a long way to make up for that loss). And this time, to make a happy story even better, Joanna's daughter Barbara had left a station wagon for us at the airport, so instead of continuing over the mountains to the lonely Ag Center, my father turned right just before we crossed the Limbé River down a short, dusty road toward our new home on the missionary compound.

He lifted one hand off the wheel to greet the neighbor women who gathered laundry from cactus hedges and the men who tipped wooden chairs against pink and green porches. At the chipped gray fountain by the hospital gate, kids beat on overturned buckets while they waited in line, the clean water splashing onto the wet concrete at their feet.

Inside the hospital entrance, women crouched in front of charcoal fires, preparing meals for sick family members, their shadows thrown long against the wall.

—*Bonswa,* a chorus of voices called out to us.

—*Bonswa,* good evening, we answered as we rolled slowly past the facilities depot, past the bamboo grove with its whispering leaves, the glaring fluorescent lights of the pharmacy and the green sludge of the fishpond, into a tidy circle of whitewashed homes under a towering *zanmann* tree. Herons squawked as they rose in a graceful arc above the breadfruit trees. We had landed in paradise.

The hallelujah chorus that I woke to every morning was a symphony sung by roosters and herons, backed by the beat of the clicking cicadas and the low whirring tick of the fan. Kicking aside thin sheets, I scratched fresh welts on my ankles and watched as a lizard flicked his tongue, then crept on padded toes toward a blood-drowsy mosquito. From the kitchen, the smell of pancakes with imitation maple syrup, carefully rationed to compensate for the sharp tang of Haitian honey. And after breakfast? An unending parade of distractions.

Feet wedged into lace-up roller skates, I tore down the long concrete sidewalk that snaked all the way from the front porch of the Hodges house to the back gate by the highway. I darted past the Rose Cottage and the wispy acerola cherry tree, from which hung tiny fruit, small as a doll's heart; past the swing set under the *zanmann* tree, past the parrot that had learned in short order how to screech my name—*Raperkrop! Raperkrop!*—in imitation of my mother's exasperated hollering. By the rabbit cages, I hurtled through a small dark forest of knobbly-armed *kakao* trees with white fairy blossoms perfectly proportioned for Barbie wedding bouquets, zipped back to the iguana cage and came to a screeching halt, then—arms wide like a levitating flamingo—I precariously turned around on tiptoe to race off in the opposite direction.

I could circumnavigate my universe in fifteen minutes and stop for snacks at any missionary house along the way.

After the dusty solitude of our desert trailer and the slow pace of the Ag Center, the missionary compound was nonstop action. My mother was an instant hit because she baked gooey cinnamon rolls and sang camp songs good and loud. She popped popcorn and hosted game nights; long after we girls had been sent to bed, we could hear the nurse volunteers slap playing cards onto the dining room table and grab riotously for the spoons.

We do take walks in the community to remind us where we are, my father pointed out in our first newsletter from the compound. I added in a postscript: *I's fun to be back in HATi, I'm glad Meadow still remembers Creole. Love, Apricot.*

Every morning after breakfast, my father walked past the *zanmann* tree and the swing set into the cluttered tree nursery with its crumbling piles of soil. The voices of the Haitian nursery workers drifted over the playground as they watered and fertilized and packed into cardboard boxes the thousands upon thousands of seedlings in plastic Rootrainers, ready to be transplanted onto the eroded hills.

There were more trees on the compound than in the rest of Limbé combined, but this was only because the Hodges family defended them so fiercely. Joanna, we learned, had planted the towering *zanmann* tree as a wispy seedling, even though the rest of her family laughed and said it would never survive. Over the years, she'd fended off the goats and children who tore at its leaves until, two and a half decades later, the tropical almond extended a quiet canopy over the missionary houses and dropped gilded red leaves twice a year for the kids to scoop up and toss into the air, pretending that it was fall.

David Hodges, Bill and Joanna's elder son, who had moved to Limbé when he was seven, still lived on the compound. He was tall and thin, with a shaggy, untamed beard, and he raced off on a red motor scooter to fire up the generator every time the national power grid failed. He was in charge of the buildings and grounds and had been known to climb power poles during hurricanes to keep the lights twinkling in the missionary houses and the vaccines at a stable temperature. He loomed over the compound like a vaguely benevolent but unpredictable giant, straight out of the Brothers Grimm; I would not have been surprised to discover that he also caught and hurled lightning bolts with his bare fists.

His wife, Emily, a full foot shorter, was an Indiana farm girl who invited the missionary kids over for book clubs in her living room. All of us had heard the rumors about how David had proposed to her—it involved the fishpond, which we were expressly forbidden to play in because sick patients had been known to tip their bedpans into its slimy depths. And yet rumor had it that when David proposed—and Emily said yes—he threw her in.

I knew vaguely of the existence of Susan and Paul, the oldest and youngest Hodges children. They no longer lived on the compound but visited every so often. Paul had a job in Mauritania; Susan lived with her family in Port-au-Prince.

Barbara Hodges had never married. She lived in a bedroom at the back of her parents' house and ran the pharmacy. My parents, who were about the same age as Barbara, never did succeed in setting her up with any eligible young bachelors, though it wasn't for lack of trying. (The rumor was that she had fallen in love with a Haitian artist, but her parents hadn't approved.) Her fingers flew over the piano keys when she accompanied the choir at the Limbé Baptist church, and she wore her long black hair twisted into a bun. She wasn't the official mother of Bill and Joanna's three adopted children, but she was the one who went with us on field trips to Columbus sites and to see metalworkers pour shimmering molten aluminum into molds and tip out cooking pots as if by magic.

In all, there were ten missionary kids at Jericho School in 1984, though the numbers fluctuated; our family hopscotched around to three different houses in two years because of rotating furlough schedules.

Joni Hodges, the youngest adopted son of Bill and Joanna, had been dropped off at the hospital as a baby with swollen hernias. After his operation, the Haitian nurses taught the little boy to say: *Bonjou, Papa* every time Dr. Hodges passed by on his rounds. Joni's mother had died two months after he was born, and his birth father already had five children to feed and care for. Joni was officially adopted when he was two. His birth father still came to visit.

Anacaona Hodges, adopted a few years earlier, had been named after a Taíno princess, and though she was only ten, she had a regal profile and carried herself with such fierce and self-sufficient dignity that I worshipped her instinctively.

Peter Hodges was eleven and quieter than his adoptive siblings. He had arrived at the hospital as a toddler with an abscessed knee, and the bones in his leg had never fully healed. I learned later that kids in Limbé mocked him for his limp, but he never teased me, even when I stormed into a fury because no one wanted to play a game of Sardines by my rules. Also, significantly, he never once called me Little Boss—a nickname perfectly calculated to tip me into outrage. I tried not to make it too obvious that I was smitten, but I couldn't have been happier when we both came down with chicken pox and were quarantined across from each other at Bernice Rogers's dining room table for an entire blessed week.

Picole, whom all the little girls on the compound wanted as an older sister, lived across the highway with her younger brother, Loren (a saucy charmer whom most of the girls were secretly in love with). Their father was a Haitian pastor named Paul Romeus who had started a trade school in Limbé with scholarships for students who couldn't afford books or uniforms. His wife, Belle, was a no-nonsense midwesterner with a dry wit and a quick smile who had worked as a nurse at the hospital for twenty years.

Sometimes Picole brought with her to the compound one of her father's scholarship students, whose mother wasn't able to take care of her. Olynda had jet-black ringlets that fell to her shoulders and long lashes. She watched shyly as we careened around the playground, shouting at each other.

Last but not least, three American girls had just moved into a brand-new house at the back of the compound, with cathedral ceilings and iron window bars welded into the shape of flowers to keep out the robbers. Kirsti, Mimi, and Carrie's father, Dr. Steve James, had come to help Dr. Hodges at the hospital. I liked Steve. He had a soft voice, and his smile turned up the corners of his mustache. I couldn't imagine him shouting at anybody. When he wasn't at the hospital, he spent hours alone with his Bible folded open on his desk.

Steve and his wife, Nancy, had both grown up as missionary kids in Burma and were best friends when they were eight years old. Their daughters were the same stairstep ages as my sisters and me. Nancy lined us up against the dining room wall in leotards and tights and taught us to point our toes and plié, after which we crammed elbow-to-elbow to sip tea in that quiet house, which breathed serenity. The Burmese teacups were pale and translucent. Grains of rice, pressed into the unbaked clay, had burned clean and left a thin sliver of glaze for the light to peek through. I had never seen anything so delicate.

Tamara, though not yet officially adopted by the Hodges family, had already been featured in several of Joanna's newsletters. Her unevenly shorn hair had been infested with lice and she was covered in running sores when she was dropped off at the missionary hospital. One eye was blind and the right side of her body was partially paralyzed. The staff at the hospital had been told that her name was *Pa vle sa*: I don't want that.

Tamara's spirit, however, was undefeated, despite the odds stacked against her, and as the nurses dressed her wounds and massaged her atrophied limbs, feeding her protein-rich mash, she fought her way to health. When the hospital chaplain made his weekly rounds, she clapped along to the Kreyòl choruses. Joanna came in to applaud her first few faltering steps, as Tamara teetered precariously, dragging her right leg along the floor. The staff at the hospital wanted a new name for her, so Bill and Joanna decided on the palm tree.

—*Yo rele m Tamara!* My name is Tamara! she'd shout to anyone who would listen, leaning on her crutch as she hitched her way down the sidewalk. When she was well enough to move out of the pediatric ward, Joanna enrolled her first in Belle and Paul's school, across the highway, paying a woman in Limbé to provide a bed for her, until Suzette, our inimitable schoolmarm, convinced the Hodges family to let Tamara join the joyful ranks of Jericho School.

As a confident transplant from the American South and the sole black woman in leadership on the compound, Suzette was—like the rest of the missionaries—called a *blan* whenever she ventured into Limbé (occasionally, people teased her for trying to hide her Haitian roots and refused to believe that she couldn't speak Kreyòl). A few of the missionaries, I later learned, were made uncomfortable by her formidable presence, but as a seven-year-old, I was blissfully ignorant of this ancillary drama. All I knew was that Suzette summoned pure outrageous joy to follow in her wake.

When I was impatient and nipped at the heels of the other kids, Suzette just gave me more writing assignments. She laughed and steered me toward my desk when I stumbled back from the library with my nose in a book, feet feeling blindly for the legs of my chair, so swept away by the power of language that I couldn't tear my eyes from the page. It was Suzette who assured me in ringing tones that I was a writer, the first time I had ever heard those magic words spoken aloud. She made me promise that I would dedicate my first book to her.

Seized by inspiration, I sat bolt upright during a game of checkers and scribbled down a spontaneous poem. My father clapped me on the back when he saw it printed in Suzette's graceful calligraphy for the *Jericho Journal* (circulation about ten):

> *The bell rang! The bell rang!*
> *Hurry, hurry, hurry!*
> *No one's got their homework done,*
> *We're all in a flurry!*

The second stanza galloped on from there.

—What a kid, what a school! my father boomed. I beamed.

Suzette was a ringleader of inexhaustible enthusiasm who donned a construction-paper top hat, red pajama pants, and the Doctor's black rubber boots for the first and only Jericho School circus.

Dr. Hodges surprised us by not only showing up but showing up in costume. He won honorable mention for his End of the World–themed hat (Joanna confided that his nickname in high school had been Gloomy Gus). One of the nurse volunteers, however, one-upped him with her prizewinning entry: Baby Getting an IV.

The missionary moms spent weeks sewing sequins onto homemade clown outfits. Peter was a juggler. Ana was a lion. Rosie and the James girls were clowns. Meadow played a snake charmer and popped out of a tall woven laundry basket with a garter snake wound around her wrist (my father had found the snake at the tree nursery and had dropped it in the laundry basket while he took a shower—the tiny creature, no longer than my sister's arm, wasn't nearly as impressive as the pair of eight-foot-long boa constrictors that he had rescued from one of the hospital wards, but my mother still screamed when she grabbed a fistful of dirty clothes and found a snake coiled around a T-shirt, tongue flickering). My mother recovered (as did the snake), and she trilled belly-dance music on the recorder as adorable, squeaky-voiced Meadow grinned shyly at the riotous applause.

Tamara wore green tights and led a trained kitty—a gangly, acrobatic medical student—around the yard by a leash tied to his ankle. At her command, he flipped into a handstand, tennis shoes dangling upside down over his head.

I balanced on the back of my father's bicycle in a sparkly clown suit, one toe pointed skyward—Amazing Apricot and Her Dynamite Dad!

During lunchtime, our games of freeze tag waited in suspended animation while we gulped down fresh-squeezed *sitronad* and *sòs pwa mayi*. Then we raced off again, mothers appeased, screen doors slamming behind us.

And if we tired of freeze tag or if the roller skates gave us blisters, there were bikes to race through the *raje* or trees to climb; shaggy black Labrador mutts to pester or swing sets to shimmy up, our legs dangling like circus performers. We caught lizards in lard cans, played Matchbox cars above the smoking trash pit, and summited the Citadel on the back of bony horses to take grinning photographs, our toes lipped over a hundred-foot drop-off—a world without safety rails.

If there is a more perfect habitat for a seven-year-old, I ask only for its address.

Musée de Guahaba

Limbé, 1984

As a wiry second-grader with skinned knees and ponytail braids, I didn't know much about Dr. Hodges except that he almost always wore red suspenders (to peg him in a game of charades, pretty much all I had to do was snap invisible suspenders and clear my throat importantly).

The Hodges house was the biggest on the compound, with a parrot that whistled from a cage on the porch in perfect imitation of the Doctor's piercing summons to the dining hall. Morning, noon, and night, a rotating cast of Haitian doctors on residency from Port-au-Prince, nurse volunteers, and international medical students crowded around the long dining room table for rice and beans and Kreyòl chicken, as well as sage pronouncements on colonial history and tropical medicine.

If we found smashed-up bits of crockery on the beach, we took it to Dr. Hodges for identification, just to watch him push up his glasses and announce that what we were in fact holding was two-hundred-year-old French pottery—most likely predating the Haitian revolution. We held the shards so carefully in our palms, it was as if they were made of diamonds.

When his long-awaited Musée de Guahaba opened just across the highway—"Guahaba" being the Taíno name for Limbé—my father took us over to see the marvel for ourselves.

Meadow and I raced past the long reflecting pool and up the red tile steps, where our father dropped a few gourdes into the donation box—the price of a large mango. Hand-painted block letters above the gleaming whitewashed rotunda spelled out *DIEU CRÉA L'HOMME À SON IMAGE*. French, not Kreyòl, was still the official language in Haiti, although only the well educated spoke it fluently—which excluded us. Dr. Hodges modestly translated: *We are created in the image of God.*

The museum housed a collection of artifacts from the pre-Columbian era to the present. Meadow and I pressed our noses against glass display cases full of carved talismans of the zemi spirits, elliptical grinding stones, a tiny bronze hawk's bell, and a delicate beaded necklace which the Doctor had reconstructed with feathers from his own parrot, alongside a quotation from Bartolomé de las Casas: *pierced with such delicacy that it seems to be a marvel.*

Hand-drawn maps detailed the Casimiroid and Meillac migrations, and a large display showed the three different cultures represented in Hispaniola: an Arawak-speaking Taíno man with earrings and a headband; an African man with a drum; and a bearded, blue-eyed European. We learned what the Old World had to offer the New and vice versa: churches, Bibles, and a cross; parrots, bananas, corn, and potatoes.

Later display cases held more disturbing artifacts: preserved in a clay brick, the clawed footprint of a giant dog, imported by the Spanish to hunt runaway slaves; a heavy iron collar attached to a thick metal chain; a broken clay hand and the decapitated head of Jesus from a destroyed colonial church; the ancient bones of a dead child, curled in the fetal position.

My father knelt beside Meadow and me and pointed up at the paintings, done by Barbara, of the caciques' first encounters with Christendom. The faces in the oil paintings were rapturous and unreal, like figures in a Sunday school flannel board. Sunlight streamed over the Admiral's squared shoulders as he knelt on the sand, holding aloft a cross. Taíno Indians clustered in the background. It was very heroic.

On the way out, I signed my name in the official museum guest book in careful, lopsided cursive. I was visitor number seven. Under place of residence I wrote Thermal, CA; Meadow wrote HBS, Limbé; my father wrote Idyllwild. We had already lost track of which world to call home.

As we emerged from the dim interior into the bright afternoon, my father shook the Doctor's hand and told him how much he appreciated all the hard work that had gone into the museum. The Doctor adjusted his thumbs under his suspenders and repeated his assertion—in his opinion, the history of Haiti was actually a microcosm of the whole human race.

Meadow and I, released from the obligatory history lesson, raced down the steps to twirl mahogany seeds on the grass.

A grand occasion, my father summarized to the grandparents after Meadow and I had skipped back across the highway to the compound. *Though Dr. Hodges did it in his humble style, with no announcement or formality, just opened the doors one afternoon.*

On the same weekend that the Guahaba Museum officially opened, Jean-Claude Duvalier, the president for life, roared down the national highway in a polished convertible. Baby Doc's glamorous lifestyle had done little to endear him to his people—his wedding was rumored to have cost $3 million and his wife flew to Paris for shopping sprees while bone-thin Haitian farmers eked out a living in the ruins of former French colonial estates—but few citizens were foolish enough to show their dislike when the president made an appearance.

For hours, there had been no one on the roads—not even the *tap taps.* I jammed my knees through the back gate of the compound to wait with the throngs that lined the highway. Then the crowd roared, and a sleek motorcade gunned through the festooned palm branches. A chubby man in a suit tossed five- and twenty-five-gourde notes to citizens who dove to catch the fluttering bills.

The gleaming vehicles swept past to the next cheering village, heedless of the bodies trapped and torn by the spinning wheels. Dr. Hodges was left to splint the broken legs and stitch the head wounds of those who had been struck down by the man who should have been responsible for their welfare. After such presidential drive-bys, the wails of mourning lasted deep into the night.

Hôpital le Bon Samaritain

Limbé, 1984

Hundreds lined up daily to seek medical attention at the missionary hospital, some of whom had walked or been carried miles in the rain or the blistering heat. In 1984, 87,936 patients received consultations: for malaria, intestinal parasites, meningitis, respiratory infection, and severe burns; separate clinics were held for diabetes and tuberculosis, which required ongoing treatment. And yet, as Dr. Hodges explained in his newsletter on triage, it was impossible to treat everyone—there were not enough hours in a day.

By Dr. Hodges's reckoning, there were only thirty-eight hospitals in all of Haiti in the 1980s, more than half of which centered around Port-au-Prince. This grim ratio afforded, on average, one doctor for every sixty-six hundred people.

An average of a hundred and fifty Haitian staff were on payroll at the hospital, most of whom had completed only a high school or a grade school education but had been trained to administer medication, bandage wounds, sterilize needles, put broken bones into traction, and set up intravenous fluids under the watchful supervision of Belle and Joanna, the nursing supervisor. Haitian lab technicians ran slides for malaria and meningitis, supervised by Herb Rogers. Haitian midwives, overseen by the sturdy, white-haired Dorothy Lincoln, tube-fed premature babies and dressed newborn umbilical cords with clean bandages torn from old sheets by Baptist women's groups in the States and flown in on the missionary plane.

Still others were hired for short-term contract work, such as the diabetics who could not otherwise afford their daily insulin shots, or unemployed townspeople who asked for help to pay their children's school fees. Cardboard boxes could be cut into tickets for triage; recycled baby-food jars arrived in clanking burlap sacks to be sanitized, filled with medicine, and redistributed as the Balm of Gilead.

Gardeners raked the brown fallen leaves and trimmed the wiry St. Augustine grass with hand clippers. Cooks cleaned the rice and hung out the laundry. Carpenters, masons, and ironworkers repaired roofs and built storage depots and furniture. Nursery workers bent over the trays of seedlings. Guards slept by the front gate at night.

Joanna worried that fewer and fewer expatriate nurses and medical students—who paid five dollars a day, room and board, for the privilege of studying tropical diseases up close and personal—were signing up to volunteer at the missionary hospital; she blamed the AIDS epidemic. A 1983 U.S. Centers for Disease Control report had given Haiti top billing in its scaremonger list of what to avoid—along with homosexuals, hemophiliacs, and heroin addicts. But even before AIDS, a medical internship in Limbé was a tough sell. Hospital staff worked long hours under stressful conditions and were susceptible to the same diseases as their patients: yellow-eyed hepatitis, hookworm, malaria, pneumonia, depression. One fair-haired volunteer from Illinois confessed that after two years in the pediatric ward, she had more freckles but smiled less often. Never had she struggled with sadness like this, though at the same time, never had she felt Jesus to be so close and comforting.

In the early years of the missionary hospital, Dr. Hodges had been able to consult with everyone who came for treatment, even if their ailments were beyond his aid. But although consultations had increased to as many as 400 patients per day, by the 1980s, a triage system had become necessary. Dr. Hodges considered the torturous sorting ritual the world's worst job.

Even before he entered the covered porch to begin the process, high-standing members of the community—a soldier in uniform, government functionaries, a Baptist pastor, or a Vodou priest—often waited to accost him.

—I know that you have many problems, *Doktè,* but I have a very sick child. You will have to see him for me.

The negotiation required diplomacy.

—But Monsieur, the Doctor might demur tactfully in Kreyòl or French, —you know that all of these people are sick; some of them very sick.

In the ensuing argument, if he deemed it necessary, the Doctor might eventually clear his throat and reach into his coat pocket to retrieve a crooked cardboard triage ticket, which guaranteed that the official's child would be seen in the clinic later that day. After this, there would be more handshakes. Only then did the true sorting process begin.

Not even a Bible verse read aloud and a morning prayer to invoke the presence of a merciful God could quell the anxiety in the room. For those without powerful advocates, triage was a high-stakes gamble. Women held rheumy-eyed children to their breasts. Men with bent skeletal chests coughed into their fists. The injustice of the situation created an unhealthy drama: Patients were obliged to prove their desperation.

The unsolvable agony was that in a perfect world, each person on the triage porch should have received treatment, but even if every IV and pill bottle in the pharmacy had been emptied, by the next morning, the lineup of sorrow would have been just as long. Dr. Hodges considered it a humiliating indictment of the modern world that so few people had devoted their lives to the alleviation of human misery.

He cut an imposing figure, brisk and professional, as he wove through the bodies sprawled across the concrete floor. Patients with tuberculosis were comparatively easy to diagnose due to severe weight loss. Chronically ill children were identifiable by their sunken eyes and reduced skin turgor, dehydrated from diarrhea. But if a child showed no outward signs of distress and he felt no fever when he leaned his hand against the small forehead, he might pause, knowing that there might yet be reasonable cause to run a lab test for typhoid or malaria. Forced, however, to weigh this possible risk against needs even more urgent, he sometimes felt compelled to move on. His weathered hands scrawled names and preliminary observations on the flimsy cardboard tickets.

Occasionally, a mother thrust a child into his face and protested: *Doktè,* my child is dying! Look at him! I haven't slept in a week.

—Madame, he might explain, the child doesn't look bad. —See, he only has a runny nose and a cold.

Patients who had already been turned aside might jump ahead of him in the queue in a frustrated bid for a second opinion. Dramatic threats were sometimes made to tip the scale of justice: If you don't see my baby today, I'm going to leave him for you in the clinic! I can't take care of him anymore. If my baby dies tonight, it will be your fault!

Others solicited the crowd for sympathy as triage tickets dwindled: Do you see this woman? Would I leave Plaisance and sit here for four days if she wasn't sick? This woman has been crying for nine days!

Another shouted: Dr. Hodges, you used to be more kind! You've changed since you first came to Haiti. You always took care of my family. Now you hate me!

When the last of the tickets had been dispensed, Dr. Hodges bowed his head and turned to go. The daily purgatory was at an end. To heed his inner conviction to love his neighbors as he loved himself required a condition of complete attentiveness to their pain, costing not less than everything. Triage, he confessed, was the acid test of his Christian faith. Disappointed voices followed him as he trudged up the path to the clinic, where he would, alongside the Haitian staff, the visiting medical students, and his fellow missionaries, resume the long, slow work of treatment, refusing to give up the fight against an unconquerable enemy.

My sisters and I, who otherwise had little interaction with the hospital, understood, at least, the agony of the pediatric ward. Like everything else in the hospital, it was patched together on a shoestring budget and held together by prayer. Staff sometimes placed two children in one bed in an attempt to turn no one away, which meant that no matter how often the nurses picked up the wailing little ones, it seemed impossible to offer truly undivided attention.

My father stopped by the pediatric ward whenever possible. As the oldest of six children, he had acquired a reputation as a baby whisperer, and he frequently brought home orphans for an afternoon or an evening. There was no formal system for this improvised foster care, but no one complained when the missionaries developed favorites. Unclaimed orphans over a year old and in stable health were usually taken to an orphanage in Port-au-Prince, but when my father heard that adorable, round-faced Eva was to be adopted by former volunteers at the hospital, he suspected that the prospective parents would be relieved if their child received extra attention.

Meadow, Rosie, and I helped give roly-poly Eva baths in the sink and giggled when she reached for our faces with soapy hands. If we stuck our faces close to hers and said: *Boo!*, she shrieked with laughter. Rosie cried when we had to take her back to the pediatric ward to sleep for the night. We tied a ribbon under her chin and dressed her in gingham and a sun hat for photographs before she disappeared into her new life, cooing into the faces of her adoptive parents in Canada.

When I was in first grade, a third of my classmates at Jericho School had been adopted by missionary parents after being abandoned at the hospital. We understood that we were supposed to be Good Samaritans—it was our job to rescue those left for dead on the road to Jericho, just like in the Bible story. We were missionary kids. We carried our benevolence like a crown, balanced delicately on our small heads. It was our obligation to be generous.

Bent over our desks at the missionary school, we always knew when someone had died at the hospital.

—*Anmwe, Anmwe! Woy! Woy!* the voices would shout, a bruised lament that echoed off the walls like gunfire. We tried not to think of them as we solved our arithmetic problems, the crumpled bodies of the mourners slack and heavy, bereft as broken Madonnas.

There was more loss in Haiti than could be wept for in a lifetime:

death for the three-pound infants in the pediatric ward and for their mothers and grandmothers; death on the highway, decapitated by a hurtling *kamyon* bus or swept away by the floods that came roaring down from the treeless mountains, bodies tangled together with the bloodred topsoil, the tin roofs, the bloated dead cows, and the bicycles all spewn out together at the mouth of the sea.

Marvels in the Marketplace

Limbé, 1984

THAT THERE WAS grief in Haiti was incontestable, but what was to be done about it often felt unclear. According to Dr. Hodges, ships in the colonial era could sail as far as fifteen miles up the Limbé River, but by the 1980s, the once proud port city boasted only poverty and a receding water table.

In the dry season, women waded across the Limbé River with bundles balanced expertly on their heads, the water barely coming up to their knees. But when the rains began, the river reawakened. Pelting rain moved across the tin roofs like pebbles thrown hard against a can. Entire hillsides washed downstream, staining the water like blood. After a truly notable storm roared down the mountains, the churning soil could turn the ocean itself an alarming shade of red a full mile out to sea from its mouth.

The only time that the Limbé River was deep enough to navigate by boat was at flood stage, when the graveled bed, usually fifty feet wide and roughly a foot deep, rose to a torrent half a mile across and up to twelve feet deep. When this happened, my parents hauled out the inflatable rafts and rode the river, bucking and hollering like rodeo cowboys (item #175544JVR from the Best Catalog, shipped in on the missionary plane and a steal at $39.97). Dr. Hodges, concerned about typhus and other waterborne diseases, did not approve, but this did not prevent my parents from recruiting the visiting medical students. After much lobbying, I, too, was allowed to join the fun. We promised to keep our mouths closed if we tipped over.

My father was in charge of our raft and put me in the middle next to Ti Cabo. Ti Cabo was one of his favorite workers at the tree nursery. He was short, like my father, and strong; he had once ridden his bike twenty miles to Cap-Haïtien to line up for the start of a bike race, then pedaled all the way back the same distance to win first prize.

I cinched my life jacket around my rib cage as Ti Cabo pushed us away from shore, one of my mother's cooking pots in his other hand to help bail. Off we sailed—a minor flotilla of yellow rafts plummeting downstream on the roiling brown current, past half-submerged vegetable gardens and banana stalks, around woven snags of mud houses that had been ripped from their foundations, until our oarsman lost control of the paddle and the raft hit a log jam, snagged, and went under. I came up spluttering, but Ti Cabo grabbed my arm so I didn't get swept downstream. My father was proud that I didn't cry.

A baffled onlooker caught the paddle and handed it back to us as we clambered onto the bank, but what he made of our gleeful idiocy was anyone's guess. We hiked back through a farmer's field, our squelching shoes leaving indentations in the carefully mounded beds of sweet potato and manioc. We laughed to hide our embarrassment.

Columbus, the very same man whose arrival in the Caribbean touched off a landslide of deforestation from which Ayiti has never recovered, may be credited with the first recorded observation that forests and precipitation are, in fact, interdependent. He noted that the daily showers which fell in the West Indies seemed to be caused by *the great forests and trees*—a cause and effect that he had observed in the Azores as a young sailor—though he noted that *now that the many woods and trees that covered them have been felled, there are not produced so many clouds and rains as before.*

These observations were, however, insufficient to protect Ayiti's magnificent hardwoods, which were pillaged by the shipload to grace the vaulted ceilings of European cathedrals, or carved into elaborate thrones for disinterested kings to lean their drinks upon.

The conquistadores, when they discovered more prosperous civilizations to plunder on the mainland, left the colony of Hispaniola to founder (French pirates helped encourage their retreat). The Spanish colonizers retreated over the mountains to the more sparsely populated Dominican Republic while French plantation owners on the western half of the island felled what remained of the lowland forests, planting slave labor–intensive crops of indigo, coffee, and sugarcane. Cedar and mahogany, resistant to insect rot, were valued by the French as *bois incorruptibles* and cut down to make the wooden beams for sugar mills.

Prior to the Haitian revolution, Dr. Hodges tallied 124 coffee plantations, 19 indigo plantations, 22 large sugar plantations, and 13 water-powered sugar mills in the Limbé Valley, all of which produced more than 4.5 million pounds of sugar annually. By the 1780s, 60 percent of the coffee sipped in gold-rimmed cups in European coffeehouses was imported from French-owned Saint-Domingue.

Ayiti, the Pearl of the Antilles, had become the richest colony in the New World under the brutal whip of slavery. Ayiti's eight hundred thousand subjugated Africans represented a third of the transatlantic slave trade. The introduced overpopulation put strains on the local environment, touching off formerly unheard-of famines and drought. Slaves, driven by hunger, hunted down the animals that had survived the wholesale loss of habitat. Colonizers who had hoped to build an empire in the New World failed to recognize that it was eroding beneath them.

When the slaves finally revolted and declared independence in 1804—the initial call to arms having been sounded half a century earlier in the fierce and unbroken north by a slave named François Makandal, who had escaped from Limbé to raise an army of Taíno and Maroon warriors—it was too late to reverse the ecological devastation. The hated plantations fell into disrepair, and ever smaller garden plots were cut into the sides of the mountains as land was divided and redivided among the descendants of those first proud, unbroken revolutionaries. But the years of abundance were over.

The forests that once released moisture into the air and caught the raindrops in their tangled branches, replenishing the hidden aquifers, had been cut down. The trees had been cut down because the farmers had no money for food, or school, or hospital bills; at least charcoal could be sold in the marketplace.

It seemed to be a riddle without an answer, but it was one that my father was determined to solve.

The two-hundred-foot expanse of trampled earth that my father managed on the compound was envisioned as a staging ground for the eventual reforestation of northern Haiti—an ambitious goal but one shared with equal fervor among the various agricultural development agencies that operated in the north, including the Food and Agriculture Organization of the United Nations as well as its Educational, Scientific and Cultural arm, UNESCO, which frequently contracted with the hospital to supply trees.

Dr. Hodges had seized on the importance of reforestation soon after he arrived in Haiti, although he'd stumbled into it indirectly, by way of archaeology. In August 1959, Bill and Joanna and their four children had discovered a spindly stand of native pine trees on an otherwise denuded peninsula overlooking the blue, peaceful Baie de L'Acul. The soil was a rich red color, and the young doctor noticed evidence of a roughly dug long-abandoned mine. He also noted a small cross etched into a rock—perhaps carved by the Admiral himself. The five hundredth anniversary of Columbus's arrival in the New World was still thirty years distant, which, he hoped, would leave him ample time to track down undiscovered sites from the First Voyage.

Hoping to preserve these archaeological relics, the Hodges family purchased the 120-acre peninsula on behalf of the hospital and began an experimental reforestation project. Slowly, against all odds, they reclaimed the barren land. Over the course of decades, thousands of drought-resistant seedlings—mahogany, pine, Haitian oak, and cedar— put down roots. Birds nested in the rustling canopy. Springs, desiccated for years, bubbled up from the soil.

The trees in this restored Eden supplied the lumber for building projects at the hospital and could be harvested to fund the retirement accounts of the Haitian staff. Once a week, my father drove thirty minutes over the mountains, followed by a motorboat ride across the Baie de L'Acul, the wind whipping his hair, to ensure that all was well on the missionary property. When one of his younger brothers back in California couldn't figure out what to do after graduation, my father recommended finding *a job that feels like vacation most of the time.*

The successful *rebwazman* of Morne Bois Pin—Pine Tree Mountain—seemed the fulfillment of the missionary dream, but what my father wanted most was to persuade the Haitians themselves to transform their own eroded land, just as the Hodges family had done on Morne Bois Pin.

And he was pretty sure he had an idea of where to start.

Sept. 20
   Went to Kreyòl Bible Study. The full moon was beautiful through tropical trees as we walked home. Just had a crazy idea. To send some guys to the market one day to sell trees.

The Limbé market roared to life on Tuesdays and Saturdays with bellowing goats, skinny kicked-aside dogs, and chickens that danced like upside-down can-can girls, their wings flapping like petticoats as they dangled from the arms of thick-wristed women. There were neat green pyramids of sweet-as-candy mangoes, sour limes, and watery *militon;* trays of red beans, black beans, rice and corn and manioc. *Machann* with wide-planted knees and inscrutable faces dangled pipes from their lips—queens of the banana regime, of the drowsy-scented pineapple.

The rest of the week, the open square of hard-packed dirt was a playground for barefoot soccer stars who, in the absence of a rubber ball, scored dazzling, heart-pounding goals between a pair of rock goalposts with a wad of tape that had been wrapped around an inflated inner tube.

In Haiti, the marketplace was where the Fates held court, where destiny tumbled like rice into a battered tin cup, where kingdoms rose and fell (the Limbé market, Dr. Hodges had learned, squatted on the two-hundred-year-old ruins of one of King Henri Christophe's many palaces). My father saw it as a staging ground for innovation. If the market was the place to introduce a new idea, then that was where he'd go to sell his trees.

Giving trees away was a well-established tradition among nongovernmental aid organizations, but my father's logic was that if a customer considered the purchase an investment, then perhaps he or she would do a better job protecting the trees.

The next morning, during staff devotions at the nursery, my father opened his Kreyòl Bible and read aloud a verse from Jeremiah about how God's people were to be like trees planted by streams of water. God loved the earth, he insisted, and wanted the empty hillsides full of trees again, so that the rains would return and people would no longer have to fear drought.

If it had been up to him, my father would have gladly spent the day chatting up passersby at the *mache* rather than beat his head against administrative details on the compound, but since he was the missionary (read: authority figure), he had to delegate.

Sem and Obed, his most trusted assistants, made it clear that they were less than pleased with my father's new scheme. As educated, gainfully employed professionals, they did not relish being chained to a tray of drooping seedlings in the midday heat.

My father, on the other hand, had no qualms about embarrassing himself for a good cause. He would even go so far as to grab a cicada off a nearby tree and roast it over an open fire to prove that it was a good protein source (he'd first experimented with cicadas in college, after he read that the Cahuilla Indians ate them roasted). If an aghast Haitian farmer tried to knock the bug out of his hands, he'd haul out his Kreyòl Bible and point to Leviticus—*cigalle* was right there at the top of a list of kosher foods that the Israelites were allowed to eat while wandering in the desert. Mostly, though, he just liked to wow an audience.

Sem and Obed, disgruntled by my father's foolhardy idea, quickly determined that Limbé was a disinterested market. When nary a soul purchased a wilting tree, my father, following Joanna's advice, decided to give some of the smaller nearby markets a go. The next day, he decided to show Sem and Obed how it was done. In a dusty village a few miles up the highway, he positioned himself next to his unwilling recruits, ready to pitch a sale to any would-be arborist who lingered long enough to get an earful. He was convinced that if the Haitians could just see the benefit of trees, they quickly would become converted to his cause. His sales pitch was that for the price of a large mango, customers could take home a tree that in just ten years could be harvested to pay for a wedding or to send a child to college.

One older man laughed and asked: Why should I plant a tree? I won't sit under its shade.

The barefoot boys in ragged shorts, still young enough to outgrow the seedlings, were even less interested: Three *centimes* for a tree? one argued. —I can buy a lottery ticket for the same price and win a fortune!

We weren't well-situated, my father wrote in his journal afterward. *Sold 4 cinnamon trees. Later some people came and bought grapefruit trees.*

Not yet willing to give up, my father staged his next trial run in Camp Coq, a modest village with a police station (though no electricity) where the weekly market bustled with vendors hawking mangoes, rice, batteries, plastic sandals, flavored ices, and bouillon cubes from burlap sacks spread out on the dirt. My father was thrilled when, after paying two men to sit in the Camp Coq *mache* for an entire afternoon, they had this meager success to report: *They sold 11 cinnamon trees and expected they could have sold 50. Two people even signed up to have trees planted on their land.*

The reason for this apparent triumph, although my father didn't realize it yet, was that Camp Coq was home to a fellow tree enthusiast who would eventually become my father's mentor, ally, and fellow renegade. For it was in Camp Coq that he stumbled across a wiry, resolute farmer named Joseph Alexandre, who introduced himself simply as Zo.

My father met Zo while he was standing beside a box of seedlings, trying to convince a few teenagers to buy his cinnamon and papaya trees. Zo needed no convincing. It was Zo who, after a day of lackluster sales at the market, led my father up a steep, crumbling hillside to see forests of mahogany, Leucaena, *labapen,* and Haitian oak that Zo had planted—without the help of missionary tree nurseries. Zo had simply scattered seeds in the dirt before the rains began.

Over the years, Zo had seen a parade of development projects come and go in the Limbé Valley, and he told my father a cautionary tale: In the 1970s, a well-meaning NGO had hosted a seminar in Camp Coq on the benefits of trees—free food, an open-air lecture, plus a box of seedlings for every participant to take home and plant on his or her own land.

The local farmers sat through the seminar as bidden. They ate the food. They even took the boxes of trees. But as soon as the farmers were out of eyesight of the well-meaning foreigners, they pitched the trees into the ravine to rot.

—Why? my father asked, incredulous.

Zo explained. The farmers assumed that there must be some hidden agenda in this foreign scheme—you couldn't expect them to trust the *blan* after a hundred other high-minded projects gone wrong.

Perhaps the donated trees were the latchkey to some secret plot; if the farmers followed the foreigner's suggestions and planted American trees on their land, the U.S. government might claim ownership. It wasn't completely far-fetched. Stranger things had been known to happen.

On the surface, the development project seemed to have gone off without a hitch—brilliant photo ops, the glossy full-page write-up for the benefit of the donors—but in the end, all that well-meaning effort went, quite literally, down the ravine. It was a bleak comedy more improbable than fiction.

Tired and beat at the end of this week, my father recorded glumly in the journal. He had sent Sem and Obed to a village called Dirisie, just down the hill from another of the hospital's tree plantations, anticipating an enthusiastic response from the local farmers. Surely, after witnessing the benefits of reforestation firsthand, the people of Dirisie would be eager to plant trees on their own land. Instead, Sem and Obed got an earful—the trees shaded out the gardens; the ground was as good as ruined if it couldn't grow food.

Discouraged, my father went to check on the compound rabbit cages before dinner. On the floor of the cage next to a female that he had bred a few weeks earlier, to no apparent success, he found two tiny skulls. He hadn't realized that she was pregnant, so he hadn't been supplementing her diet. The ravenous mother had consumed her own offspring.

My father took a shovel to the thick, rubbery grass in front of our volunteer cottage. If he couldn't convince the farmers to plant trees, then at least he could help the kids at Jericho School appreciate the pleasures of gardening. He stabbed bamboo stakes into the dirt to make raised beds. He was, however, predictably disappointed by our work ethic. *They got hot pulling weeds,* he noted irritably after a solid hour of reminding us not to get distracted.

—Come on! he berated Meadow and me after the rest of our classmates had slunk home. —Don't you know how to work? Whose daughters are you, anyway?

If my father's shoulders were starting to stoop under the weight of the accumulated disappointments, Joanna's chipper enthusiasm, miraculously, never appeared to waver. When bean stalks curled up the trellises at the Jericho garden, she wrote a thrilling newsletter about all the new skills that the missionary children were learning.

Truth be told, we were pretty pleased with ourselves, despite my father's scolding. Meadow's green beans were as long as her outstretched arms, and my sunflowers were taller than anyone else's in the garden—even taller than Peter's, whose sheer proximity when we knelt beside each other in the dirt was enough to set off a hurricane in my thumping rib cage. He didn't seem annoyed when I chattered away about the story that I was writing in class—a dramatic mythology about coconuts—and when I tried to organize everyone into a game of tag at recess, he gave a quiet shrug and said it sounded fun. I tore around the *zanmann* tree, cheeks flushed, as the fine, silty dust turned to wet paste between the toes of my sandals—cheap blue glittery plastic from the marketplace, but they made me feel like a warrior princess.

I did not in a zillion years expect Peter to return my affections. My knees were perpetually scuffed from chasing lizards around the yard, and no matter how fervently I wished to be cute like Meadow, with her soft voice and bright blue eyes that squinted shut whenever she was embarrassed, I was bossy and opinionated and couldn't for the life of me learn to keep my mouth shut.

Rosie had it easiest—at three, she was blond, feisty, and adorable. In the evenings, while Meadow and I jostled at the kitchen sink and took turns twirling a soapy washcloth over the plates, our father slung Rosie onto his shoulders and took her for walks around town, just as he used to do with me when we lived in the California desert.

One of his favorite rambles with Rosie was to the garbage dumps at the edge of town, where they liked to catch toads, but sometimes they detoured through the empty Limbé market, littered with mango husks and discarded bags of syrup-ice, to watch the boys play soccer. It was on one such night, having left the dusty square to walk under the mahogany trees behind the museum, that a realization dawned on my father: the Limbé market was almost entirely devoid of tree cover.

The barest outlines of an idea began to coalesce in his mind. What if the entire town could be replanted, starting with the marketplace?

Rosie was as excited as he was when they returned from their walk, for he had just taught her to spell her first word. She proudly performed for us, perched on his shoulders with the canopy of night at her back, to the applause of the cicadas. For several weeks running, she signed her name T-R-E-E instead of Rose.

By the end of October, my father's wilted enthusiasm had begun to revive. With Zo at his side, he presided over a revival meeting in Camp Coq with the goal of converting the local farmers to the gospel of trees. At least sixty people, most likely inspired by Zo's example, professed that they wanted trees on their land. *This is a harvest of sitting in the marketplace,* my father noted in his journal, euphoric.

Confident that his incremental efforts had already begun to make a difference, my father moved the dusty, treeless Limbé market to the top of his agenda. He strategized with Obed until they came up with what felt like a foolproof plan. First they paid house calls to local officials: the mayor of Limbé, the police chief, the leader of the Boy Scouts, the pastor of the Baptist church. Next they measured the market, which incited curious conversations among the onlookers.

—Is the *blan* buying the marketplace? small boys asked, watching my father and Obed lay out measuring tape. —Is he going to build a bigger one?

One elderly gentleman with white hair and watery eyes informed them that when he was a boy, there had been many, many trees in the marketplace; he had been afraid to hike alone into the mountains for fear of what might be hiding in the forests.

Obed, his memory stirred, also remembered two tall trees that once spread their branches over Limbé, though they had long since been cut for firewood.

Perhaps, my father dared to hope, this symbolic act of replanting shade trees in the market would be the turning point.

It was to be a day like no other, full of fanfare and ceremony, a day for photographs and handshakes with shovels in hand; a day for the newsletters—the day the missionaries bequeathed a canopy of trees to the Limbé market.

On the appointed afternoon, now long weeks in the planning, the mayor himself tossed the first shovel of dirt over the tender roots. A choir from the Limbé Baptist church lifted their voices to bless the day, and the sun shone benevolently on the straining necks and arms of the Boy Scout leaders in their neckerchiefs and knee socks, not to mention the glad-to-be-escaping-our-schoolwork missionary kids of Jericho School.

We scooped handfuls of rich dark earth around the trunks of two hundred drought-resistant seedlings that my father had purchased from a small backyard Haitian nursery started by one of his former employees (he didn't want to repeat the Camp Coq misadventure and plant American trees).

No detail had been overlooked. There were designated caretakers to water the trees in the dry season and bamboo slats to keep the goats at bay, though it seemed an unnecessary precaution; even goats didn't like the taste of neem trees.

The heavens themselves seemed to vouchsafe a happy ending: as soon as the ceremony was over, a few light clouds blew over the sun and danced a minuet above the just-planted trees, sprinkling raindrops on the heads of the jubilant schoolchildren, who skipped home aglow with the conspicuous pleasure of benevolence.

Or at least that is how I remember it.

As it turned out, one or two details had been overlooked. The local officials had been consulted, but the barefoot soccer players, loath to lose their playground, had not. Nor had my father thought to check with the women who peddled their wares twice a week in the blazing sun.

The day after the tree-planting ceremony, when he came back to check on the seedlings, the *machann* told him exactly what they thought of his lousy idea, complaining that full-grown shade trees were the perfect habitat for snakes, and they didn't fancy the idea of one dropping on their heads while they worked.

Moreover, the entire project was seen as a hateful compromise to which they had not given their assent. One of the candidates running for *député* had promised them a proper covered market like the Iron Market in Cap-Haïtien, but with the new trees, they were afraid he'd never deliver on his campaign promise.

In his next newsletter, my father conceded defeat.

SPECIAL EDITION newsletter "Haiti"
by Jon & Flip Anderson:
February 2, 1984

This country certainly needs more than trees and rabbits. Haiti has been called the "graveyard of development projects." We can add my idea of planting trees in the market place to the list of failures. It appeared to start with success. The holes for planting the trees were all dug one morning by a crew supplied by the Magistrate. In 5 min-

utes the work was done. It is incredible what a little organization can do. That night a big rain fell which seemed a confirmation of success. The trees started to grow a little and I could envision the shade they would be giving within a year's time. Now, 3 months later they are all gone. For some reason people started breaking the heads off the trees and then taking the bamboo pickets for firewood. I guess my vision of a beautiful shady place was not shared by the people who bake in the strong tropical sun. I don't like to give up though and there were many people very supportive of the project so I think we'll try again, organizing from a different angle. What other lessons wait to be learned? Is there a possibility for success here?

———————

Like a long line of others before him, my father's missionary efforts had faltered, but it may be that the wasted time was not completely in vain. The shade-dappled marketplace never materialized, but a few of the local residents appeared to be inspired by the idea and planted trees in front of their own houses. The seedlings in the marketplace didn't survive the year, but those planted by ordinary citizens—*si Dye vle*—still stand in Limbé like sentinels, their leafy branches perfectly suited for equally stubborn birds to build their nests.

A Hundred Ways to Get It Wrong

Limbé, 1984

M Y FATHER'S CURE for the stress of Haiti was to collapse onto the living room floor for a quick thirty-minute nap after lunch, his back slumped against the cool concrete, oblivious to our feet scampering past his head. All that was necessary was to stop and let the body revive itself, then back to work again.

He was learning the hard way that reforesting Haiti was not going to be as straightforward as he'd hoped. Torrential tropical storms could drop up to twelve inches of rain in a single night, washing away months of work. And then there were the goats, who could happily chomp their way through hundreds of seedlings in a matter of days.

When my father took a group of visiting Canadians to visit a rural school where they'd planted two hundred and thirty trees the previous year, only one had survived. In an attempt to salvage the visit, he helped the church group plant more trees along the Limbé River, but when he returned the following day to check on them, a few seedlings were already gone.

—Such a place, he muttered as he kicked at the disturbed soil. The wear and tear of altruism, seen up close in all its bewildering inconsistency, was enough to grind a man down.

My father was even more exasperated when Obed asked permission to attend a weeklong agricultural seminar in Port-au-Prince and instead emigrated to the U.S. Obed later wrote, semi-apologetically, to say that he had found a good-paying job in Connecticut—though he was surprised that he didn't see many other people on the road when he walked to work. My father was frustrated. Haiti badly needed men with Obed's drive and vision, and yet success so often seemed to be equated with escape. (The painful truth: that no matter how hard Obed worked, he could not have risen to a position of authority equal to my father's or earned an equivalent salary—even at our meager income of several hundred dollars a month—was a tension unacknowledged by most missionaries.)

And yet when it came time to hire new workers for the hospital tree nursery, even for part-time jobs, my father waded through piles of politely worded requests—some of them from applicants who had gone to the extra trouble of translating their letters into English in the anxious hope of winning his favor.

> *2 Avril 84*
> *Mr John*
> *Agronomy*
> *Limbé, Haiti*
>
> *My dear*
>
> *I've great honeur to salue you and to make you to think to me perfectly.*
> *I want you send your new to me and the walking of your work.*
> *With your love the kindness to recover my letter with a great pleasure.*
>
> *I remain your affectionate*
> *M- Charely*
> *Student of Department's Agriculture*

Had my father been able to read French, the candidates could have shown off their fluency, but even among those whose families had scrimped and saved for the best education they could afford, the worry was palpable. The missionary hospital, subsidized by churches in the

U.S., was the largest employer in Limbé. But there weren't enough jobs to go around.

My mother, stuck at home with Rosie, felt the frustrations of Haiti to be nearly endless. Most of the other missionary wives, who worked in the office or as nurses in the hospital, hired cooks to help in the kitchen, but my mother's Kreyòl was faltering, and giving instructions grated against her independent streak. Also, she wanted her daughters to learn how to wash dishes and keep their rooms clean, like other American girls. But everything in Haiti took extra time. Fresh cow's milk, delivered by a local farmer in a rinsed-out rum bottle, had to be pasteurized. Yogurt meant setting the canning jars in a warm bath and checking on them every few hours. Whole wheat flour, which wasn't for sale even in Cap-Haïtien, had to be sifted from the *son de blé* (more commonly used for animal feed, but my mother wasn't picky).

As she slapped, folded, and leaned hard against the flat of her palm, kneading the bread for dinner, she daydreamed about being able to push her grocery cart down an air-conditioned aisle and buy whatever she needed straight off the shelf, in English. The prospect of returning to the U.S. after three intense years in Haiti felt like a cold glass of water after a twenty-mile hike. It was hard to even imagine a life where there would be time to play recorder and take walks by the creek in Idyllwild; a world without so many needs clamoring for her attention.

Joanna, having decided that my mother enjoyed too much free time, had put her in charge of the hospital doll project, which meant that at any moment there might be a knock on the door with a request for help. Joanna sold hundreds of the cheery cloth Haitian dolls when she went on speaking tours, and diabetic women at the hospital hand-stitched the eyes and mouths to pay for their daily insulin shots. My mother was in charge of fixing crooked embroidery and restocking the little gold baubles that doubled as earrings. She purchased fabric for the doll dresses from *machann* with carefully balanced baskets on their heads, who confidently measured the cloth by the length of their arms.

My mother also volunteered with Meadow's kindergarten class at

Jericho School, and helped my five-year-old sister learn to ride a bike. When Meadow could wobble, with a wrinkled forehead and fierce concentration, the entire length of the compound with my mother running alongside, she suggested that my father take her out for a spin, just to see how well she was doing.

My father held the bike seat while Meadow balanced her feet on the pedals, then sent her flying with a good strong push, only to stand back and watch as she veered with a scream and a crash into the rabbit cages behind our house.

—Jon! Why didn't you help her? my mother yelled as she ran to pick up the bike and the crying daughter.

He threw up his hands and stalked into the house. —That's how my dad taught me!

With our parents' attention fixed elsewhere, we missionary kids competed for any scrap of attention we could find. I hated and loved it when Ana pinched my cheek and told me that I was cute before escorting me through the back-door entrance to the Hodges house to play Barbies. The next day, with Kirsti at her side, she'd inform me that I was too hotshotty and American. I was a pest, and my nasty jelly sandals made my feet look ugly.

—I didn't want to be friends with you anyway! I'd shout, sticking out my tongue and kicking at the dust as the screen door banged shut behind them.

When it was Kirsti's turn to be picked on, she didn't yell or fight back. She just retreated inside her quiet house, into the arms (so I imagined) of a serenely attentive mother, which did little to soothe my jealousy. For at least a week—or was it longer? it feels, in memory, like a year—we made a pact not to speak to her or even acknowledge her presence. Within days, Kirsti had morphed into a pale, frightened shadow. Only Picole would play with her at recess. Peter, sensing danger, made himself scarce, as did Meadow.

I, on the other hand, rather liked the way that Kirsti's lower lip trembled and her brown eyes blurred with unspilled tears. Now that I was no longer the one being humiliated, it felt delicious to pile on the scorn. This newfound hatred tasted sweet. I belonged. She didn't.

Most of the parents, distracted by a hundred other crises, never even noticed, but when Suzette caught wind of our game, she dressed us down in a white-hot fury. I could not meet her livid gaze. Kirsti hid under Suzette's arm as we lined up miserably to beg forgiveness. Kirsti patted our backs tentatively, murmuring absolution, which only made it worse. I slunk home with my chest heaving.

We had created, on the missionary compound, a world unto ourselves: communal living—but only for the expatriates. Only in rare moments did we recognize our poverty. We had only each other to turn to. Our enclave smacked of scarcity, not wealth.

All of the missionary kids had learned to belt out the lyrics to "Ayiti Cheri," thanks to Laurie Casséus, who drove over from the nearby Baptist seminary to direct the Jericho School choir. Laurie's long blond hair swayed across her back when she raised her arms and summoned our voices into the air, and we threw ourselves into that rousing love song for Haiti—*Ayiti cheri, pi bèl peyi pase ou nan pwen*: Beloved Haiti, there is no more beautiful country than you—but aside from trips to the beach or church on Sundays we rarely left the compound.

We seldom saw our Haitian and Dominican friends in Cap-Haïtien, and though my mother played the autoharp with a Baptist choir in Limbé and joined a Kreyòl Bible study with Pastor Tomas, my participation was limited to Sundays, when I pulled on my white socks with lace fluttering around the ankles and, in my scuffed church shoes, doing my best to avoid the mud puddles, walked the half mile to the Limbé Baptist church.

The sanctuary held more than a thousand worshippers, even without the balcony that hung half-constructed from the far wall, whose rose window Dr. Hodges had helped design. Women with starched white doilies balanced on their heads arrived throughout the service to squeeze onto the long wooden benches, but the thin flutter of air from two small oscillating fans behind the pulpit barely reached the front rows.

During the brow-wiping sermons, Meadow, Rosie, and I were expected to pay attention like the Haitian girls who sat so quietly in their Sunday dresses. My father allowed no fidgeting. He refused to let us bring colored pencils or books, like the other missionary kids, so I flipped through the Old Testament, which, luckily enough, was chock-full of drama—Absalom dangling by his long hair from a tree as his horse raced off without him; Ruth slipping under Boaz's cloak at night; Onan, who was supposed to provide his widowed sister-in-law with a son but instead *spilled his seed upon the ground, for which offense the Lord slew him* (a sufficiently vague descriptor but one that I nevertheless hid furtively if my father happened to glance over at the page).

Had I been asked, I would have piped up proudly that of course I was a Christian—I had gotten down on my knees and prayed to ask Jesus into my heart when we lived at the Ag Center, during a Children's Bible Hour radio broadcast. It was nice to know I had heaven to look forward to, maybe even some stars in my crown if I behaved just right. It was just that the flowery sermons and long-winded prayers in Kreyòl went on so long. At least in English church we got to sing silly songs with hand motions.

I didn't mind Sunday school on the compound with Suzette. She had us memorize her favorite Psalms, which I rather liked. When I climbed trees and recited Psalm 139 under my breath—*Oh Lord, You have searched me and You know me, You know when I sit and when I rise*—I could almost feel God shimmering in the leaves. I felt more or less the same frisson of glory if I fell and got the wind knocked out of me and my mother put her hand on my forehead and prayed a shimmering waterfall of words in a language spoken by nobody, as far as I could tell, but her and God. Baptists got nervous when people spoke in tongues, but my mother's glossolalia was an incantatory song, a burbling babble of comfort. If church could have included a little more of that close and holy darkness, it wouldn't have been half bad.

Instead, church seemed to mostly be about sitting still and trying to impress God (or other people). When it was time for the French hymns, I stood up alongside everyone else, a thousand feet shuffling on the bare concrete. Most people in Limbé spoke no more French than I did, but the women dutifully adjusted their head coverings and cradled their thumbed and wrinkled songbooks as we blundered along together. Sometimes my mother stood up front and strummed her auto-harp while severe-looking men with tightly cinched belts passed the collection baskets. Only when we got to burst into the harmonies of the Kreyòl version of "We Shall Overcome"—*nou va triyonfe yon jou!*—did the enormous room swell to its full echoing capacity.

Finally, after what felt like three torturous hours, the pastor raised a hand and squinted his eyes shut, using his other hand to mop his fore-head with a starched handkerchief as he pronounced the benediction. And then, mercifully, it was over. The congregation crowded into the aisles to catch up on the latest gossip; I retreated through the side door with the rest of the missionaries. Even in church, we kept to our own.

On the long walk home, Dr. Hodges trundled past on his bicycle, having pedaled in early to teach Sunday school. His bike bell clanged a polite warning, his hand lifted slightly in hello. Sometimes a car full of missionary kids drove past waving, with Barbara at the wheel, but my father insisted that we needed to walk because it would help us meet our neighbors—as if that alone could bridge the chasm we'd created.

My mother held Meadow's hand, and my father hoisted Rosie onto his shoulders. I walked as quickly as my too-tight church shoes would carry me.

The road from the church was treeless and hot. Women shelled pea-nuts in their front yards. Men tipped back woven chairs to listen to the radio. A girl, pinned between an older woman's knees with her scalp pulled back at a sharp angle, met my eyes as the comb yanked backward.

Neighbor kids yelled *Blan! Blan!* but I hated it most when they called Meadow and me *Cheve wouj! Cheve wouj!* (our red hair being the ongoing joke because, despite our obvious wealth, it looked as if we suffered from protein deficiency). Watching each other from a distance, we jumped to conclusions and got it wrong at least half the time. It was a relief to finally reach the front gate of the compound and retreat under the cool shadows of the overhanging trees as Haiti dissolved be-hind me into a clamorous song.

Ti Marcel

Limbé, 1984

Two years into his unplanned career as a missionary agronomist, my father wrote to Grandma Lois: *You said not to wear ourselves out taking care of Ti Marcel. I think in a way it's therapy for me.*

At nine months old, Ti Marcel had neither hair nor teeth and could not sit up. She weighed under eleven pounds. My father brought her home from the pediatric ward so that my sisters and I could shout some life into her, but she didn't smile or giggle like other babies. Her skeletal arms jutted out from her distended abdomen, and she had wide, unblinking eyes and a rib cage like a shuddering kite frame, ready to catch in the slightest breeze and lift her out of our hands, drifting beyond the horizon, lost to the world.

A visiting American nurse had pointed out the tiny foundling to my father because of the simple astonishing fact that she kept not dying. More than once, the doctors had performed emergency venous cutdowns on her ankles to connect an IV to collapsed veins. My father suspected that her chances of survival were slim if she remained in the overcrowded ward, untouched for hours. He wanted to give her a fighting chance, as he would have wished for any of his daughters.

Rosie, who was four years old and eager for a younger sibling, leaned in close and tickled Ti Marcel's feet. I was eight and aware of all the attention I had already lost. I turned away. Her papery skin reeked of scabies medicine and urine.

She had no name. The Haitian nurses at the hospital called her Ti

Marcel, little Marcel, and this name—the name of the father who had apparently abandoned her—was one of the few things we knew about her. The fragments of backstory, which we acquired piecemeal from uncertain sources, were as follows: Her mother was said to have died soon after giving birth; unnamed relatives fed her watered-down tea instead of milk, then left her at the missionary hospital. They had not been in contact since that time. Her father, Marcel, was rumored to have fled the country only to be thrown into detention once he arrived in Florida. It was an old, tired story—yet another survivor with a strong body and shrinking options who had risked everything for a chance at *Peyi Bondye,* God's Country: where coins could be found on the street, free for the taking; where all the children had enough food to eat and all the fathers had three-car garages; a distant realm from whence the missionaries hailed; mythical land of the minimum wage.

My father brought Ti Marcel home from the pediatric ward every chance he could find, and took her out in the rain to feel the sharp sting of raindrops on her bare arms. Cradled against his chest, her ungainly head listed awkwardly on a thin neck. In the waning and humid dusk, my sisters and I raced in breathless circles around their two-headed silhouette under the *zanmann* tree, playing freeze tag in the dust.

As the months whirled by, my father's letters radiated pleasure. Ti Marcel learned to sit up. She grew hair. She developed a taste for my mother's home-cooked dinners, mashed into gruel by my doting father. *Baby Marcel is everyone's example of a miracle,* he boasted to Grandma Lois. *Yesterday she held a bottle all by herself.*

Even I couldn't deny the transformation. My father had always insisted that she was a smart kid—he could tell by the way her eyes followed us around the room—and within a few short months, she had blossomed into a determined, curious child. She could follow all the prompts in the *Pat the Bunny* book when she sat on his lap: Lift the handkerchief to play peekaboo, pat the man's scratchy beard, put her finger through the gold wedding ring.

She began to spend entire weekends at our house, which my father chronicled in his weekly letters to faraway California.

> Dec 8: *We had Marcel over again last night. She really has a lot more hair . . . In just the last few days the older girls have decided she really is neat. They said last night that they're starting to like her more.*

> Dec 15: *Good morning, the chickens are crowing, the crows cawing, the cat meowing, Marcel squeaking, and the sky is a pretty color . . . Marcel has spent the last two nights here. She always sleeps straight through and wakes up to be no trouble at all.*

My father adored Ti Marcel. I still considered her a menace. I hated how gently he spoon-fed her gulping hunger, as if he would do anything to rescue her. He never seemed exasperated when she soaked the bed with diarrhea, but if I sassed back instead of setting the table like Mom asked, he'd slam open the drawers in the kitchen and yank my arm while paddling mightily with a wooden spoon. Ti Marcel didn't have the strength to defy him, and no matter how little attention he gave, she turned to him like a sunflower.

Even now, I can remember the texture and shape of my jealousy, wadded up like a loose sock under the heel of my roller skates, grating against my anklebone every time I rounded a corner. Jealousy jarring and black-heat-abrasive, like the skid of sweaty knees and palms on jagged concrete when I hit gravel and my skates flew one way and my arms another—blood from broken palms and a skinned nose leaking into my sobbing mouth.

At eight years old, I didn't care what became of her. I wanted my father back.

By Christmas, Ti Marcel had her own bed at our house, to my mother's growing exasperation. My father never gave any warning before he brought home a baby from the pediatric ward, which meant that the burden for the rest of us girls fell to my mother. Still, she helped me pick out an embroidered yellow dress from the marketplace as a Christmas present for Ti Marcel—reminding me firmly that God wanted us to be kind to everyone, but especially to those without families to love them.

I listened resentfully to my mother's Sunday school lesson, then lost myself in making an elaborate card, mesmerized by the confident arc of my crayon as it swept across the page.

On Christmas Eve, the missionary kids lit tissue-thin Haitian *fanals* and carried the swaying candlelit cardboard churches through the hospital to sing carols to the patients. We plonked out a pretty decent rendition of "Hark! The Herald Angels Sing" in Kreyòl, but had to revert to jolly old English for "Good King Wenceslas." Dr. Hodges's deep baritone rumbled under my mother's soprano—*as the snow lay round about, deep and crisp and even.* The families of the patients, not having understood a word, leaned against the doorways and shouted *Amèn!*

The annual Christmas pageant at the seminary, by contrast, was performed only in Kreyòl. For once, we weren't the stars of the show and didn't have to sit in the front row, which felt like a relief. Mary, played by a young Haitian seminary student, rode in on a live donkey, and five-month-old baby Andrew, recently adopted by Steve and Nancy James, was awarded the place of honor in the manger. The shepherds did their best to gaze meaningfully at the Christ child while wrangling a herd of squirming goats, but the bleating animals startled poor Andrew, whose parents passed forward his bottle as an entire flock of angels danced down the aisle singing hallelujahs. I agreed with my parents: No Christmas pageant in the States could hold a candle to that chaotic joy.

As soon as we got home from the pageant, my father brought Ti Marcel over from the pediatric ward for Christmas dinner. She smelled of Vaseline and sulfur powder, but he didn't seem to mind—scabies being, as he put it, a small price to pay for life itself. The electricity had been flickering on and off all evening, and the kerosene lantern wouldn't stay lit. When our dinner guests arrived—fellow tree-hugger expats who worked for an NGO in Cap-Haïtien—my mother tried to make small talk while slicing a fresh pineapple and checking on the rolls in the propane oven as my sisters and I, hopped up on all the excitement, raced around her ankles shouting at each other. My father was too busy to help; Ti Marcel needed a bath.

Joanna knocked on the door in the midst of this commotion to inform my father that some well-heeled Haitian visitors wanted to purchase poinsettias so he needed to open up the greenhouse for an after-hours sale. He promptly handed my mother the dripping baby, still crying and cold from her bath. My mother never did find the elusive bottle of formula—which my father, in his hurry, had dropped into an empty chicken-feed container just outside the front door—so my mother spent twenty minutes trying to placate a wailing baby while Christmas dinner grew cold in the dark.

But it all turned out quite alright, she concluded with a sigh in her weekly letter home to the Divine grandparents.

With only six months to go before our two-year contract at the compound was up, it was unclear what our future might hold. Joanna had already informed us that her daughter Susan would be moving back to Limbé with her family; Susan's husband, Ron Smith, would resume management of the tree nursery. A visiting American Baptist Foreign Mission Society representative, impressed by my father's work ethic, had encouraged him to apply to seminary, since the Baptists required all full-time missionaries to obtain a master's degree or higher, but the Fuller School of World Mission in California had yet to reply with an acceptance offer. Nor were my parents sure how they'd pay for a seminary degree if my father did get in. The crop of spaghetti squash that my father had tilled into the soil in California had eaten up a good portion of what they'd saved while working at the Ag Center, and our income at the missionary hospital, subsidized by supporters in the States, capped out at a few hundred dollars a month—which was more than enough to live on in Haiti but wouldn't stretch very far in California. He might be able to pick up a seasonal Forest Service job, but it would be too late to plant vegetables. And besides the cabin in

Idyllwild, whose pipes wouldn't last through a winter, we didn't have anywhere to live (the trailer in the desert, to my mother's great relief, had been sold at a steep discount and hauled away by a friend even poorer than we were).

But no matter how daunting our own challenges might seem, tiny Ti Marcel was a living reminder that we could always find someone who had it much harder than us—and if she could stare down those odds, then surely we could do no less.

By the time the end of January rolled around and a letter from California arrived with the news that one of my father's sisters was willing to adopt Ti Marcel so we wouldn't have to leave her in Haiti, the argument that had been silently brewing for months spilled out into the open. My father, swept along by the hope that this borrowed Haitian daughter would soon become a part of the family—even if only as a niece or cousin—wanted to move her out of the pediatric ward permanently. My mother reminded him that Ti Marcel already had a father, even if he hadn't yet returned for her.

This, at least, was sufficient to force my father to stop and consider his actions. He drove the next day to the Teleco office in Cap-Haïtien and placed a collect call to his sister. Shouting over a badly connected line in a sweltering phone booth, my father explained that as fond as he was of Ti Marcel, it didn't seem right to uproot her from her family. We would just have to trust that God would continue to protect her.

He was, however, moved by his family's generosity. *We still can't get over what a wonderful family you are to be willing to adopt a kid mostly for our sakes,* he mused reverently on a cassette tape for the Andersons.

My mother, on the other hand, found the public drama humiliating—particularly as it reflected poorly on both my parents' meager finances and their hazy plans for the future. *Apparently they thought Jon couldn't live without that little baby so they were going to adopt her for us,* she explained to the Divine grandparents. *However, it isn't something one enters lightly.*

Even after the conversation with his sister, my father continued to pamper Ti Marcel without any hope of permanence, bringing her home every night for dinner, until Meadow and I complained. Even Rosie was tired of playing with her. Couldn't we do something else for a change?

For once, my father relented; that night we played checkers. Meadow, who didn't appreciate getting skunked by my two kings, tipped over the board.

The next night, Ti Marcel was back. She had just gotten her first tooth—which, my father pointed out proudly, hadn't even made her grumpy—and we celebrated her first birthday with a chocolate cupcake and a candle that we helped extinguish.

Exactly one week later, like a character in a mystery novel, Marcel, the rightful father, reappeared. It was an otherwise unremarkable Monday afternoon. Herons squawked in the trees, and missionary kids raced on roller skates around the bumpy circular sidewalk as Marcel, still dusty from his three-hour *kamyon* ride, made his way in silence to the pediatric ward. He had arrived without fanfare, but he had returned to claim his own.

The prison cell in Miami had apparently been a fabrication. As it turned out, he was a farmer with a small plot of land outside of Gonaïves, and he had left his cows and fields for the day to reclaim his daughter. No explanation was given for why, if he owned milk cows, his daughter had been left at the hospital in such dire condition. The Haitian nurses, bristling with condescension, showed him his transformed little girl, who could now stand against the rail of her crib and bounce with chubby arms. They explained that she had become a favorite of a missionary named *Agwonòm* Jon, who wanted to adopt her.

Marcel's response was adamant, as the nurses later reported to my father: I don't want the *blan* to take my baby!

This assertion should have been enough to settle the matter, but by so blatantly demonstrating our affection for Ti Marcel, we had wandered into uncertain territory. Given the historic imbalance of power, it was widely understood that if a *blan* decided to take custody of a Haitian child, his will could not be thwarted, even by the rightful father.

Indeed, before Marcel was allowed to take his daughter home, he was sent first to speak with Dr. Hodges, who cleared his throat and decreed that the child—for her own protection—was not yet healthy enough to leave the confines of the hospital.

Marcel reiterated to the nurses in the pediatric ward that his daughter would *not* be raised by a white man, then melted back into the obscurity from whence he came.

My father, who heard about the encounter only after Marcel had left, readied himself for the impending loss. *It seems very right that she should have a real father,* he penned in a letter to his mother later that afternoon. But there was already a catch in his throat—so much so that he added later, as an afterthought scribbled in the margins: *I'm glad she didn't go today. I will miss her when she does go.*

As far as I was concerned, the crisis was over. Now that Ti Marcel had a home waiting for her, I could cuddle her without envy. I wove her hair into soft braids and read her fairy tales on the cicada-humming porch while she sat on my lap and reached for the pages.

Life was looking up again. There were newborn baby bunnies to smuggle from their cages, a kite-day competition at Jericho School, and my new Easter dress, which spun like a gilded teacup when I whirled around the living room. Grandma Lois had even heard rumors that my father had been accepted at Fuller Seminary, though the news wasn't official yet. What did it matter that our passports were missing? We were seasoned adventurers by now. The world was full of surprises.

On our last Easter morning in Haiti for the foreseeable future, my father shook us awake in the dark. We clustered around Mom's autoharp and stared down from a ridgeline as the sun spilled over the mountains into the Limbé Valley. Flocks of cattle egrets lifted from the mangroves. Far beneath us, like a glittering promise, curved the blue, quiet Baie de L'Acul, into which jutted the triumphantly reforested Morne Bois Pin peninsula. My father and the Haitian nursery workers had just planted an additional 960 trees on that restored Eden. My mother clasped her autoharp to her breast and sang like an angel.

The Limbé Baptist church celebrated Easter with a long, slow rhythmic march to the river where the baptismal candidates, robed in white, waded into the water singing. The missionaries celebrated with an all-compound potluck. Ti Marcel sat on my lap while my parents grabbed each other's waists and barreled across the grass with their legs tied together, taking a noisy first place in the three-legged race. I came in second in the sack races. Meadow, who had just learned to jump rope, whisked around our volunteer cottage, humming to herself. Rosie licked the icing off a pan of cinnamon rolls. Ti Marcel, rechristened Marcelle in my father's letters, trilled her sweet-voiced gurgle of *Da-da-da-dah*. She had just broken in three new teeth, as sharp as diamonds. She was almost crawling.

As my father had already pointed out to Grandma Lois, Marcelle's dramatic recovery was a useful counterweight to other disappointments. For though the Morne Bois Pin peninsula appeared, from a distance, to give off an inspirational glow, my father understood that all was not well in the missionary forest. He had long suspected that the local employees, who received no direct oversight during the week, were not only falsifying their time sheets but even cutting down trees and pocketing the profits.

Determined to set things straight, he set out a few days after Easter to catch the suspects in the act. He did not, as he usually did, cross the bay in the small wooden motorboat that belonged to the hospital, which he knew could be heard from across the water; instead he drove to a black sand beach directly across from Morne Bois Pin and paid a fisherman with a tattered sail to drop him off on the opposite shore without anyone knowing that he had arrived.

As it turned out, his suspicions were justified. The workers were not at their posts, nor even on the peninsula, although they came running as soon as they saw his stoop-shouldered silhouette through the neglected trees. On further investigation, he found hastily scattered branches over tree trunks that he had not authorized the men to cut.

He fired them on the spot, then hiked along an unpaved road to catch a *tap tap* back to where he'd left the vehicle, pulling into the compound just before dark. Only too late did he learn what he had lost.

My mother was up to her elbows in greasy soap bubbles, the bread pans clinking in the sink, when she heard the knock at the door. She had been trying to get the house in order after a frantic morning during which she had baked cinnamon rolls while babysitting three additional missionary kids, cooked lunch for a friend, then welcomed surprise visitors who were more than happy to bite into the sweet candied bread melting with homemade butter. After her guests finally left, she was about to settle Rosie down for a much-needed nap when a gang of missionary kids banged on the door to ask for my help catching a garter snake. Meadow and I raced off after them, and the commotion yanked four-year-old Rosie out of her drowsiness. My mother had to go back in and rub her shoulders until she finally got quiet.

My mother felt vaguely irritated as she left the dishes in the sink to respond to yet another interruption. Opening the screen door, she was startled to find Ti Marcel in the arms of a stranger. Marcel, whom we'd never met, explained that he had brought his daughter, Cherylene, to say goodbye.

Marcel and his sister had already made a careful, diplomatic tour of the hospital, though it had taken him almost an hour to convince the skeptical Dr. Hodges that his recently malnourished daughter would not relapse under inattentive supervision. Marcel was polite but firm. He would make sure that his daughter received proper care. Before he left Limbé, Marcel stopped to thank each of the missionary doctors and nurses, the Haitian staff—and, of course, my family.

My mother, thrown off guard by the sudden announcement, had just sufficient wherewithal to assemble her own scattered daughters (Rosie poked her head out of the bedroom as soon as she heard voices; Meadow and I were under the *zanmann* tree, the snake having gotten away). My mother explained to us that Ti Marcel had a new name and that we might not see her again, then helped us gather up the books and toys and clothes we'd amassed over the previous seven and a half months of pretending that she was our sister.

We gave hugs and one last kiss. Rosie cried, but I didn't. Everyone on the compound—except the Doctor and Joanna—left sooner or later. It was safer not to get attached.

My sisters and I tagged along as far as the carport to watch Cherylene leave. She seemed happy enough, tucked against her aunt's hip, her chubby legs showing under her dress as her father, straight-backed and purposeful, strode out the hospital gates.

Joni was kicking a soccer ball by the fishpond, so Meadow and I drifted over to join him. Rosie climbed up on a row of propane tanks by the carport, punchy and a little off-balance without her afternoon nap. When she jumped, the hem of her dress snagged on an empty propane tank and it tipped over in slow motion on top of her. I came running as soon as I heard screaming. Meadow tore down the sidewalk for Mom.

Rosie ended up with a big red welt on her forehead and a few scrapes but otherwise seemed fine.

—You darn kid! my father shouted when he got home and heard the news. —What did you think you were doing?

It was just as well I didn't read his letters until years later.

April 16, 1985 letter to Grandma Lois:

> Well my trip to MBP went well . . . Sure enough no one was working . . . There's more to the story but I'm tired and am really writing about something else. When I got back I found out that Ti Marcel was gone. Her father and his sister had come to get her . . . I'm glad I wasn't here. I would have cried.

When I opened that letter for the first time, in my mid-twenties, I was surprised at how the dust-winged specter of jealousy fluttered out at me from the page. I had to blink angrily to keep its claws out of my eyes.

My mother, predictably, had a different take on the situation.

April 16, 1985 letter to the Divine grandparents:

> *Dear Divines, Greetings from your faraway but not forgotten daughter. We received two letters from you on Saturday so I better return the favor. Well the big news is that Ti Marcel is on her way home to Gonaïves with her father and aunt. Her new name is Cherylene! That was mighty tough news for Daddy Jon and Rosie . . .*
>
> *I took Rose through Pediatrics to look for another baby to love and there were plenty of little, hardly alive, bony kids . . . Jon beat me to bed so will see you tomorrow.*

Ti Marcel had received her allotted miracle—she had gone home with a father who wanted her. Meanwhile, back at the hospital, the lineup of brokenhearted babies was just as long as before.

Maddening, beloved Ayiti Cheri, land of myriad contradictions: the orphans who appeared half starved and abandoned on the hospital doorstep, only to be reclaimed later by smiling, guileless parents; the reforestation projects mangled by goats; the donated infant formula pocketed on the sly by opportunistic employees.

Each frustrating scenario held a yet more complicated layer hidden underneath. Peel back the mattress of the donated hospital bed and find a nest of cockroaches. Peel back the pages of the missionary account books and discover no one willing to pick up the tab for malnourished orphans except little old ladies in American Baptist churches who knit garish yellow and pink sweaters for children in the tropics.

Demand change, by all means. Yet know this—you will not be the first to fail. Such endeavors look easy only from a distance. It is only after the clouds have evaporated that gritty reality holds sway.

With little more than a month to go before our imminent departure from Haiti, my father tried to cram in as many farewell adventures as possible. He was ready to be done with compound life, which he saw as a burdensome luxury; if we did ever return, he had promised himself that we'd find a small house in a rural community where my sisters and I could grow up speaking Kreyòl and playing with Haitian friends. My mother agreed—at least initially.

In the tiny village of Soufrière, along a river called Suffering, our truck broke down and we had to roll a flat tire across the dirt for an hour and a half before we could flag down help (the spare was flat, too). On a sailboat ride to Île de la Tortue, hunkered down between bags of charcoal and rice, my mother and Rosie both got seasick. I panicked when the wind caught the mast and tipped the overcrowded fishing boat so far that we nearly capsized. When the storm subsided and the sails went limp, men grabbed the oars to heave us through the rocking waves, the knotted muscles in their backs straining and easing, straining and easing, as the passengers sang us to shore, an invocation to the spirits to carry us over the depths.

My father's enthusiasm never faltered; he was convinced that the whole trip had been worth it just to see the color of the sea after the storm—*absolutely the most beautiful deep blue*—but my mother's wanderlust was spent. By the time we made it back to Limbé, after flagging down a *tap tap* and leaving the Daihatsu parked on the wrong side of a swollen river, each of us girls taking a turn on the backs of strangers while my mother waded across alone, my mother had concluded that America might be boring, but Haiti was far too stressful.

My father, however, wasn't about to leave until he'd seen for himself that Ti Marcel was being properly cared for. She had missed her first checkup at the hospital, but he and my mother returned pleased from their surveillance mission. Some of Cherylene's relatives had emigrated to Canada, and the money they sent back helped to pay the living expenses of the rest of the family. Marcel had been tending his gardens a few miles outside of town, but Cherylene stayed during the day with one of her aunts in a well-kept house with cement floors, electricity, and a television—which was more luxury than my father allowed us. Meadow and I were at Jericho School and didn't get to see her, but my mother assured us that she looked cute and healthy and had barely recognized them after a month away. She was crawling all over the place and strong enough to stand and inch along the wall—it wouldn't be long before she was ready to push off and walk on her own strong legs.

Rose was so happy to see her. We all were, my father updated the grandparents.

Having finally located our missing passports, I leaned down and whispered into the ears of the black Labrador retriever: *tell Peter I will miss him.* We leaned our heads out of the car windows and waved frantic goodbyes as the missionary compound disappeared behind us, and inhaled one last deep breath of *kasav* roasting over a charcoal fire. A *kamyon* swerved around us going the opposite direction, the blare of its bugle-call bus horn followed by the clamor of chickens as they fluttered away from the thundering tires. Men on the roof straddled shifting bags of mangoes and manioc, their laughter exploding and then fading to silence as they hurtled past us toward an uncertain future.

As we lifted above the runway on a missionary plane, Haiti receded, the dense green thickets of bamboo, Leucaena, and cactus giving way to barren hills.

Into one of our going-away cards someone had tucked an unexplained pamphlet: "Are Missionaries Unbalanced?"

———————

We read Joanna's next newsletter under the scrub oak tree at our cabin in Idyllwild, which announced that the Jon Anderson family had moved out at noon on a busy June day in 1985; by three p.m., Joanna's daughter Susan, husband, Ron, and their six children had moved in to replace us. It was a bona fide Hodges reunion, and their ranks were growing. Paul Hodges, Bill and Joanna's youngest son, flew in from Mauritania with his wife and nine-month-old son a few days later, and settled into an apartment above the museum. David's wife, Emily, gave birth to their second child. And Barbara agreed to take in eleven-year-old Olynda,

whose beleaguered mother had begged the Hodges family to give her
daughter a chance at a better life.

Steady, quiet-voiced Peter was so jealous of his newly adopted sister that, during a game of catch, he threw the ball as hard as he could
against her thin chest.

Dr. Hodges was sixty-one years old, and Joanna was sixty-two. With
four children, five adopted children, and umpteen grandchildren gathered about them, they decided to purchase land a few miles outside of
Limbé, as it appeared that they would be spending the rest of their lives
in Haiti. Dr. Hodges explained to a friend from medical school that he
still hoped, after his retirement, to dabble in medicine, archaeology, and
museology—*the latter being a nice quiet occupation for befuddled old men.*

He was being modest. A reporter from the *New York Times* had recently spent five and a half hours in Dr. Hodges's study to find out
more about the La Navidad excavation, and a two-page article was
about to be published in that illustrious newspaper: "Columbus's Lost
Town: New Evidence Is Found."

Bill and Joanna's retirement property overlooked the very same
two-headed mountain that Columbus had christened Dos Hermanos,
the Two Brothers, and which was known in Kreyòl as De Tèt. The Doctor had unearthed zemi amulets on the summit, and found petroglyphs
carved into rocky outcroppings, an experience that had inspired him
to poetry:

> *During the rainy season dark gray, scudding clouds are drawn
> to the mountain, plunging it into deep shadow, and on the heights,
> a cold penetrating wind makes one forget that the foot of this peak
> stands in the tropics. As on all cloud-wreathed summits, where the
> ground recedes in all directions into a boiling mass of vapor, the im-
> pression is one of mystery and grandeur.*

In the shadow of these mountains, Dr. Hodges surmised that perhaps he might finally escape into relative peace, working intermittently
on various subjects that had piqued his curiosity. *The years here haven't*

really been what you might call easy, he mused. *When we sailed off into the blue those many years ago . . . I had many misgivings. I believe, however, that God has been faithful to our vision.*

To read those letters now, knowing precisely how that vision unraveled, is to tempt my own missionary impulse—I want to reach back and shake his stooped shoulders.

Surely, I tell myself, if he had known what was coming, he could have found a way to walk away before it destroyed him. But perhaps I am too optimistic. Even if we could foresee our own demise, would we really have the strength to prevent it?

BOOK TWO

On the last day of the world
I would want to plant a tree.

W. S. MERWIN,
"PLACE,"
THE RAIN IN THE TREES

We, content at the last
If our temporal reversion nourish
(Not too far from the yew-tree)
The life of significant soil.

T. S. ELIOT,
"THE DRY SALVAGES,"
THE FOUR QUARTETS

The Burned Village

Ayiti, 1493

O N HIS SECOND voyage, Columbus returned to the New World
flush with fame. The ships that accompanied him were crowded
with men eager for their share in the wealth—former prisoners freed
by the crown to help civilize the islands, priests eager to convert the
heathens. But of Columbus's proud first settlement, La Navidad, only
burned timbers remained. None of the thirty-nine men had survived.

The gracious Guacanagarí pled innocence. Fragmentary stories
emerged that the Spaniards, savage with infighting, had commandeered
as many as five Taíno women apiece. Death came by disease, by sword-
point, and, it was rumored, at the hands of Caonabo, a cacique from
the south of Ayiti who—having sworn no loyalty to the Spaniards—
was rumored to have administered the judgment that the lawless men
brought upon their own heads.

Enraged that his vision had so quickly unraveled, Columbus ordered
retribution. Caciques were captured and sold as slaves, or hanged, like
the poet Anacaona, Caonabo's widow, whom the Spaniards believed to
be in alliance with the devil because the feast that she served her un-
grateful guests included roasted iguana—which the superstitious colonizers mistook for dragons.

The cacique Hatuey from the province of Guahaba ordered his
people to throw their gold into the murky depths of the Limbé River
and flee. But even this precaution could not save them. Hatuey, targeted
by the conquistadores as an incendiary symbol of native resistance, was

eventually hunted down in the mountains of Cuba and condemned to
the stake. A Franciscan priest urged Hatuey first to be baptized; Hatuey, tied to his funeral pyre, asked if there would be any Christians in
heaven. Assured that there would be, Hatuey proclaimed that he had
no wish to go to such a place. At these blasphemous words, Spanish
soldiers set him alight, and Hatuey's enslaved people were condemned
to the mines.

The gaping irony, that those who claimed to speak on behalf of God
seemed to be concerned only with wealth and power, did not escape
the ire of the Spanish priest Bartolomé de las Casas. Outraged, he wrote
a blistering *Short Account of the Destruction of the Indies* and demanded
protection from the Crown for indigenous peoples. He described how
two Taíno boys brought parrots to the conquistadores—*and the ones who
call themselves Christian took the parrots and just for the fun of it, cut off the
heads of the two boys.*

Less than thirty years after the arrival of the gold-hungry Europeans
on Hispaniola, the Taíno population—their garden plots destroyed by
free-ranging Spanish cattle, vulnerable to smallpox, and weakened by
famine—had shrunk, according to a 1519 census, from an estimated
one million inhabitants to only twenty-five hundred.

Spanish settlers accused Columbus of having inflated his stories
about the great wealth of the New World, and he was removed by the
Crown for failing to keep order. He was taken back to Spain in chains.

Ironically, it was Bartolomé de las Casas, the passionate defender
of the Indians, who suggested that the shrinking Taíno labor force be
replaced with imported African slaves—though he later repented of
his advice. For what followed was unimaginable. Cramped slave ships.
Bodies fed to the sharks. Brutalities that defied comprehension. When
Spain eventually abandoned the western half of Ayiti for more profit-
able colonies in the New World, and ownership passed to the French,
an eighteenth-century etching by a shocked gentleman witness showed
a punishment designed by plantation owners: a hole dug just deep
enough to cradle a pregnant woman's belly so that the owners could
beat her as close to death as possible yet still harvest the unborn slave

she carried. That this same colony poured such vast wealth into the coffers of Europe made the depravity that much more chilling.

On the night of the great slave uprising in 1791, in a dark stretch of woods along the north coast of Haiti, the rebel leader Boukman rallied his fellow slaves to seize their destiny and fight for their freedom.

Boukman's fierce cry was later imagined and set down in words that every Haitian schoolchild would recognize:

> *The God who made the sun, who stirs up the sea and makes the*
> *thunder roar, is ordering us to vengeance.*
> *He will help us throw down the image of the colonist's God,*
> *who is thirsty of our tears.*
> *Listen to the freedom that is speaking to our hearts.*
> *I swear I will never let the blacks live in slavery.*

A thousand plantations in the rebellious north—including Limbé and Acul—burned to the ground. The slaves carried as their standard a spear with the impaled carcass of a white baby.

Ayiti's soil was thick with blood: slaves, colonizers, Taínos, missionaries, all heaped together in their torment. The land was torn apart by their suffering. Hills, topsoil, forests gone, washed out to sea or burned until nothing remained but charcoal. Ashes to ashes, dust to dust. The Christian conquest of the New World had accomplished a desecration so profound that five centuries would be insufficient to heal the scars.

There Goes My Life

Idyllwild, 1989

MOM AND DAD say we're going to Haiti by the end of the summer — or whenever we get the money, whichever comes first. There goes my life!

I put down my pen and closed my journal. When I turned thirteen, my father had dug out the dirt under the porch of our Idyllwild cabin so I could have a room of my own. The damp earth floor had been tamped down and covered with a sheet of plastic and a carpet remnant, and there was one tiny window that the raccoons rattled at night. My head almost grazed the five-foot ceiling, but when I clicked on the lamp and curled up in my sleeping bag, it was the perfect place to decompress my whirling brain.

I had whole notebooks full of various attempts at stories and poems, although I rarely finished any of them, frustrated that I couldn't force the words on the page to match the fierce rhythm in my head. I hadn't forgotten my promise to Suzette to dedicate my first book to her, but my seven-year-old confidence had fizzled out.

My little sisters, ages eight and eleven, still slept upstairs on bunk beds in the one-room cabin, while my parents had the loft. I was careful never to invite classmates over to the house, having won a scholarship to a prep school in Idyllwild that offered Latin and rock climbing; I would have died a thousand deaths if any of my friends found out about our pit toilet. Nor did I disclose that my father's idea of a good time was to drive out to empty campgrounds on the weekends and raid the dumpsters.

My father's excuse for these excursions was that he wanted me to learn to drive stick shift in the green pickup, which backfired constantly and had rust holes under the passenger seat, so that I had to scoot the floor mat in place or get splattered with muddy runoff from the wheels.

In the empty parking lot of the Pinyon Flats campground, I hunched behind the wheel, mortified, while my father swung one leg over the metal lip of a dumpster and jumped inside. I could see the top of his head as he clambered over bedsprings and flattened cardboard.

—Come here and give me a hand with this! he called moments later, his voice echoing against the metal. —Perfectly good clothes, he grumbled, handing down a ripped plastic trash bag. —What people in this country throw away!

I talked him out of bringing back a skirt for Mom, but he still made me spin doughnuts in the empty parking lot before he drove us home. I clenched one hand on the steering wheel and the other on the gear-shift as he tried, exasperated, to explain how to shift into second gear without stalling out.

—C'mon, he chided. —You're not even trying.

—Dad, I *am*!

How and when to argue without tipping him into violence was a skill I was still perfecting. He had recently pushed over the dining room table when I refused to take a bite of fish at dinner.

As he drove back up the mountain toward Idyllwild, his callused hands palmed the wind. Far beneath us, green polo fields and golf courses marched down the dusty Coachella Valley toward my grandparents' date ranch. Quail skittered through the chaparral, their voices a furtive *pit-pit-pit* in the dusk.

I chose the moment when it looked like my father's guard was down to make my case: I could stay behind and board at the prep school while the rest of the family went back to Haiti without me. I was old enough to be on my own.

He laughed and kept driving. No chance.

Apart from my father, no one in the family wanted to sign up for another year and a half of missionary service (which was the shortest time frame that my father seemed willing to accept and the longest span of time that my mother would agree to; she was adamant that I should be able to finish my last two years of high school in the U.S.).

My mother certainly seemed happy enough in Idyllwild, aside from our too-small cabin and the absence of an indoor toilet. She served corn dogs to my sisters at the elementary school cafeteria, and led music at the Idyllwild Bible Church. Her best friend loved to hike and pray. She had cut her hair short, and drove down the mountain once a week to take a drafting class at a community college, drawing endless blueprints for the real house she had not yet given up on, though my father had threatened not to build it unless we first went back with him to Haiti.

He had dropped out of Fuller School of World Mission after only two years; he hated being stuck in a classroom. My mother, who would have given anything to be a student again, could audit only one class a term because she'd never finished her bachelor's degree. Instead, she got a job as a checkout clerk at Ralph's grocery store and typed up my father's papers, snapping at him when he leaned over her shoulder to point out a word she'd gotten wrong.

Without a master's degree, my father wasn't eligible for full-time missionary work with the American Baptists, and all of the other organizations that he'd applied to had turned us down. The Mennonites asked whether he'd defend his family if there was a threat of violence; when he said yes, they told him they found his peace stance lacking. A mission agency in Irian Jaya had changed their mind after they found out my mother spoke in tongues. (I wasn't exactly sure why that should disqualify her, but I wasn't overly disappointed: missionary friends in Irian Jaya boasted of roasting sago grubs instead of hot dogs, the soft, squishy bodies exploding in their mouths like lard.)

The only reliable work that my father had been able to find in Idyllwild was cleaning toilets at Forest Service day use areas and crawling under vacation homes to install plumbing. He had also spent a few backbreaking weeks replanting native seedlings on a logged hillside, which was the closest he'd come to happiness since we left Haiti.

What he craved, my mother explained, was work that mattered. He had hoped to return to the mountains as a full-time forest ranger, but with budget cuts and affirmative action quotas, he hadn't been hired back. Reforestation in Haiti, despite its challenges, at least felt consistent with his vocation: to care for the earth.

The only trouble was, my sisters and I were no longer quite so gung-ho about being uprooted. During tense conversations around the dinner table, Meadow, Rose, and I agreed that we would be willing to go on a summer trip to Haiti, to see old friends and relive old memories, but that was the extent of our curiosity.

Rose had been four when we left and barely remembered Haiti. Now a dimpled second-grader, blond as a beauty queen, she wasn't ready to leave the mountains where she had been born. Meadow, whose curly red perm bobbed against her shoulders when she giggled, had a gaggle of girlfriends who performed gymnastic tricks together on the playground at recess, and she was reluctant to say goodbye to that sweet camaraderie.

The very last thing I wanted, as a thirteen-year-old, was to move back to a conservative missionary compound in middle-of-nowhere Haiti, where, instead of Halloween, we'd celebrate Bible Dress-Up Day; school dances, it went without saying, would be out of the question—positively immoral.

I was also more concerned than my father seemed to be about the letters he read aloud to us from the missionaries who still lived in Limbé. Baby Doc had fled the country soon after we moved away—newspaper images showed him in exile in France, plump, in a white suit, his $900 million Swiss bank accounts padded with stolen aid money. After decades trapped under a repressive dictatorship, the country had exploded into anarchy. Closed schools. Uprooted gardens. Charred businesses. Pastor Tomas at the Limbé Baptist church grabbed the pulpit and urged his congregation to stand together and act as responsible citizens; political freedom did not mean the freedom to avenge grudges. Susan Hodges, Joanna's eldest daughter, supplemented her mother's more optimistic newsletters with fatalistic updates: *Medical people have all left the country and other clinics and hospitals are unreliable (closed half the time because of politics). Good ole L'Hôpital le Bon Samaritain is open every day come hell or high water!! Port-au-Prince is a WAR ZONE.*

To *dechouke* once meant to pull out a stump by its roots in order to clear the land, but as Dr. Hodges explained to his supporters, the old word had taken on a more sinister meaning. In the face of such violence, the powerless learned to keep their heads low until the newly powerful had executed their vengeance and the *dechoukaj* was over.

My father assured us, before he and my mother flew to Haiti for a one-week fact-finding trip over spring break, that things were already starting to settle down in Haiti, but while they were in Limbé, yet another attempted coup shut down all the airports and they were three days late getting home. The following day, the very same missionary plane they'd just taken out of Cap-Haïtien was hijacked.

And this, I wondered skeptically, was a safer place to raise three girls than Godless America?

When we finally agreed to take a family vote, my father reminded us of all the things we'd loved about Haiti as kids—the beach trips, the green-throated lizards on the dining room wall, our friends at Jericho School.

I folded my arms, unconvinced. My mother wavered. When it came time to vote, she confided her reservations in lopsided, uneven pencil: *Meadow, our tender and cautious child, doesn't want to leave her friends and familiar surroundings. She says she doesn't care whether we go or not but I suspect going back will be hardest for her.*

After the votes had been counted, I added an unsolicited note beneath my mother's words: *Apricot, our noisy and obnoxious child, says she doesn't care whether we go or not. I wish we could afford to send her off to boarding school.* To myself I added, as if in consolation: *I am pretty sure I will survive no matter what we do.*

The final tally was four to one against moving back to Haiti, yet somehow my father still overruled us.

Trees: A Sign of the Kingdom

Idyllwild, 1989

B Y DECEMBER 31, 1989, our bags were all but packed, our goodbye parties planned. I woke to the howl of coyotes as they circled a rabbit den in the meadow. My sisters and I dressed for church in skirts and delicate sling-back shoes that threatened to slip as we gingerly made our way over the icy deck to the car. My father was still working on his sermon notes. At the top of each typed page, he'd scrawled a reminder in blue ink: *Don't sniffle!*

After our commissioning service at the Idyllwild Bible Church—hands laid authoritatively on our bent heads, earnest requests for God's protection, followed by syrupy piano music under the pastoral prayer—we stood in the foyer to shake hands and hand out prayer cards.

Our typed support letter explained that Haitian Christians needed missionaries to help them be salt and light in their communities: *They want to see how they can restore their land so it can adequately feed their families and be preserved for future generations. Mothers want to raise up godly children in the midst of a culture that doesn't understand marital fidelity.* (The assertion that we had anything to teach Haitian Christians about morality was not yet painfully ironic.)

Restoring the land was, at least, a subject on which my father was reasonably knowledgeable. At Fuller Seminary, most of his papers had focused on deforestation. Long after the rest of us had gone to bed, he'd sat up at the battered Formica table with his tongue clenched between his teeth to scour the concordance for Bible verses about trees.

He found four hundred separate entries. Of the fifty different instances of the word "forest" in the Bible, he noted that only *one* was found in the New Testament. Ditto for "streams," which showed up seventy-six times in the Old Testament but only four times in the New—evidence of deforestation in the Promised Land.

Hackles raised, he launched in like Smokey the Bear going after a casual litterer who had just tossed a match down on the forest floor:

> *This paper is written from the premise that trees, the earth and people were all created by God for good and that he remains concerned over the condition of all of them; that he loves all peoples and all lands. Christianity has been blind to the necessity of concern for the environment. We have been guilty of abusing the provisions of God's good creation.*

He even, presciently, found a way to weave the threat of climate change into his twenty-seven-page paper, "Trees: A Sign of the Kingdom," complete with bibliography (the only problem was, it was 1985, and evangelical America was still decades away from giving a damn).

He wasn't much of an evangelist aside from the gospel of trees, but he reminded his readers that it was bad theology to separate the spiritual from the physical and cited Ezekiel 24:19 to end, bang, with a flourish:

> *Must my flock feed on what you have trampled*
> *and drink what you have muddied with your feet?*

Pleased, he got up from the dining room table, stretched, and stepped outside, having heard on the radio that there was supposed to be a lunar eclipse that night. But the glare of the city was so skittery and frantic for attention—car lot searchlights probing the foothills, Los Angeles a neon time bomb on the horizon—that even at midnight the moon was 100 percent invisible.

When Halley's Comet did a fly-by a few months later, he drove us all the way to the date ranch, several hours away, not about to miss it just because city folk didn't have the good sense to turn out their lights at night. He and Mom tucked the three of us girls onto a mattress in the back of the pickup, then shook us awake at two a.m. to watch the faint flare of white along the horizon. In open spaces, he felt as if he could breathe again.

When my parents first floated the idea of going back to Haiti—before they asked my sisters and I what we thought—they agreed that they didn't want to just live among missionaries, isolated from our Haitian neighbors.

On their fact-finding trip over spring break, they were pleased to discover that Jules Casséus, the president of the Baptist seminary, was supportive of my father's vision and even invited us to live rent-free in a house just across the road from the seminary campus in Haut-Limbé. This time, instead of cushioning ourselves within the confines of a missionary compound, we would be surrounded by Haitian neighbors. At Casso's suggestion, my father would organize reforestation and erosion-control gardening projects in a small community about an hour's hike into the mountains. In this way, my father hoped to bypass the foreign-run tree nurseries and convince rural farmers to plant their own seeds on their own land—just as Zo had done years earlier.

A few of the missionaries were skeptical of this low-budget scheme, but the one thing my parents had acquired from Fuller Seminary, even without a degree, was a determination to at least make new mistakes; Projè Pyebwa, for which my father had supplied hundreds of thousands of trees when he ran the hospital tree nursery, had planted twenty-five million trees in Haiti in the 1980s, although during the same period, as many as seven trees were cut down for each new one planted. It was time for a new paradigm.

My parents' one concession for having yanked me out of prep school was to allow me to stay behind for a two-week scuba-diving course, so while I packed my bags for Baja, the rest of the family stepped gingerly around sewer-clogged gutters in Port-au-Prince. My sisters, unwitting test cases in this missionary experiment, walked for hours across the city to buy bus tickets. They ate sugarcane peeled and split by machetes, and bought fresh-cut oranges and fried sweet potatoes from women who hunched over charcoal *rechos*.

The next evening, their bus ground to a stop at the end of a dirt road in Haut-Limbé. My father shouted up at the men on the roof for the suitcases, and strangers swung the dusty luggage onto their heads and strolled alongside, goading him with questions. Roosters and gaunt, timid dogs skittered across dirt courtyards. Goats bleated behind cactus fences.

There was no food in the house when they arrived, and no stores nearby to purchase bread or milk. By bedtime, Meadow was trembling from hunger, unable to hide her tears. My mother held her and stroked her hair, insisting that my father at least knock on Laurie and Casso's door, at the Baptist Seminary across the road, to borrow a cup of powdered milk and some rice.

My sisters' discomfort was no more than that of other nearby Haitian children who had ended the day without a meal. That night, on the other side of the cactus hedge, a wake was held for a neighbor who had died. The relatives sang hymns late into the night. My sisters fell asleep to the sound of wailing. Haiti was troubling in this regard—no matter how broken we felt, another, greater sorrow loomed just over our shoulders.

We are pleased with the house, my father wrote to me a few days later. The stationery featured a cartoon pig that snorted: *Forget you? FAT chance!*

Opening the letter in Idyllwild, I took a deep breath and prepared myself for the worst.

My mother and sisters had just returned from taking the *tap tap* to the Limbé market to buy household supplies, and I was to add to my suitcase a serrated knife, vegetable peeler, a whetstone, and a hammer. My mother's take on our housing situation in Haut-Limbé was, predictably, rather more ambivalent than my father's: *The furnishings are mahogany wood and uncomfortable to sit on very long. So far, I haven't seen any cockroaches, but we've cleaned out lots of their droppings. As you can imagine, there's not much privacy.*

My father concluded: *You'll make kid number 6 in the high school. People are amazed at how grown-up you are and how beautiful too from your picture.*

The compliment, a rarity, I dismissed as a bribe, but I wondered nervously which picture he had shown them—most likely the one from our prayer card (now stuck to every church member's refrigerator): all five of us squinting into the sun in front of Suicide Rock. I had worn my favorite teal shirt and brocade vest. I had been too heartbroken to smile.

Cynical City

Idyllwild, 1989

*W*ELCOME TO CYNICAL CITY, I wrote on the title page of my eighth-grade journal. *The mixed-up feelings of a very mixed-up girl in a mixed-up world (from a person who is only human and who likes certain things to remain confidential).*

A short list by Apricot Michelle Anderson of things that I have survived thus far: (not very impressive, I know, compared to what other people have survived, but hey—it's my list):

- Pinworms, most likely picked up while running around barefoot at the Limbé compound, though no one figured it out until we were back in California. My father didn't want to waste money on medical care, so he turned me facedown on the bed and picked the itchy, wriggling worms out of my anus while my mother busied herself in another room. He told me to quit crying and hold still. I was nine. In that moment, I hated him. Hated her. Hated Haiti for infecting me.

- Home alone on robbery night. Well, sort of. We lived across the cul-de-sac from a crack house while Dad was in seminary in the Los Angeles foothills (he had turned down the apartment complex with the rest of the missionary families because he said he needed a garden).

Mom called in what looked like a robbery, then left me to babysit my little sisters while she and Dad drove across town for a Focus on the Family event with James Dobson (ironic). When the police pounded on the door, I didn't know what to do. I knew better than to open the door to strangers but wasn't sure if this also applied to police. Meadow and Rosie huddled behind me in their nightgowns, wet hair dripping onto the floor. I was ten. I didn't open the door. Apparently, the police complimented my mother afterward on my excellent manners.

• Four new schools in as many years. You'd think I'd have it all figured out by now.

Fifth grade: Franklin Fox Elementary (Altadena). My sisters and I were some of the only white kids in the school, but everyone spoke English so it felt way easier than Haiti. Lots to catch up on. I figured out how to leap between the whapping double-dutch ropes but couldn't keep up with the flash-footed girls on the playground who knew all the words and dance moves to "Thriller" (my only exposure to Michael Jackson being the Weird Al Yankovic version of "I'm Fat," which we had listened to in music class in Limbé, all of the missionary kids cross-legged on a woven grass mat on the floor). It sucked being the odd one out.

Sixth grade: Woodrow Wilson (Pasadena). On the first day of middle school, all the kids from my neighborhood were bused across town to be integrated with the white school but I didn't know which bus to take home and was too ashamed to ask. I guessed wrong. More than a mile from home with my uncle's oversized trumpet case banging against my shin bone, a sketchy-looking man with a paper bag told me I wasn't allowed to walk through the neighborhood and made me go past a chain-link fence and knock on a stranger's door to get permission. The woman who yanked the door open didn't think it was funny, but at least she yelled at the man with the paper bag, not me. Her thick arms bent at her hips as she roared: *Don't you be messin with her!* My mother called her my guardian angel.

Seventh grade: Idyllwild Elementary. The year that I burned my first journal and my father told me I looked like a slut for wearing pink stretch pants under a sparkly silver butterfly belt.

Eighth grade: The Elliott Pope Preparatory School, Idyllwild, where seniors lounged in acid-washed jeans in the smoking lounge, casually comparing trips to Bali and Mount Everest as Bon Jovi yowled in the background. Eighth-grade boarding students were invited to drop acid their first weekend away from home. I wasn't sure which was worse: the prospect of moving back to Haiti in the midst of political uprisings, or the misery of being the only prude at the prep school. Meanwhile, my mother accused me of being The Devil's Handmaiden when I "provoked my father" by writing in my journal instead of participating in family devotions. He threw a Bible through the window. I picked up the broken glass.

The story that I did not confide to anyone, not even to my journal—and certainly not to my parents—was that during the loosely chaperoned scuba-diving trip in Baja, a cocky nineteen-year-old had unrolled his sleeping bag next to mine while we camped out under the stars. Unable to stop him from touching me, I assumed, mistakenly, that my father must be right: I really was a slut. My shame was a smell I couldn't wash from my skin.

Time to Try Out Our Dreams

Haut-Limbé, 1990

At the LAX airport, having just celebrated my fourteenth birthday, I waved goodbye to the grandparents and walked alone onto the plane. To steel myself, I pretended that I was a world-famous author heading off for an international book tour.

I made a few attempts to flip casually through the in-flight magazine (careful not to let on that I hadn't been on a plane since I was nine), but as soon as we lifted off, I scrapped my dignity and pressed my face to the glass. The plunging weight was like the sudden drop of a roller coaster. Mountains flattened to wide, arid deserts. The world at my feet. If I could just keep going, preferably to somewhere I'd never been before, I could subsist, if necessary, for at least a month on peanuts and ginger ale.

Reality sank in as the tiny missionary plane banked low over the sugarcane fields and hillsides empty of trees, the Citadel a defiant fist against the sky. At the Cap-Haïtien airport, ceiling fans caked in a layer of dust rotated uselessly while customs officials rummaged through my luggage. The breeze from the sea smelled of rotting fish and garbage.

My sisters, whom I had not seen in weeks, threw their arms around me, their thin cotton dresses blowing in the wind. My father had a Haitian straw hat shoved over his ears and a faded blue backpack slung over one shoulder. He looked sunburned and relaxed. For once, he seemed genuinely glad to see me. I noted with disappointment that my carefully teased bangs, shellacked into place with Aqua Net, were already starting to wilt in the tropical humidity.

My mother kept turning around in the front seat of the new-to-us blue station wagon as we inched through the soot and noise of Cap-Haïtien, telling stories about the disaster of a birthday cake that they'd tried to bake for her in the solar oven in the front yard: one side of the cake had been lumpy and undercooked, the other was blackened to charcoal.

Children tapped at the windows of the car and called: *Blan! Blan!* as bare-chested men strained against wooden carts piled high with discarded tires and sugarcane.

I could almost convince myself in the States that we were the ones who were barely scraping by, with our pit toilet and hand-me-down clothes raided from a dumpster, but all it took was an hour in Haiti to yank things back into perspective. We were unmistakably privileged. The inequity felt glaring and uncomfortable.

As my sisters led me up the steps to our new home in Haut-Limbé, a squat yellow concrete building surrounded by a few spindly croton bushes, neighbor children peered through gaps in the cactus fence. Inside was a stiff wooden couch; a leaky sink not quite lined up against the bathroom wall; and two metal bed frames in the room that my sisters shared.

—We'll have to take turns sharing a bed, Meadow explained, trying not to giggle. I looked around, horrified, until Rose laughed and pushed open the door to a former broom closet. There was just enough space inside for a single bed, a shelf, and ten inches of floor.

I tossed my bags onto my bed and collapsed. After a strained click, the cassette tape whirred to life, and the Little Mermaid echoed down the hallway. *Wouldn't you think I'm the girl, the girl who has everything?*

As soon as we finished lunch, my mother drove the four miles into Limbé so I could meet the other missionary kids at Jericho School. I stared out the window at hazy blue mountains and green-fingered mango trees. It felt familiar and surreal.

The compound was more or less as I remembered it—the *zanmann* tree a little taller, the playground slide a little more dented. The other teenagers in the one-room high school scraped their chairs back from their desks to stare at me. I felt suddenly aware of how very American I looked with my noisy earrings, ratted bangs, and teal mascara. Clearly an outsider.

—Hello, we all mumbled self-consciously.

Olynda had been adopted after we left, but I knew the rest of the teenagers. Ana, at eighteen, was as regal and unreadable as ever. Peter, about to graduate, had the same wry, quiet smile. (Did he remember, I wondered sheepishly, my schoolgirl crush?) Reuben, Susan's oldest son, had the classic Hodges intensity—ready, at a moment's notice, to battle out an argument or repair a broken engine. Kirsti and I were the only ones not related to the Hodges family. We'd written a few sporadic letters over the years, mostly complaining about our conservative parents, but it felt awkward to see each other in person again; we weren't nine years old anymore.

Bernice Rogers, now the high school superintendent, broke the silence by holding out her arms for a hug. Her round midwestern face was stretched into a smile: Look at how much you've grown! she crowed. Her reading glasses dug in to my neck.

When my mother suggested that maybe I'd like to help shelve books in the Jericho library until school let out, I nodded and slipped outside after her. Across the grass, Haitian nurses crossed the raised walkways of the hospital. Gardeners leaned against the fishpond, its tepid surface thick with algae.

—I think you'll be really happy here, my mother said, squeezing my shoulders. I stiffened.

She peeked inside the other classrooms so I could say a quick hello to Meadow's and Rose's teachers: dimpled, guitar-strumming Mary Hays in the four-student middle school; white-haired, widowed Ms. Whitt. In all, twenty-eight students were tucked inside the freshly whitewashed walls of Jericho School, sixteen of whom were the adopted children or grandchildren of Bill and Joanna Hodges.

In the dimly lit three-foot-by-three-foot school library, stacked floor to ceiling with musty paperbacks, I sat down on the floor with one of the Jim Kjelgaard adventure series that I had read and reread in grade school—each new heart-stopping climax centered around heroic dogs who raced to rescue their hapless humans, complete with an obligatory happy ending. The pages were more fragile than I remembered. The story threatened to disintegrate in my hands.

Today Apricot arrived safe and sound, my mother wrote to a friend in Idyllwild. *I can't believe how much more relaxed I am, all my little chicks are back in the nest. Sometimes I can't believe this is really happening so smoothly. God is certainly going before us. We are so thankful for the time we have to try out our dreams.*

The Rock in the Water

Haut-Limbé, 1990

IN THE MORNINGS—HOT, humid, smelling of hibiscus and smoldering charcoal—my father headed off into the hills with a backpack full of seeds, a jug of water, and a Kreyòl Bible from which he read aloud Bible verses about trees. When strangers asked him what he carried in his *makouti* he answered: I'm carrying hope.

The week I arrived in Haiti, my father insisted that the whole family join him for a two-hour Kreyòl church service at a tiny outstation church in the mountains, an hour's walk from our house. Afterward, during his interminable visits to check on the gardens of wrinkled old women with toothless smiles who pulled out their best chairs while they squatted beside us on the dirt, my sisters and I sat down gingerly, irritable in the heat, on wooden chairs that wobbled beneath us, the palm-frond seats softly disintegrating, testimony to the ceaseless, invisible ministrations of the termites. Obeying our father's mute orders, we sat still, listened without comprehending, without interest, to the blurred cadence of language, the ritual formality. First the greetings, then the polite inquiries about the health of distant relations; a discussion of crops, trees, the weather; a smattering of politics.

If we were particularly unlucky, my father would ask us to sing a song before we left. His cracked but earnest voice chased the melody while my mother soared above us on the descant: *Eske ou vle ale lakay Papa mwen, lakay Papa mwen* . . . Do you want to go to my Father's house?

The song, like most spirituals, described with foot-stomping, hand-clapping yearning the Sweet Hereafter that we all longed to escape to, but if you had asked me, at fourteen, what I thought of *lakay Papa mwen*, I would have told you that I wanted nothing more than to escape his tyranny.

Rey, the village where my father focused his reforestation efforts, was, like many others in Haiti, a small cluster of houses along a dirt path, not particularly close to a streambed but within walking distance. The gardens were small and subsistence-based, and the farmers survived by impossibly slim margins. Most families tried to supplement their income by planting cash crops such as manioc and peanuts—well suited to the brutal tropical climate—or by cutting down trees for charcoal.

My father quickly gained a reputation as a rare *blan* who wasn't afraid of walking, whether in the rain or in the sun, and flush with possibility, he organized field trips to expose the farmers in Rey to innovative ideas that were already being used across the north of Haiti. Wedged into the battered blue station wagon, they drove an hour and a half to peruse the vegetable market in Saint-Raphaël. They hiked six miles to see a fish project in Vallières. More than once, he took farmers to Camp Coq to see his friend Zo—his oldest ally and fellow tree lover. Zo had not only survived the *dechoukaj* but had redoubled his reforestation efforts, proudly leading visitors through forests of cinnamon trees, and showing off cages of sleek, healthy rabbits.

At least initially, the farmers seemed inspired. My mother hiked up to Rey twice a week and helped demonstrate how to mix animal manure with unused vegetable trimmings to create compost, though at first the women only laughed when my mother asked permission to collect the dried cow patties from their gardens: *Mezanmi! Gade blan yo!* Look at what the *blan* are doing now! My mother shrugged and explained that in the U.S., people paid good money for manure. The women only laughed all the harder; they'd heard some hard-to-believe stories about the *Gran Peyi,* but this was too much.

Meanwhile, my father handed out new vegetable seeds for farmers to try in their gardens and drought-resistant *kasya* trees, which coppiced readily—even when harvested for charcoal, the stumps sent up new offshoots. Tiny seedlings began to unfurl tentative green-fringed leaves. Hope was in the air.

When my father came home at night to a hot meal and an indoor shower, heavy-laden with gifts of guavas, pineapples, mangoes, *kasav,* and bananas, he recited one of his new favorite Haitian proverbs: *Wòch nan dlo pa kòn mizè wòch nan solèy.* The rock in the water doesn't know the misery of a rock in the sun.

I don't go to bed hungry with mosquitoes buzzing around on a grass mat, with some kids sick and no hope of income for weeks to come, he wrote to our supporters. *I am getting to know people who have even more misery than I've suggested above. They are teaching me about courage.*

When I came home from a long day of filling out mind-numbingly boring correspondence courses at the missionary school while my parents were off saving the world, I wished aloud, repeatedly, that I had been allowed to finish high school in Idyllwild.

If my father insisted on a family Bible study after dinner, I shoved my chair into the corner of the living room and crossed my arms, a contemptuous look on my face, while, through the screen windows, as if in mockery of our failure, hymns drifted over the cactus hedge. One of our Haitian neighbors, a Boy Scout leader and stalwart member of the local Baptist church—clearly a hundred times holier than we were—could be heard praying aloud with his four daughters. I smirked: *No pressure, Dad.*

A Wall of Mountains

Haut-Limbé, 1990

WHEN THE MISSIONARY mail plane floated in from Florida with letters and care packages full of things that couldn't be purchased in the north of Haiti—melted-together M&M's, Kool-Aid packets, chocolate chips, tampons—it was a delicious torture to imagine climbing into the cockpit and quitting Haiti for good.

Sweat dripped down the back of my knees as unemployed Haitian teenagers lounged in the shade of the one-story terminal, their voices rising and falling like heat on the runway. When the pilot finally unlatched the cargo hold, the teenagers swarmed over the mail sacks like ants over sugarcane, vying to carry the heaviest boxes—whatever meager tip they might earn presumably being the difference between eating or not eating that day.

When the missionary letters and boxes were safely stowed in the back of the station wagon and customs duties paid, my father slammed the hatchback shut and pulled down the dirt road toward Limbé. A few younger boys raced behind to leap onto the bumper. My father accelerated and they jumped off, shouting. Overhead, the plane circled once and disappeared over a wall of mountains.

My mother carefully rationed the care packages sent by our supporters. My father tried to convince the church to stop sending them. *I don't see why a missionary flight should be used for candy and goodies,* he grumbled irritably in the margins of one of my mother's letters.

If a care package included a cassette tape, my sisters and I sat around the dining room table and leaned in close to hear the voices that tumbled out. Grandma Marian, in Nebraska, told us that she was sewing tea cozies for her ladies' Bible study group on Thursdays; our cousins were going to Disney World for their summer vacation; Uncle George was buying a new car. Occasionally, Grandpa George recorded an inning of a ball game or a selection of big-band music, complete with shrill radio advertisements for life insurance.

I traced the lines of the plastic tablecloth with my finger as they described the remodeling they were doing on their sun porch, Grandma's soft voice nearly drowned out by a shovel scraping against a pile of gravel outside. Goats bleated as trucks ground past on their way to market. A radio blared *konpa* music in a language I had no wish to understand.

My father's newsletters from Haiti were, nevertheless, optimistic.

> *Bonjour zami yo! The Anderson family has arrived safe and sound in Limbé. One of the girls' first comments was, "There are lizards in our house!" And it is true. We have lots of lizards. They must think this house is their home as they creep along the walls and window screens in the Chameleon colors of bright green and brown. We consider them welcome guests because of all the bugs they eat.*
>
> *And I guess for similar reasons, we too are considered welcome guests by the Haitians. We are a curiosity to them and as they get to know us better, they realize we have come to help them as we can.*

In a handwritten postscript to one of his relatives, my father conceded that my sisters and I had readjustment blues, but added, *We are still very glad to be here.* It was early in the game. He was confident we'd come around.

I wasn't. *At least during the week I can keep busy with school and see other Americans, even if they despise me,* I confided to my journal, *but weekends are miserable in this deserted hellhole. Everyone is at a soccer match now. Talk about a dead sport.*

My mother, torn between her homesick daughters and her husband's determination to transform Haiti—one eroded hillside at a time—by some miracle talked my father into attending a weekend pool party in Cap-Haïtien with the rest of the missionaries. (*Wasn't restful. Enjoyable although expensive* was his peevish conclusion in the day planner that doubled as his journal.)

For once, I could kick off my confining missionary-kid clothes and slip into the deep artificial blue of a hotel pool. Waiters in white uniforms served us cold Cokes on linen tablecloths. I ordered french fries and stretched out on a towel next to the other missionary girls to gossip in the sun. When they pestered me about which boy I liked, I tugged my bathing suit into place and dove into the pool, my hair billowing out behind me. When I came up for air, my father announced that it was time to go, pronto—then got sidetracked telling a volunteer about his tree projects.

I pulled a T-shirt over my head and wrung out my wet hair. He didn't notice when I slipped on a pair of shorts and begged Meadow to wait with me out by the car, where we could at least read novels while we waited for him to stop talking.

Two bare-chested Haitian teenagers sauntered over to chat us up.

—Hello bay-bee, what ees your name?

I pretended to ignore them.

—What time ees eet? one asked, then careened off into a dizzying patter of Kreyòl I couldn't begin to follow.

—I luf yoo. Fuk yoo.

I laughed and flicked back my hair.

Meadow, growing alarmed, fumbled with the car keys and disappeared into the station wagon, locking the doors behind her.

My father rounded the corner, took one look and marched over, his shoulders rigid. The teenage boys scattered.

On the drive home, I glared out the window. When I felt the sting of salt in my eyes, I angrily wiped away the tears. I archived my growing list of parental injustices:

My parents SUCK. They have these stupid "dress code rules"
that they come up with off the top of their heads whenever they feel
like it. It was just another case of some lame, horny guys trying (I
repeat, trying) to pick up a girl but Dad told me that it was because
I was wearing shorts. He was serious! He really thinks I am a slut.
I got this huge, 45-minute lecture about "decency" and "being a
proper example to our community." And after that, Kirsti and Ana
walked out wearing even shorter shorts than I had!

We returned to a huge pile of letters with, once again, none for
me. Sometimes I feel so confused as to where I really belong.

Weekends in Haut-Limbé held a cavernous loneliness. Our house
was separated by a dirt road from the main seminary campus, and every
time I pushed open the metal gate, I felt like an idiot trying to stammer
out greetings in Kreyòl, my grammar as clunky as a six-year-old's. The
Haitian seminary students were all older than I was, and few spoke
English.

Nine-year-old Rose, at least, had a friend her age—Laura Rose,
Ivah's granddaughter, who was fluent in both Kreyòl and English—
but Meadow and I had only the novels we borrowed from Casso and
Laurie's bookshelves. Casso, who always seemed to be in conference
with someone about the administration of the Baptist seminary, would
nod politely and hold open the screen door when we knocked. Laurie
was usually at the piano giving music lessons, but being a missionary kid
herself, she understood what we were after. We could at least imagine
ourselves into other worlds: St. Petersburg, Prince Edward Island, the
Warsaw ghetto, Omelas. A book was a door in the wall. An escape.

My father, exasperated that we appeared so uninterested in learning Kreyòl (it was not taught at the missionary school), hired a tutor
named Manno, an ambitious young man in his early twenties whose
dark eyes, under long, curling lashes, held my gaze and did not look
away.

At first I reveled in this attention, but when Manno held my hand in
his and insisted that we go on a walk to practice my Kreyòl, something

about his confident refusal to take no for an answer made my chest tighten. Unable to admit even to myself what I was afraid of (I could not explain to my unconscious mind that Manno—although persistent and older than I was—was not the nineteen-year-old on the scuba trip), I instead ducked out the back door when I heard him coming.

After weeks of my evasions, Manno finally exploded to Meadow: You do realize that your parents are paying me for this?

In a rare show of solidarity, all three of us eventually managed to convince my father that it would be irrelevant to continue language lessons; all our friends on the compound spoke English. Worn down by our complaining and embarrassed on Manno's behalf, my father eventually threw up his hands and gave up.

I never knew what to do with male attention once it had been won, and in that respect I was very much like the heroines in Jane Austen novels, whom I admired and longed to emulate. I adhered, unquestioning, to a dualism that my faith professed to deny but that every rule of propriety had etched in stone: My spirit might be pure, but my body was corrupt, an untamed beast that I must bring under control or risk unimaginable consequences. The missionary parents hinted at the terrifying specter of pregnancy, which lurked at the edges of unchaperoned teenage gatherings, but beyond that we did not discuss it. Birth control was anathema; abstinence was our iron-clad rule of law. (Ashamed, I hid my period for months until my father realized that I was stealing my mother's tampons.)

No one stopped the teenage boys on the missionary compound if they set off for a long bike ride in the hills, but the feminine ideal seemed to imply that one should suffer beautifully in silence, disappearing into an inner landscape of muted colors and soft edges, safe within a gilded cage—a standard of self-restraint I could never quite live up to. I shrieked and howled and cavorted during volleyball games at Jericho School, wore gold hoop earrings as big around as my neck, and hung my head backward over my chair and laughed until I could not breathe, making a fool of myself just to make everyone else laugh. If prizes had been awarded for trying too hard, I'd have won a chest full of clanking medals.

Only when I was alone did the frenzy subside into loss. Sent to the hospital pharmacy after lunch so that I would not distract the other students, I bent over an electronic scale and counted pills into recycled baby-food jars while Barbara Hodges leaned back in her office chair to argue effortlessly with the drug reps in either French or Kreyòl over the cost of prescriptions. Behind us, at dimly lit windows, Haitian pharmacy workers filled orders and dispensed the donated milk powder.

If I turned right past those windows and went down the raised pathway along a narrow courtyard lined with benches, past market women with bright lengths of cloth and enamel dishes, past beggars and stray dogs and foraging chickens, I would arrive at the pediatric ward, from whose overcrowded cribs my father used to bring home orphans for my sisters and me to love.

The pediatric ward was a magnet for expatriate female volunteers to the hospital, who spent hours patiently rocking the babies and playing with the abandoned children in the urine-stained wards. Even dour, sarcastic Susan Smith, Joanna's eldest daughter, who wore a permanent scowl and her gray-blond hair twisted into a knot at the nape of her neck, was transformed. She complained when Joanna hounded her into writing a newsletter—*I have been requested to write a HAPPY story!*—but her pride was evident when she described a boy named Aristole, suffering from *kwashiorkor,* who had been dying slowly of starvation until his mother brought him into the hospital.

> *Well, you should see my little family now! Aristole is sitting up and chugging down plate after plate of food. He smiles . . . and Jesus's love just <u>glows</u> around their corner of Peds, like a halo! <u>Although</u> a stranger may only see rags, and dirt, snotty noses, and a bad smell, I feel sorry for that person's blindness.*

Susan, for all her prickliness, was a devoted, generous nurse. I was one of the blind. On the one and only visit I paid to the pediatric ward, at fourteen, a boy with white-blue cataracts grabbed my dress and kept trying to pull me down to his arms. A girl who looked to be my age, with vacant eyes and atrophied arms, moaned softly, leaning against a wall. The smell of urine and diarrhea was thinly veiled by disinfectant. *I wish, I just wish that they could all have homes, a place to love and be loved,* I wrote in my journal, but I did not return.

I weighed pills and tallied patients' charts and helped count the thin and wrinkled piles of gourdes on Friday mornings in Joanna's crowded mayhem of a payroll office, but I could not bear to look into the faces of the orphaned children. Our meager kindness, as missionaries, felt so limited and unsubstantial. It hurt less to turn away.

Some days, while I waited for my mother to pick us up after school, I'd climb the *labapen* tree just to be alone with my thoughts. Occasionally, Tamara would keep me company, perched on the edge of the picnic table, her blind eye white and staring. I remembered the outlines of her story—how she'd been left at the pediatric ward and adopted; how she had willed herself back to life—but we had never talked about it.

—I feel like God isn't really there, she confided once when the two of us were alone in the yard. Sometimes her laughter had a cold, sharp edge.

I didn't know what to say. *Was* God actually watching over us? My own family's return to Haiti seemed less ordained by God than strong-armed by my father. I could still recite the Psalms that Suzette had us memorize when she lived on the compound—*If I rise on the wings of the dawn, if I settle on the far side of the sea, even there your hand will guide me, your right hand will hold me fast*—but they no longer felt a talisman against harm. Tamara had seen so much more suffering than I could begin to imagine. Why did she feel so alone? Why did I? Surely God must have noticed.

Tamara sat on the bench of the picnic table and dug her cane into the dirt. I rearranged my back against the *labapen* tree.

It was hot and muggy—it was always muggy—and leaves circled down from the *zanmann* tree. A wash lady sat behind the Hodges house, folding laundry into a wicker basket. A pair of broad pink underwear shook on the line. Tamara changed the subject for me.

—Don't drink coffee, it will stunt your growth; you'll end up like me! Her crutch smacked the sidewalk like an exclamation mark as she limped away.

To be able to forget, if only for a few hours, the heartbreaking lament of Haiti—a scratched and broken record, endlessly stuck on repeat—was in part why I climbed trees and barricaded myself behind books.

Trips to the beach, though far rarer, achieved the same effect. On the few and glorious afternoons when the missionaries loaded sunscreen and cameras into sisal bags for a ride on the hospital's wooden motorboat, the sea grew wild as the fishing villages and the curved Baie de L'Acul receded behind us. For an afternoon, the tiny island of Île-la-Rat—once a buccaneer stronghold, now a stranded white hillock of sand—was ours alone to savor: a serene and undefiled oasis. There were no forlorn children to linger and stare at our pleasure, no voyeurs to make us wonder why we'd come. The gently splashing waves throbbed a siren song to which we gladly surrendered.

My mother grabbed a snorkel and slipped into the water. Meadow and Rose hunted for hermit crabs along the shore. I folded my journal open on my knees, burying my toes in the warm sand.

Sometime later, I glanced up and realized that Peter had wandered over to join me. I was startled when he sat down beside me and asked how I was adjusting to life in Haiti. I confessed that it all felt a bit confusing.

He admitted that he, too, was anticipating culture shock—he'd be leaving for college at the end of the summer and had never lived in the States before. I sympathized; it could be disorienting to move back and forth between such different worlds.

We sat for a while in companionable quiet, then found snorkels and drifted over the coral reefs. Blue and yellow fish darted beneath our feet.

It wasn't uncomfortable silence, I noted in my journal afterward, as if trying to decode a mystery.

On the trip home, my father, one hand on the outboard motor, pointed out a distant flock of pink flamingos. I was perched in the prow beside a five-year-old girl, recently adopted, who was learning to speak English. Angelina and I dangled our feet over the waves and laughed whenever a wave leaped up to splash us, then she fell asleep in my lap, lulled by the rocking waves. I watched her sleep and wondered what sorrows she had already faced and what courage she had found to pull around her.

Dèyè Mòn, Gèn Mòn

Haut-Limbé, 1990

THREE MONTHS AFTER my family moved back to Haiti, in March 1990, protests erupted in Port-au-Prince demanding that General Prosper Avril step down as president. I didn't understand that he had been accused of human rights abuses, or that the demonstrators were agitating for justice. I knew only what my father told me—that there might be roadblocks in Cap-Haïtien, which was why he took back roads from the airport after picking up the mail. My sisters and I, along for the ride, were far more interested in an upcoming movie night on the compound: a chance to forget for a few distracted hours that Haiti might be on the brink of yet another military uprising. By the time we reached the Limbé Valley, all danger, we assumed, had been left behind.

We had just crossed the bridge over the Limbé river, cattle egrets lifting from the rice paddies, when my father slammed on the brakes. Boulders and burning tires blocked the national highway. Through the smoke, gun-toting soldiers waved us to a halt.

My mother began praying aloud in tongues. I hugged my sisters in the back seat. My father leaned his head cautiously out the window and, after a brief negotiation, was told that we could proceed. Soldiers grabbed bystanders by their clothes and shouted orders to heave the rocks from the road. Heat crackled from the burning tires as we crept forward through the inferno on our fool's errand.

Safe on the missionary compound, we heard more stories of violence. Ken and Debbie Heneise had been caught in tear gas in Cap-

Haïtien but had managed to get away. Port-au-Prince was in chaos. By the time we summoned up the courage to drive back across the bridge and down the highway to our home in Haut-Limbé several hours later, my father was careful to offer rides to three Haitian acquaintances at the hospital so that we wouldn't simply be perceived as the privileged *blan*, sailing heedless through the wreckage of Haiti's political aspirations.

That night, my mother sat on my sister's bed and strummed her autoharp, singing praise songs to keep the fear at bay. Her high, clear soprano echoed down the concrete hallway. *Poor Meadow cries herself to sleep at night*, I noted in my journal. *I wish there was something I could do.*

Even after martial law was declared, my father continued to hike several days a week up to Rey, until a truck full of armed men intercepted him, demanding an explanation for the notebook in which he took down the names of local citizens and made notes about their gardens. Apparently, the police station in Limbé had heard suspicious stories about an unknown *blan*, a possible agitator, but the farmers along the path to Rey rushed to my father's defense and no charges were made.

—Well, you should be glad I'm not in prison, he announced as he kicked off his shoes by the door.

If he was afraid, he did not let on. My mother's reaction was equally unreadable. In theory, I understood that yes, we were protected by God, not to mention our American citizenship, but I felt an uncomfortable tightening in my chest when I thought about our Haitian neighbors, most of whom had no means to escape should the situation escalate. When my father hinted that there might be more political unrest to come, Meadow's forehead scrunched into worried lines. Rose, at nine years old, seemed willing enough to trust that we were going to be okay, but I couldn't figure out how safe we actually were.

Nor was there any discussion of whether or not Haiti could, in fact, be helped by our feeble efforts.

Letters from our supporters were full of concern. *Calm here*, my father updated the grandparents. *But no guarantee it will remain.* My father's run-in with the Limbé police only seemed to strengthen his determination to make a difference, but the stories he retold around the dinner table were increasingly bleak. The lay pastor in Rey, Frè Reynold, supplemented his meager income by buying and reselling *kasav* (a local Taíno delicacy, pounded manioc leached of its toxins and baked into a chewy flatbread) in the capital. Usually, Frè Reynold could expect a profit of fifteen U.S. dollars for a four-day round trip, but he had arrived in Port-au-Prince just as the military coup was unfolding. His unsold merchandise rotted in the streets. He lost fifty-eight dollars—two months' wages—and instead of the usual five-hour *kamyon* ride home, it took him twenty-four hours to get past all the roadblocks.

Other farmers in Rey were already uprooting their withered green stalks of corn to feed hungry livestock. The early rains, which had lured them into planting their seeds too soon, had come and gone, leaving only dust. A woman with seventeen children called my father over to her three-rock fire to let him taste the only food she could find to cook: green bananas with dried fish and onions.

My journal, written in pink and teal ink, could not have been more different from my father's:

> [Jon journal] 3/12/90: *Started raining early this AM. Just what is needed to calm country down. Planted sugar cane and papaya and kudzu seeds. Also planted Kajou seeds. A few Pele are finally germinating. Went with Reynold to show him Zo's rabbits and visited his tree plantings. Impressive. He loves trees. Cinnamon flowering.*

> [Apricot journal] 3/13/90: *The country seems pretty stable. We saw not even one glimpse of a soldier. This morning I received another extremely demeaning lecture. This time it was informing me how spoiled I was (now <u>there's</u> a confidence builder) because I didn't eat breakfast. See if you can figure <u>that</u> one out! I HATE Haiti.*

My mother, meanwhile, admitted to a friend:

This has been an extremely hard week for me. Usually Jon gets a hold of my letters and writes all over them. But this week's letter is just between you and me. I could use a good friend right now.

Tomorrow is supposed to be big day for revenge in Cap-Haïtien. They want to dechouke (uproot) all the old Duvalier people who are supposedly armed.

The girls are missing the things we left behind in America. There have been days when I've cried and cried. Mostly I think it's because I'm trying to balance the needs of both husband and daughters. Jon has such high expectations for all of us.

The more my father immersed himself in the agony of the Haitian farmers, the further he retreated from our family, as if embarrassed by our luxuries. My mother seemed dismayed but I, for one, was glad that he wasn't around—he only criticized. As far as I could tell, he believed that our family's only purpose was to serve Haitians, which meant that Mother's Day was neither remembered nor celebrated, until my mother burst into tears and he hastily threw together a shell-collecting expedition. Tenderness was an emotion he reserved for delicate vegetable starts, seedling trees, and babies.

Only once was my mother able to convince him to drive to the beach for an afternoon swim after running errands in Cap-Haïtien. At thirty-seven, she still had the body of an athlete, lean and strong. She slipped off her dress and dove in, pulling her arms through the water in long, even strokes, the wake rippling from her shoulders. She wanted him to forget Haiti, if only for an hour. Instead, he sat with his straw hat jammed onto his forehead as if, by denying himself this one indulgence, he could make amends for having taken time off work in the middle of the week. When they got back into the car to drive home, she refused to speak to him.

Flip is not happy with me was all that he would admit to his journal. *She says I am only a companion. When she has expectations, she gets disappointed.*

And yet sometimes, in spite of their stubbornness, my parents found a way to reach across the chasm that Haiti had opened between them. I can picture them standing in the doorway of the kitchen in Haut-Limbé, his arms around her waist, laughing about something I did not then understand. His hands were always stained with dirt, no matter how long he scrubbed them, and his tangled hair hid sunburned ears; her eyes sparkled like a girl's.

It was my mother who finally convinced him to let my sisters and me bring home two fuzzy, round-bellied Labradors when Laurie and Casso's dog had puppies. I cuddled the puppies on my lap on the porch during a lightning storm, as torrents of rain poured off the tin roof. Inspired, I penned an ecstatic letter that Grandma Lois promptly typed up and mailed on to the relatives (gathering courage from this, I secretly submitted it to *Youthwalk* magazine without telling anyone):

> *A brilliant flash of lightning would split the sky, leaving every single blade of grass and drop of rain outlined for an instant; burned in your memory, the silhouette on your eyelids. And with a mighty crash, a roll of thunder would pound out a celestial rhythm in the skies, seemingly loud enough to tear the earth in its sheer power. It is an incredible feeling to be lightly brushed with the same winds that took place in that unearthly display while feeling the comforting warmth of a slumbering puppy. And yet the most soothing—and the most frightening—fact is that it is the same God. The God of the storm is the same as that of the snuggly, furry puppy—he's big enough to protect us, but gentle enough to care for us individually. How lucky we are!*

Both puppies stopped eating a few weeks later. Missionary friends suspected that they might have contracted worms. After the first puppy died, my mother—against my father's protests—drove us all the way to Cap-Haïtien with a towel stretched across the backseat of the station wagon to try to find help, but the only veterinarian in town was on vacation in the States and wouldn't be back for weeks.

We dug a double grave under a dead orange tree in the yard. The knowledge that we had wasted time and money trying to save a puppy when so many around us faced far greater losses only added shame to the grief. I played a lament on my mother's recorder. My sisters held on to each other.

By Father's Day, my father and I could barely tolerate each other. He refused to even consider my suggestion of an elegant family luncheon in Cap-Haïtien, as the thought of sitting down to an expensive meal while farmers starved on the nearby hills made him irritable. Instead, he decided that we should visit Cherylene in Gonaïves.

It had been five years since we last saw Ti Marcel, and the whole premise felt ridiculous to me—a two-hour drive over dusty, miserable roads to find a child who might or might not be living in the house where we had last seen her, years earlier. I didn't want to admit how much it hurt that my father would rather spend the day with a Haitian girl he wasn't even related to than have lunch with his daughters.

We couldn't call ahead; there were no phones. Meadow and Rose groaned at the long, hot car ride ahead of us. My mother told us to at least try to have a good attitude—it was Father's Day.

Cherylene's aunts were sitting on the front steps when we arrived. They remembered my parents and pulled out their best furniture, sturdy iron chairs with plastic seat covers, and a child was sent running to buy us Cokes. My sisters and I sat stiffly upright, the backs of our legs stuck to the sweaty plastic, while someone else fetched Cherylene. Neighbor kids crowded into the open doorway to stare at us.

My father, ever impervious to awkward social dynamics, made small talk. He asked after Cherylene's father only to learn that Marcel had taken a new wife in the country; he seldom visited. Cherylene had been badly burned when a can of kerosene tipped over and her clothes caught fire. She had beaten out the flames but spent months in the local hospital recuperating.

She stepped through the front door nearly an hour later, her hair freshly plaited in tight braids tied with white ribbons. She was wearing a bright blue skirt festooned with sailboats. She didn't remember us, but she had heard stories.

She walked toward us, smiling, her hand held out. —What did you bring for me?

My mother looked embarrassed, but dutifully pulled out a bag of Rose's hand-me down dresses.

We watched, horrified, when one of the aunts summoned Cherylene to her side and lifted up her shirt to show us the scars from the cooking accident. Her skin from waist to neck was puckered with taut pink splotches. I realized, ashamed, that I didn't know how to say "I'm sorry" in Kreyòl—for her pain; for our foolish insistence on barging in on her life, reducing her once again to a recipient of our generosity; for the gulf between our lives and hers.

Before we left, my father tried to persuade my sisters and me to sing a song in Kreyòl, but we gave him thin-lipped smiles. Instead, Cherylene turned up the radio and danced alone in the middle of the room to klank-a-dank *konpa* music. When she asked to keep my sunglasses, my parents smiled and raised their eyebrows at me suggestively. I said no.

In the photo that my mother snapped of the two of us, saucy six-year-old Cherylene hams it up in my thick-framed dark glasses while I watch from the chair, a strained smile on my face.

From my father's perspective, the day was a smashing success, even if he found the Pentecostal prayer meeting at the end a bit unnerving. Cherylene's relatives handed out hymnbooks and head coverings, and everyone started praying and singing at once, the din of our overlapping voices like a holy ghost cabal; my mother rather liked it.

As soon as we got home, my father dashed off a letter to Grandma Lois: *It's a wonder she is alive. Her burn was worse than I can describe but she was in good health. I'm sure we'll see her again.*

When my sunglasses broke soon thereafter, he said that it should be a lesson to me for hoarding.

I despised my father's faded, rumpled clothes, his dirt-stained fingernails, and his unpredictable temper. I avoided sitting next to him at dinner so that I wouldn't have to hold his hand during the prayer. But even I could tell that his enthusiasm had begun to falter. By late summer, the rainy season still had not arrived. Farmers called it the worst drought in seventeen years. Creeks that had never run dry slowed to a trickle, then evaporated. In the village of Rey, there was barely enough water for people to drink, let alone irrigate their vegetable gardens.

After fifty-three days without rain, most of the seedling trees that my father had given to the farmers had withered and died. He spent weeks trying to capture a spring from a nearby gully and paid a local mason to construct a cistern in a last-ditch attempt to save the vegetable gardens. But the cement was faulty, and in the middle of the night, the walls collapsed. Terrorized farmers were jolted awake in the dark by a shuddering explosion of water across parched soil.

Two thousand dollars of donated funds evaporated into the dust.

My father's record keeping was a litany of failure:

> *Joseph's garden hit by chickens.*

> *Reynolds' family of 8 had 6 bell peppers for dinner. Nothing else to eat.*

> *Yesterday a vehicle struck school kids above Limbé, quite a commotion. Driver ran for his life. Car stoned, burned. Kid from mob came in to hospital, ear nearly severed by flying rock.*

> *Dr. Hodges sees only a grim future here.*

My father couldn't bring himself to visit when a family returned from a consultation at Hôpital le Bon Samaritain with the news that their six-month-old baby was dying of AIDS. Instead, he slipped off his backpack in the thin shade of a guava bush and tried to pray. Across the flood-scarred valley, he could just make out the faint blue edge of the sea. *Dèyè mòn, gèn mòn.* Behind the mountains, more mountains; behind one problem, another loomed. He hid his face in his hands.

When I read this entry in my father's black day planner for the first time, decades later, I was surprised by the grief that welled up in me. There was so much to mourn: the drought. The AIDS epidemic. The farmer in Rey who left behind forty-three descendants, yet his land was sold to pay for a lavish funeral. But it was the news from Adeline, our first cook at the Ag Center, that pushed my father over the edge.

Adeline used to bring her son, Nosben, over to sit next to her as she stirred the rice and beans, while my sisters and I played nearby. Nosben was a year older than Meadow, and Adeline had hoped to send him to live with his father in the U.S., but a visa had never materialized. Instead, at thirteen, Nosben had died of sickle cell anemia—a disease that could have been managed had he been born into different circumstances, or had he made it safely out of Haiti. Adeline was inconsolable.

After the funeral, my father picked up a wooden statue of a peasant woman struggling under an impossibly heavy load and hurled it across our living room. The statue shattered when it hit the wall, the basket splitting open along the wood grain, the woman's broken arm flying from her body. My sisters hid behind my mother. I watched my father crumple into a chair. At fourteen, I knew only that his rage, even if it stemmed from grief, was a poison that was seeping into all of us. If we did not find a way to survive sorrow, we, too, would self-destruct.

On Belonging

Limbé, 1990

HOW QUICKLY WE turn away from the pain of others when a distraction is offered. My sisters and I felt like escapees from a monastery when Steve and Nancy James offered to let us house-sit their airy four-bedroom in Limbé while they took a three-week summer vacation in the States. We hurled ourselves into the frenzy of compound life: movie nights in the upstairs lounge, pizza parties, Slip 'N Slide races across the lumpy grass lawn. No one stared when we flopped down in our sagging swimsuits and shot along the slippery plastic, wet hair in our mouths. We could even wear shorts as long as we didn't leave the compound—which we hardly ever did anyway, as the political upheaval had triggered a fuel shortage.

Our universe had shrunk to the size of a polo field, circled by barbed wire. The Doctor's and Joanna's mad genius son, David Hodges, boasted that he had stockpiled a forty-one-day supply of diesel in a hidden depot to keep the missionary generators running even if the rest of the country exploded into anarchy.

Free at last from my father's high-minded expectations, I watched back-to-back movies with the other teenagers, or hung out at the picnic table under the *labapen* tree with Olynda. After five years on the compound, Olly's English was as confident as her Kreyòl. Even when we were annoyed with each other, she had a teasing, playful way of turning conflict sideways, and she could almost always make me laugh. We were forever scandalizing Susan Smith by flirting with boys.

We were about the same age, but Olynda seemed somehow older. During slumber-party confessionals, I learned that her story was even more complicated than I had imagined. Her father—an American man whom she could barely remember—had died when she was four. She thought his name was Richard. She'd never actually seen a photograph of him.

Her birth mother, Bernadette, small-boned and petite, had been one of his employees at a sequin factory in Port-au-Prince. Only after his death did Bernadette learn that he already had a wife and children in the U.S.; one son came to Haiti for the funeral. Bernadette lost her job at the factory soon after. Olynda remembered neighbor kids calling her a devil's child and pinching her to see if she felt pain because her skin was lighter and her hair was different.

She was six when her mother explained that she would be spending the summer with relatives in Limbé. After her mother left, Olynda's aunt informed her that Bernadette would not be coming back.

Shaken awake before dawn to fetch the water for her cousins' breakfast, Olynda carried the rest of the family's laundry down to the river to wash. She cooked rice and beans and swept the dirt courtyard. She fell asleep on a mattress stuffed with rags. She could still remember the sting of the long cowhide whip.

Paul Romeus, the Haitian pastor who ran the school in Limbé that Olynda's cousins attended, pressured the family to let her attend as well. Paul offered a scholarship to cover Olynda's school fees and uniform; his daughter Picole brought her over to the missionary compound to play. The first time Olynda visited the compound, she was startled by the slide and swing set. She'd never seen a playground before, and was amazed by the missionary houses full of Barbie dolls and tiny Barbie shoes. She had never even imagined that such things existed.

She learned only later the reason that her mother had left her. Shunned by her family, Bernadette had sunk into a deep depression, but when she returned and discovered the welts on her daughter's back, she took Olynda back with her to Gonaïves. There, the taunts from the neighborhood kids were unrelenting. Olynda couldn't stop talking about the missionary compound in Limbé: a dreamworld where everyone was happy and there were always friends to play with.

Bernadette eventually convinced Bill and Joanna Hodges to adopt her daughter.

—We talked about it and agreed that it would be better for me, Olynda explained. —More opportunities. Piano lessons, trips to the States.

Joanna's newsletter announcement of the adoption had included a photograph of Olynda with her chin tucked shyly, her long hair curled against her shoulders.

—It was like getting my childhood back.

I nodded as if I understood.

—But when my mom got pregnant again later, when I was fourteen, and kept the child, I was so angry. Why couldn't she have kept me? Why couldn't I be with her, too?

We had no answer to this question. We lay on our stomachs and tried to imagine what it would have been like to be in her mother's shoes.

Bernadette visited every few months, perched stiffly on the edge of a sofa in the living room of the Hodges home, but the conversations always felt strained. Olynda wished she could just sit down on the floor and play with her baby brother, but she didn't know how to put her mother at ease.

The compound had seemed like such a paradise when we were little, but we were teenagers now. Overwhelmed by paradoxes we couldn't resolve, Olynda threw a pillow at my head.

—It's ridiculous! I won't even be allowed to wear makeup until I'm eighteen! she groaned.

I laughed and threw the pillow back.

We never talked outright about the unspoken hierarchy on the compound, how the adopted children were given keys to the pantry in the kitchens and had to unlock them for the rest of the Haitian staff. When Barbara had to be in Port-au-Prince for the day, I found it both flattering and absurd (though I never challenged it) that I was considered responsible enough to be put in charge of Haitian employees twice my age.

Even I had noticed that the missionary kids who had friends in

Limbé seemed to invite them over only when no one else was around. Once, I pushed open the door to the TV lounge and found Ana surrounded by Haitian girls I didn't recognize, combs and fingers tangled in her hair. She made no attempt to introduce me, just glared over her shoulder until I backed out of the room mumbling apologies. I wasn't sure which of us was more embarrassed.

Manno, our former Kreyòl language instructor, must have been aware of the compound's implicit bias, but he ignored it, showing up unannounced one summer afternoon when the teenagers were camped out under the *labapen* tree, debating whether or not the pirated Janet Jackson album that I had picked up at the open-air market, with crooked photocopied lyrics in Spanish, was appropriate for the younger kids to listen to.

Manno looked as proud and poised as a rooster in a cockfighting ring when he drove up on his red motor scooter. The other missionary kids tried not to laugh when he asked if I wanted to go for a ride. I was mortified by what I interpreted as his unabashed interest in me (compound rules dictated that such things should never be disclosed openly). When he tried talking to me in Kreyòl, I answered in English, lest I humiliate myself even further.

If I had written the script, Peter would have put his arms around me and sent Manno packing like some hoodlum in a 1950s musical, all of us in hoopskirts and leather jackets. Instead, while I half-mocked his broken English, I noticed that Peter was starting to edge away from the picnic table. When it became obvious that no one else wanted to talk to Manno any more than I did—he was an outsider; he wasn't one of us—he left abruptly, clearly as offended by the encounter as I was.

As soon as he was gone, I tried to lighten the mood by making fun of him. My friends were oddly unresponsive.

—He's just trying to get to know you. You should have some Haitian friends, one adopted teenager told me.

—But he doesn't want me for a friend; he only wants to get to know me because I am a *blan*! I protested, trying, unsuccessfully, to make everyone laugh.

—You have no idea what it's like to be Haitian, my friend said coldly, then walked away. It struck me with a sudden wave of embarrassment that because we were all missionary kids, I had imagined that our experience of Haiti was essentially the same. I had assumed too much.

Olynda followed Kristin. Peter was already gone.

Lizzie and Tamara stayed to argue over whether Barbara had any right to turn off *The Mickey Mouse Club* in the middle of an episode just because it was immodest. I played with the peeling paint at the edge of the picnic table, trying to appear unconcerned. A screen door slammed and I could hear laughter. I could only assume that they were laughing at me.

As missionary kids, none of us had any wish to live on the compound for the rest of our lives, but we resented those who reminded us how very isolated we were in our petty kingdom suspended between worlds. We closed ranks to keep them at a distance: Manno, the visiting expatriate volunteers. The night before Ana and Peter left for college, all of the teenagers somehow ended up in the tree nursery, perched on bags of sawdust while the rain tinged against the metal roof. The warm half-dark smelled of earth and pinesap, and we cracked jokes about where we'd put a swimming pool on the compound, or who among us was most likely to end up married to a potbellied American with a Southern accent.

I had never felt so close to finding my tribe. For the first time in as long as I could remember, something buried in me began to unfurl, like a seed, long dormant, turned toward the light. For one night, at least, we were home to one another.

Just after ten p.m., we scattered reluctantly. I lingered under the *zanmann* tree with Olynda, not wanting the night to end, until Barbara slammed open the screen door, her voice tight with warning: Where were you? Your father was looking all over for you!

I could just imagine him stalking through the shadows, his shoulders hunched and angry. I would have to keep to myself what I had discovered in the dark. I slipped through the moon-white trees, my sandals slapping the sidewalk. The night insects whined a shrill chorus and I wanted to burst into song with them: *I'm alive, I'm alive, I'm alive.*

When our allotted three weeks of house-sitting came to an end, even my father was disgruntled about moving back to Haut-Limbé. *(I wouldn't mind getting to play ranger for a while,* he confessed in a postcard to Grandma Lois, *I'm getting burnt out here.)*

One of the teachers at Jericho School had quit abruptly, leaving the elementary school in the lurch, and my mother agreed to take the job if no one else would. Joanna offered us a two-bedroom volunteer cottage on the compound. I'd have to share a room with my sisters, but it was worth it. Only my father lobbied half-heartedly for returning to the Baptist seminary. This time we overruled him.

When we drove back to pack up our things, we felt a momentary flicker of guilt when we realized that Rose's friend Laura Rose, along with our youth group leader, Kathy Brawley, and the middle school teacher, Mary Hays, who all lived on the seminary campus, had decorated our walls with balloons and hand-lettered posters: *Welcome back!*

We explained with chagrin that it just made sense for us to move to the compound—there was a fuel shortage, after all, and it was anyone's guess when things would improve. But the truth, as my mother let slip in a letter to a friend, was rather less noble: *Jon is a rather austere type, but not us girls.*

My father bought a mountain bike, cheap, from the open-air market and pedaled the six miles back to Rey to check on the gardens, but his idealistic experiment had been effectively vetoed. He had wanted us to live among Haitian neighbors, thinking that perhaps, eventually, we could muddle through and find our place in the seminary community. I would like to believe that I was capable, at fourteen, of trading condescension for curiosity. When Laura Rose became a teenager, she joined a local Haitian karate team, which I would have loved, and I'd give anything now to be effortlessly fluent in Kreyòl (though perhaps the adverb betrays me—a still-adolescent longing for a world where no sacrifice is required).

The question I can't escape (the question that underlies every missionary experiment) is: Should we have kept trying, even if we were doomed to fail?

A Leaky Roof Can Fool the Sun

Kay koule twompe soley, men li pa twompe lapli

Limbé, 1990

THE FIZZY EUPHORIA of the compound did not take long to wear thin. Under the watchful gaze of the missionaries I was not permitted, at fourteen, to watch PG-13 comedies unsupervised, much less *The Color Purple.*

Meadow borrowed library books and disappeared inside herself. Rose schemed and squabbled with the other ten-year-olds who tore down the twisting sidewalks on bikes and roller skates. I escaped onto the flat, unfinished roof of the school. Olynda hated it when I disappeared to be alone, but no one had bothered to remove the rickety wooden ladder after pouring the cement for the roof, making it the perfect hiding spot; all I wanted was time by myself to think.

Peter had left for college, taking with him whatever unspoken kindness it was that leapt between us. I had been tempted, at odd moments, to climb onto the luggage rack of our station wagon and shout to the world that I loved no one else but him, but I worried that it would embarrass him. I was too loud, too impulsive. He was so very unreadable.

I could never quite convince myself that he regarded me with more than avuncular fondness, though I clung to any offhand comments that might be teased into a double entendre (the most romantic thing he'd ever said was to offer to take me avocado picking in the moonlight). In one letter, written soon after he left Limbé, he confessed that he felt like a fish out of water in the dorms of his small midwestern Christian college, and told me that I should have started working on him much earlier to become more sociable. He didn't, however, go so far as to admit that he missed me.

In his absence, I took to watching *The Mickey Mouse Club* every afternoon at four p.m., wedged onto a couch in the back room of the Hodges house with Olynda and a passel of bug-eyed younger kids. The Mouseketeers wore silk shirts and swooped across the stage with a soulful bravado that I could not begin to muster. As missionary kids, we studied their dance routines with religious fervor. Occasionally, one of the Hodges grandsons, a fourteen-year-old named Ryan with a square jaw and piercing blue eyes, squeezed in next to us. My father, hearing rumors of lewd dancing, decided to monitor the scandal for himself.

I was livid when he yanked open the screen door to the TV room and sat down uninvited. I jumped up and switched off the television, but he turned it back on to watch while Olynda and I beat our fists against the tetherball in the yard and Ryan rode his bike in aimless circles around the *zanmann* tree.

That night I slammed the dinner plates onto the table. My sisters skedaddled to the bedroom. I seethed in silence while my father enumerated his concerns, then shouted at him: I don't *care* what you think, I *want* to be worldly.

I wanted to belong to this great, wide, reckless world, not just sit back in judgment of it, but having no words for this, I burst into tears. My father was sufficiently dumbfounded that he had no comeback.

My father was not at all pleased when he learned a few days later that Ryan and I had slipped out alone for a quiet walk along the Limbé River. Neighbor kids had followed us to hold my hand and ask for my watch and earrings, but even with an entourage, it felt like a breath of freedom.

Ryan and I poked around a small shed on the Limbé River full of rusting gears from the defunct hydroelectric dam that his father, Paul Hodges, had helped to construct, and which I hadn't even known existed. The dam, built in the late 1960s, had supplied electricity to the hospital for a few years, until the river jumped its bank in a storm and tore out a swath of gardens on either side, washing thirty thousand dollars of donated funds out to sea. There were people in Limbé who said the *lwa* of the river had given his daughter in marriage to the god of the sea, and that the spirits had not been pleased with the dam. For once, the U.S. Army Corps of Engineers seemed to agree.

When we tired of poking around the ruins, Ryan taught me how to skip rocks across the Limbé River. Then we saw a hill on the opposite bank that looked like it needed climbing. We'd seen market women wade across with heavy baskets balanced on their heads, but the soft silt sucked at our feet. Within seconds, I had water up to my thighs and was laughing hysterically. Deciding it was best to dry off before we returned to the compound, we found a grassy bank and flopped down next to each other in the sun. A breeze fluttered a tangle of morning glories in the *pengwen* cactus. Ryan squinted up at the sky. His eyes were a deep blue-gray like the underbelly of storm clouds, with long lashes that curled to gold at their tips.

—You know, I don't really like most people, he admitted.

—That's nice of you! I said, tossing a piece of grass into his hair.

—I only like interesting people, he explained, flicking his eyes over my face before looking away.

I could feel the giddiness in me trill to a fevered music, like an orchestra winding up for an opening song: timpanis and snare drums and high, breathless flutes. I was hoping for a kiss, but grinning old men on the way down from their gardens shooed us off.

My unchaperoned walk with Ryan, a dangerous breach of propriety, was among the many instances of adolescent misconduct discussed at the next emergency meeting of the missionary parents, after which I was forbidden to leave the house without parental permission, much less the compound.

I know my limits, I wrote furiously in my journal after my new curfew was announced: six p.m. My father remained impassive.

Since we could no longer spend our evenings gossiping on the swing set, Olynda and I started planning a trip to the beach with the other teenagers for Dessalines Day, when schools across Haiti would be closed to honor the man who had declared independence from the French and solidified the revolt of the world's first Free Black Republic. But when the day arrived and my mother left for a retreat with the other teachers, my father announced that it was to be a family trip; Olynda was not invited.

—But we've been planning this for weeks! I argued. —You promised!

(In all likelihood, my father had been careful to promise nothing. "Wait and see" was his proud and stubborn mantra.)

—It's not happening, he said.

I protested. He ignored me.

I put my hands on my hips and insisted that I was *not* going.

—I'm tired of waiting around. Your sisters are outside ready to go, he said, turning toward the door.

—You expect us to obey you as if you're some all-wise, all-knowing parent, when all you do is just change your mind at the last minute like some cruel dictator! Why should I have to respect you if you don't even keep your promises? I'm not your slave!

His left hand jerked toward me. I assumed he was going to grab my arm and drag me to the car.

His palm landed square on my jawbone as my face hit the wall. He had never hit me before. He had spanked us as kids, and sometimes rattled the wooden spoon drawer for effect, but it had been years since he had laid a hand on me.

I staggered, then stood up again, my head spinning.

We stared at each other, hearts pounding. I could hear my sisters crying outside.

—Now get in the car, he said.

—I'm not going.

He slammed the door behind him and yelled at Meadow and Rose to stop waiting around. I slipped down to the floor and leaned against the wall.

It was important for each of us to pretend that we had won this standoff. I boasted to my journal that when he slapped me, I was numb like Novocain, like the Ice Maiden; he had not broken me. The deeper wound, that the man whose affection I once longed for could convince me—even for a moment—that I was to blame for his assault, was a grief I couldn't bear to acknowledge.

My father, equally unrepentant, was careful to tell my mother over dinner how much fun he'd had with my sisters. In his journal, he went so far as to adopt the passive voice, as if to sidestep responsibility: *Apricot gets stubborn about going to Bas Limbé as family. Gets slapped hard on side of face. Still won't go. We did have fun. Girls rode on top of car on way back. Lots of rain in the night.*

We did not speak of the incident again. A few days later, I was lunging after a volleyball with Olynda and Ryan when he announced that I needed to get home and change; he needed a family photo for the newsletter. I followed, sulky with disgust.

Windows down, without air-conditioning, we drove in our Sunday best up a twisting mountain road while I tried to hold my hairsprayed bangs into place. He wanted mountains in the background, so we drove past wooden tables piled with tomato paste and Chiclet gum, past farmers with rusty hoes balanced across their shoulders.

When we finally pulled over and composed ourselves into a strained tableau—the cheerful, smiling ten-year-old; the beleaguered mother; the awkward middle-schooler; the brooding teenager with a hairbrush gripped in her fist as if she'd prefer to shove it down her father's throat—the sun appeared from behind a bank of clouds and streamed across the panoply of green-shouldered mountains like a veritable sign from heaven.

A perfect missionary family.

The newsletter for which the photo had been taken was not one of my father's most hopeful missives. He had compiled bleak updates on the impact of the AIDS epidemic in the local villages—dying gardens ruined by drought; fuel shortages; parents unable to afford *tap taps* for their sick children; unpaid loans and nonexistent electricity—then concluded: *Such are my reflections for the day: long, repetitive, depressing, not much Christian thankfulness. You can pray for Haitians and for us, that I won't be overwhelmed or get calloused, that we can help in our time here.*

My mother ripped the newsletter in half. We were the sent ones, the ones paid to provide uplifting stories.

But real life seemed to supply far more disappointments than triumphs. It was hard to find God in the pain.

After my parents' shouting match over the newsletter, the latest among many such arguments, I winced as the door to their room slammed shut, followed by my mother's muffled sobs. I dragged a pillow into the tiny closet of the room I shared with my sisters and curled up in the fetal position, my knees tucked under my chin.

Two doors down on a faded queen-size mattress, my mother was curled into the same clenched parenthesis.

Love, if it is to survive, is a patched-together tent of whatever you have on hand to protect yourself from the wind and the sun. We were trying, but there was a Haitian proverb for our doomed dance: *A leaky roof can fool the sun, but it can't fool the rain.*

That night, when my father insisted that we play a board game as a family, I locked the closet door and refused to come out. He found a screwdriver and removed the hinges.

—This is a punishment for your disturbing behavior! he said as he lifted the door onto his shoulder and carried it from the room.

—I still have a bruise on my face from where you slapped me! You beat your own children, and then you say that *my* behavior is disturbing? You're completely blind to your own hypocrisy!

My mother positioned herself between him and me. —Jon! I will not allow you to hurt my daughters! I want you out of this house until you can control yourself!

My sisters cowered behind her.

—Apricot is the one who is out of control! he yelled over his shoulder as he stormed off to work in the garden.

I grabbed the closet door and hefted it back into place while my mother pulled Meadow and Rose into her arms and prayed aloud to Jesus. My hands were shaking, but no one stopped me. With each turn of the screwdriver, I tamped down my hatred, counting down the days until I never had to see him again.

My father's journal entry for the day, characteristically brief, read: *Took door off Apricot's closet. Everyone upset about that. Flip's last comment before bed was she was thinking about suicide with a note saying it's my fault.*

I tried writing a letter to him, the only way I could think of to reflect back the hurt he was causing, to force him to listen to us. A week later, having tipped over the dining room table and shattered the candlesticks that we'd bought Mom for Mother's Day, he shoved a reply under my door.

Dear Apricot,

Since you tried writing last week I'll try it tonight. Such a dis-appointing and destructive end to the day. Alas. Sorry it happened, and sorry if I blamed you for my actions. Seems that we both have situations that we are incapable of handling properly.

I know for me that the more overtired and overstressed I am the less control I have. The way you were curling up on the chair while Mom and Meadow were reading I suspect you were tired too.

When I threw the book and tipped the table I was in a rage. It was something happening through me but I wasn't in charge. I was caught off guard and didn't realize what was coming. Usually when that happens I feel very sorry and regretful afterwards. Last night it took some time to feel that way. Not that I was glad I had done it, but I guess I was feeling that it wasn't my fault. A dangerous way to be.

He reminded me that he had been disappointed by my behavior, then continued:

I ask you to forgive me. If you find it is a spirit of rebellion that controls you and you are absolutely unable to participate I will for-give you also, and pray that you will be freed, just as I hope myself someday to not have fits of destructive anger.

Love, Dad

I had to reread the letter several times before I could work up the courage to answer. By the time I had slipped a reply under his door, he had already fallen asleep. Exhausted by the emotions I had struggled to put onto the page, not yet able to imagine that these tense preliminary paragraphs marked the beginning of a slow reconciliation that would take us years—perhaps a lifetime—to complete, I eased open the screen door and settled myself onto the back step.

Rain pinged against the tin roof, and the frogs were wailing. One voice would begin alone, low and insistent, only to be joined by others, summoned into song in the wet night.

I wanted to climb onto the roof of the school, but I was not quite brave enough to risk my father waking to find me gone, and the roof would only be sopped with puddles.

I felt weighed down by my parents' expectations for me as a missionary's daughter, always on display, but it was they who had first taught me to trust myself to wild spaces. I could only imagine that they felt equally trapped by the absurd expectations hanging over all of us. Where did they turn for solace?

The roof of the school was my cathedral. It was the only place on the compound—the only place in Haiti—where I felt utterly alone, free to sink into a deep well of silence, seen and heard by no one. Flat on my back under a blue-black sky, scalloped breadfruit leaves and royal palms swayed against the stars. The bamboo rustled and sang. I flung out my arms and drank in the glory, held by a mystery greater than myself.

I was an acolyte at the temple of beauty, although I did not yet have words for this, and no doubt would have considered it heresy if I had. Beauty was a luxury that, as a missionary kid, I had been taught to mistrust. It was not useful. It could not save anyone. But when I was alone with beauty, something in me felt reckless with joy. I was in the presence of something that I could not name, but when it spoke to me, I wanted to answer: *Here I am.*

Dust Doesn't Rise Without Wind

Pousyè pa leve san van

Limbé, 1990

I DID NOT piece together until decades later that at the same time I was trying to negotiate my independence from my father behind the closed doors of our volunteer cottage, the Hodges family was embroiled in parallel conversations with the board of the American Baptist Foreign Mission Society.

The Foreign Mission Society, which had changed the name on its letterhead to International Ministries to reflect the changing times even though the original title was retained on legal documents, had dropped increasingly forceful hints over the years that it would prefer to see more cooperation between the missionaries and the local Haitian Baptists. Dr. Hodges, by way of argument, pointed out in carefully typed letters that his daughter Barbara played the piano and directed a church choir; he himself taught Sunday school at the Limbé Baptist church. As for the suggestion that members of the Haitian Baptist Convention be given a titular role at the hospital, the Doctor pointed out firmly that the pastors had no medical training.

This potential conflict had rumbled just below the surface for decades, with negligible impact, until Dr. Hodges turned sixty-five years old. At which point the board of International Ministries, whose official policy eschewed any authority structure that smacked of colonialism, asked Dr. Hodges to either choose a successor or relinquish financial control to national leaders, as mandated by mission policy.

The initial conversations were cordial, until Dr. Hodges announced that he saw no need to tinker with a system that had more than proved its efficacy, and he had no immediate plans to retire.

The American Baptist Board of International Ministries, thrown back on its heels, reconsidered its strategy. The men on the mission board visited once every few years for official ceremonies, but had no precise role in Haiti. They could not claim to have carried the foundation stones for the hospital; nor could they boast of patients healed, generators fixed, or trees planted. And yet they were, technically, Dr. Hodges's superiors, conduits of the monies that poured in monthly from distant supporters. And in rare cases of extreme insubordination, the American Baptist Board of International Ministries had the power to strip errant missionaries of their title and authority—although such a thing was never mentioned in polite company.

My father overheard enough to understand that the Hodges children feared losing their homes and responsibilities should the leadership at the hospital change hands. (The Hodges children were not shy in voicing their opinions.) But as the date for the presidential election in Haiti approached and the missionaries gathered in the evenings to listen to Voice of America radio broadcasts in the Doctor's study, the far more pressing conflict seemed to be the escalating violence in the Haitian countryside.

When I was fourteen, my understanding of Haitian politics was ill informed and filtered through cynicism. I had noted in my journal, just after we'd been caught in the roadblock in March: *A woman president (temporary for three months—until the "election") was sworn in at 10 a.m. (well, it was scheduled at 10:00, but it ended up happening around noon. That's Haiti for you!)*

What I did not understand until years later was that three days after the coup d'état of Prosper Avril, General Hérard Abraham, the acting head of state, had ceded power voluntarily, and in his place a provisional president had been sworn in, with a mandate to organize what some were calling the first free and fair elections in Haiti's history.

Ertha Pascal-Trouillot, who had already made history as the first female justice appointed to the Haitian Supreme Court, admitted that she preferred the solitary pleasure of books and classical music to the public eye, but declared that she would accept her heavy task in the name of Haitian women. Democracy, for the first time in decades, was poised to take her seat at the National Palace.

Over the next nine months, twenty-four separate candidates for president vied for the favor of first-time voters—including the former head of the Tonton Macoutes, a man named Roger Lafontant, who had returned from exile and made no attempt to hide his Duvalier connections. The two front-runners were Marc Bazin, a former World Bank economist who had worked as the Haitian minister of finance and believed that a stable economy was the key to prosperity; and his ideological opposite, Jean-Bertrand Aristide.

Aristide, a Roman Catholic priest with strong connections to Vodou and social justice, had made his name in the slums of Port-au-Prince, with fiery liberation theology sermons about how it was long past time for the rich to share their wealth with the poor: *We must end this regime where the donkeys do all the work and the horses prance in the sunshine.*

Dr. Hodges, during his three decades in Haiti, had done his best to steer clear of politics but he was concerned that Aristide's rhetoric seemed to place missionaries on the wrong side of the divide. Instead of being seen as generous benefactors, missionaries, for the first time that Dr. Hodges could remember, were cast as privileged oppressors with access to foreign funding.

When the more politically conservative presidential candidate Marc Bazin swept into the hospital yard on a campaign stop, the Doctor cleared his throat and shook his hand uncomfortably; he did not want to appear to be taking sides. Aristide, however, showed no interest in hobnobbing with the missionaries. His supporters danced through the streets of Limbé shouting—*Oh! Ah! Oh! Ah!*—as they swayed to the rhythm of drums and whip cracks. My father caught a glimpse of the bespectacled priest through the barbed-wire fence behind the tree nursery. For a moment, the two men locked eyes, then the flatbed truck rolled on, past the water fountain, as the slim priest was swallowed up by the ecstatic crowd.

My father, like Dr. Hodges, was skeptical of Aristide's campaign promises; redistributing wealth sounded like a slick way to justify more violence. Aristide promised a new and prosperous Haiti, but to my father it seemed like the only real social agenda was to target new scapegoats. And if owning four *karo* of land—about twelve acres—instead of one tiny garden plot was enough to make someone a target, then Haiti was in trouble.

Better to skip the campaign speeches and do something useful, my father grumbled as he pedaled his bicycle up the highway to visit Zo. Another round of violence was the last thing the country needed right now. People were already too nervous to plant trees or plan for the future.

Wading across the Limbé River, my father was startled to find an open basket where the paths forked at the *kafou*. Flies buzzed over the strange apparition: short, glossy brown hair, a dark mane. A horse's severed head, the glazed, milky eyes flung open.

As my father stepped closer to study it, a swarm of flies erupted into an erratic spiral. It looked like it had been a beautiful horse. Possibly a revenge killing. Or maybe a threat? Surely people wouldn't sacrifice their own animals to appease the *lwa*; they'd have to be desperate.

My father was, at least, pleased to find that Zo's trees, even in the midst of the drought, were thriving. Zo had clearly been hauling water out of the river. Even the vegetables looked lush and vigorous. Zo waved my father over to see the new cedar tree he had just planted. *Sèd*, Zo explained, was used to make coffins. It kept the spirits at bay.

When my father asked about the offering at the crossroads, Zo was circumspect. He lived in a small community; he had learned to be careful. —It is easier to make a snake stand than to change a Haitian, Zo offered by way of a reply. A proverb that my father was free to interpret as he wished.

My father turned Zo's words over in his mind as he pedaled his bicycle back to Limbé.

The proverb could certainly be read as a criticism of the violence, but it was also true that the snake, though hunted, had figured out how to survive—refusing to stand when it already knew how to glide along the surface of the earth, to drink in the sun's heat, and to slip between the rocks for protection.

On the long-awaited and historic date of Sunday, December 16, 1990, citizens across Haiti took to the polls to elect a president. The results were to be announced the following afternoon, a day that my father and his fellow nurseryman on the compound, Ron Smith, spent disciplining a thief who had been caught stealing trees on missionary land.

The Morne Bois Pin peninsula, just as it had been when my father was in charge, was distant enough from the oversight of the compound that an enterprising opportunist, sizing up the situation, might hope to harvest a tree or two and escape detection. A pile of freshly thinned logs on Mon Bwa Pin had gone missing, and when local authorities informed the missionaries that they had the suspect in their custody, Ron, who had managed the backbreaking reforestation project for the better part of two decades, wasn't about to let Aristide's share-the-wealth speeches give people the idea that they were entitled to steal the hospital's trees.

Ron didn't want the man thrown in prison or beaten for his crime, but he also didn't want to lose any more trees, so he convinced my father and a visiting medical student from Australia to help him stage an improvised charade to give the accused a good scare.

Ron, claiming to have close personal connections to the head of the Haitian army after his years in Port-au-Prince (he was bluffing), promised that terrible things would happen if any more trees went missing. My father held up a broken camera to make it look like he was taking photos. The accused man was forced to hold in front of his chest a piece of paper on which was written *Volè*. Thief.

The intimidation routine was something of a gamble. If Aristide followed through with his campaign speeches and power swung to the powerless, this kind of hazing could put the missionaries in considerable danger. Nor was the heavy-handed bullying a very Christlike example. Christ, like Aristide, had preached on behalf of the poor. And he had expressly forbidden his followers from repaying evil with evil.

As Ron, my father, and the visiting medical student drove back to the compound, having successfully executed their staged drama, my father felt edgy and exhilarated, like a sheriff in some Wild West frontier town, tracking down a cattle thief. The three *blan* were still laughing about the scared expression on the face of the accused when Aristide supporters closed in around the missionary vehicle, chanting a victory song. The election results had been announced: Aristide, just as he'd campaigned, had won by a landslide.

The medical student from Australia slid down his seat in terror, having heard horror stories about mobs bent on *dechoukaj*, but no threats were made as the missionary vehicle inched through the dancing throngs who swayed and clapped, waved palm branches, and blew on conch shells, seized with elation that the long wait was over—that a new and more just society was, after all this time, about to begin.

The View from Dancor

Limbé, 1990

THE PRESIDENTIAL ELECTION, which the missionaries had fretted over for weeks, had come and gone without violence (though my father and the Hodges men still insisted that things could turn sour at any moment). Drumbeats echoed down the dirt streets of Limbé to celebrate Aristide's triumphant victory. He had secured an overwhelming 67 percent of the popular vote; Bazin, who came in second, garnered only 14 percent.

Meadow cut delicate paper garlands of lords and ladies dancing. I helped my mother weave strands of ragged pine branches to hang from our ceiling by a red ribbon; another missionary family had given us five chopped-in-half candles to use for our Advent wreath.

It was as restful a Christmas break as I could have wished for, aside from my anxiety over how I would feel when Peter stepped off the plane after his first semester at college.

I hung back when he stood on the front porch of the Hodges house with the other missionary kids. Those just home from boarding school carried a brash, confident energy that felt distinctly, disquietingly American. They lugged suitcases full of new CDs and talked casually about trips to Chicago to visit car shows. Belle and Paul's son Loren, who had been away at boarding school his entire high school career, made even the missionary moms swoon with his broad shoulders and easy banter. Whatever uneasiness these fellow missionary kids had felt while masquerading as average American teenagers was now unrecognizable under their sleek haircuts and clothes that anyone could tell hadn't been purchased at the open-air market or from a mail-order catalog. Even Peter and Ana, expatriates for only three months, seemed transformed. It was I who now felt foreign, overshadowed, awed.

I climbed alone onto the roof of the school after a noisy welcome-back game night around Bernice Rogers's dining room table. I couldn't stop thinking about Peter. He'd asked what books I was reading, what I thought of the elections, what the chances were that I'd be able to beat him at a game of spoons. He'd met my eyes and hadn't looked away. When he listened to me, he seemed so serious that I told him he was a sixty-five-year-old man poorly disguised as a nineteen-year-old. I was relieved that I could still make him laugh.

I leaned back against the roof, my head in my hands, and took in the high chirruping notes of the night insects, the dank undertone of desire in their discordant song. Silence was a mirage, a memory I couldn't quite put my finger on. A shimmering insubstantial thing that I tried to remember between the murmur of an unseen radio, a trumpet-call *kamyon* horn from the highway, the scuff of a dog's feet trotting across the dried leaves, the roosters that crowed at all hours. In six short months, we would be leaving Haiti so that I could finish high school in the States, just as my mother had promised, but at this precise moment I did not wish for any other life but this.

The 1990 Christmas edition of the *Jericho School Journal* included a tongue-in-cheek wish list of gifts that we students would have liked to be able to bestow: for Angelina, tap shoes and a dress; Olynda, lots of cats; Apricot, the largest pair of hoop earrings in the world; Flip, a good night's rest for a year.

On Christmas Eve, Steve and Nancy James popped out of their kitchen with a flaming plum pudding, singing: *Please put a penny in the old man's hat, if you haven't got a penny then God bless you!* Then we dashed off, jolly as you please, for the annual pageant at the Baptist church in Haut-Limbé. Mary perched atop a bony donkey, and shepherds chased a herd of live goats down the aisle. King Herod, who had a tendency to steal the show, draped himself in Christmas lights and plugged himself in. Steve James, the resident pacifist, was particularly pleased when the soldiers sent to kill the innocents in Bethlehem instead dropped their fake guns in front of the manger and worshipped the baby Jesus.

We played board games and watched *White Christmas*. My mother made caramel corn. My father read John Muir.

Olynda and I, calculating that the parents were sufficiently distracted, found bikes and pedaled to the open-air market. We told Tamara, perched on the front porch of the Hodges house, that if anyone asked for us, we were out of toothpaste.

We'd been friends for almost a year, but it was the first time that the two of us had escaped the compound without adult supervision. I fell off my bicycle in front of the Catholic church and plowed into a woman with a basket of soap balanced on her head. Olly apologized for me in fluid Kreyòl, then laughed all the way to her aunt's house. I had never met her aunt—I hadn't even realized that she still lived in Limbé—but the soft-cheeked matriarch welcomed us with a kiss on each cheek and pulled out her best chairs in a cool, tiled front room.

If Olynda felt any resentment over how she had been treated as a child, she didn't show it. She was her warm, gregarious, teasing self—even more at ease, it seemed, than when we were on the compound. Nephews and neighbor kids flitted in and out of the open doorway, and I discovered to my flat-out surprise that I could follow the flow of the conversation—a spirited, comfortable banter, mostly about school and relatives and food.

I waded in once or twice. Kreyòl seemed to be a language of interrupted monologues and interjections that functioned as a Greek chorus would: commentary; call-and-response. An emphatic language, honed over the centuries to communicate what could not be openly declared, punctuated by accusatory music. Startled laughter deepened like a hollowed-out drum that bounced and rumbled even after the mallet had been set down.

When we reluctantly said our goodbyes and biked home, it struck me that for one gorgeous afternoon I had not been trapped in the role of the *blan*—the giver of gifts; the visiting expert. I had been no more than a member of the choir.

I felt giddy with possibility: if Olynda and I could explore Haiti on our own terms, without parental interference, maybe I could actually learn to feel at home here. Was such a thing even possible?

Even my father seemed to be in a temporary good mood when he slipped back into ranger mode to organize a hike on the last day of December. I couldn't talk Olynda into coming with us, but Peter said that he wasn't about to let me beat him to the top of Dancor.

Cool mountain air from the summit filled our lungs as my father pointed out, three thousand feet beneath us on the valley floor, the black-sand beach of Bas-Limbé and the green promontory of Morne Bois Pin. Île-la-Rat was a speck along the blue edge of the sea. The stone Citadel, to the north, jutted from the horizon like a raised fist; to the south was Crête Rouge. At the time of the Haitian revolution, twenty-two fortresses had perched, unconquered, along the mountains' spine, an unbroken line of defense.

As we hiked down, it dawned on me that exactly one year earlier, upon learning that we'd be moving to Haiti, I had scrawled: *There goes my life.* I had been wrong. I had been yanked into a wider, more complicated world where sorrow and beauty lived under the same leaky roof.

I had wasted most of a year in self-absorbed drama, but there was still time. When I got home, I updated my journal: *I never did think I'd admit to loving Haiti, but I am glad I'm here.*

After the Dance, the Drum Is Heavy

Aprè dans, tanbou lou

Limbé, 1991

M Y FATHER CELEBRATED New Year's Day by hiking across the worn hillsides to wish his farmer friends *Bòn ane* (unlike my sisters and I, who spent the afternoon watching movies on the compound). At every house, he was offered a thick, steaming bowl of traditional soup jomou, pumpkin soup redolent with shallots and garlic and, if the harvest had not been too lean, goat meat. In return, he handed out New Year's *zetrèn:* batteries, toothpaste, nail clippers, scissors, toy cars, and seeds. More than one farmer clasped his hand and said: *Sa se yon jou mwen pa t panse mwen ta wè.* This is a day I never thought I would live to see.

A widow in her fifties pulled aside a thin curtain to show my father the single room she shared with her seven grandchildren, as wide as a double bed. He prayed with her and read the Psalms from his well-thumbed Kreyòl Bible, then gave her a gift of twenty-five dollars—enough to pay a year's rent—plus a forty-dollar microloan so that she could buy material to resell at the market. She had worked as a *machann* in the Limbé market before she lost her children to AIDS; worry over her remaining grandchildren had cost her livelihood.

My mother, back at the compound, had opened our door to find a woman whom my father had met some months earlier in a small village near Zo's house. Cleanne's feet were dusty and her dress was torn. She looked to be only in her late twenties but already seemed broken by life. My father had given her money so that she could visit the hospital, but it hadn't been enough to pay for the consultation. My mother supplied the remaining nine dollars. Cleanne's daughter, in torn sandals, waited beside her like a shadow.

The next visitor who knocked was a more frequent caller. She made the rounds every few months, complaining that none of the Haitian Christians would give her even one gourde to buy charcoal; no one showed compassion, only the *blan*. If no gifts were forthcoming, she would declaim loudly: Lord have mercy on us all! My mother sent her home with a bunch of bananas.

My father made it back to the compound just in time to catch the last few minutes of the Rose Bowl, televised live from Pasadena. *What a trip to see sunny Southern California,* he wrote in a postcard to Grandma Lois. *Forgot there was such a thing as the Rose Parade.*

Although it went against my father's better judgment, my mother insisted, and my sisters and I were elated when, for my fifteenth birthday, I got to bring home a floppy-eared gray puppy to replace the ones that we had already lost. I buried my nose in her impossibly soft fur and named her Squash.

My father, keenly aware that most animals in Haiti were lucky to scavenge whatever they could find—he knew families where even the children weren't guaranteed more than one meal every few days—decreed that the dog would under no circumstances be allowed to sleep inside, but she whimpered and scratched at the door on her first night away from her litter mates. At two-thirty a.m., he rolled over and grumbled to my mother that this hadn't been *his* idea.

I'd already carried the mewling pup inside when my mother pushed open the door to the room I shared with my sisters. Her tiny body burrowed against my chest as I pulled the sheet over us.

—Don't wake up Dad, my mother whispered.

Three days before Christmas vacation was supposed to end, my mother announced that she would be driving to Port-au-Prince with whoever wanted to join her for a weekend stay at a missionary guest house with a pool. My father was predictably exasperated. Milos and Christa, who didn't own a car, had talked her into it.

Christa and Milos both worked at the hospital, but it was Milos who was the joyfully unrepentant troublemaker. A Czechoslovakian nurse with a wild, dark beard, he kept reproductions of Orthodox icons in his wallet, in case he had to call on the saints for help. When he went jogging along the highway, he was famous for reaching up to bump the carefully stacked baskets on the heads of market women, just to hear them swear at him. On several different occasions, my father had overheard Haitian onlookers debate in serious tones whether or not Milos was in fact crazy—a *moun fou*.

Some of the missionaries were horrified by Milos's antics, but when he was scolded, he frowned and looked down at his clasped hands, then announced with an impish grin that there was not enough joy in the world.

The kids on the compound adored him. Chaos followed in his wake. He gave away chocolate on his saint's day but would tell no one his actual birth date. In the fairy tales he wrote and distributed to friends, strange figures wandered in and out of the surreal, like characters from a dream. He seemed haunted by secrets.

My father, although fond of Milos, was not at all pleased with the plan: Flip, are you crazy? There's a gas shortage!

—We'll just use some of the gas we have stored; better to use it than have it stolen!

My father stormed off to the garden. She kept packing.

I had been briefly tempted to stay when I mistakenly assumed that both of my parents would be away for the weekend. I could invite Olynda over and we could stay up late and bake brownies; the puppy could sleep inside and no one would even know. I changed plans in a hurry when I realized that I would be stuck at home with my father.

My mother honked and waved as we drove out of the compound the next morning. My father planned to ride his bike up a steep dirt trail to a village called Suffering, then take a *tap tap* to Gonaïves to visit Cherylene. We agreed to pick him up on our way back. He promised to feed the puppy.

Even with nine people crammed into a five-passenger station wagon (Meadow and I curled up on pillows in the back, Rose on a lap), the four-hour drive was—without my father's dispiriting presence—everything I could have wished for in a road trip. We stopped along the highway outside of Gonaïves and took goofball pictures in front of bizarrely formed cacti, and ate lunch at a serene beachside restaurant in Montrouis—indulgences we never would have dreamed of if my father had been driving.

I love Haiti! It's a tourist's dream! I rhapsodized after eating peanut-molasses candy and raspberries in Fermanthe. Milos talked my mother into brunch at the Olaffson, the fanciest hotel I had ever seen, then swept us off to visit the Haitian art museum in Port-au-Prince. Mom laughed more than I'd heard her laugh all year. We even stopped at an air-conditioned supermarket (air-conditioned!) in swanky Pétionville and bought real Granny Smith apple juice—each cardboard box with its plastic sippy straw a tantalizing reminder of a life we'd nearly forgotten.

My mother, unused to driving in the city, hunched her shoulders and gripped the wheel nervously when she had to pull into Port-au-Prince traffic: a honking jumble of motorcycles, kids in school uniforms, overloaded *kamyon* buses, and snow cone vendors clanging the sides of their carts. She was even jumpier when we walked out one afternoon to buy fried sweet potatoes from a hissing pan of oil.

—Rose, you're standing too close to the street, get behind me!

—Mom, I'm fine! Rose snapped back. She was ten years old. Of course she knew how to walk down a street.

My mother kept grabbing for Rose's arm, and Rose kept yanking it away.

—Here, Rose, I'll protect you! I cried, leaping in front of her the next time we had to cross a road. I held up my hands like a badly trained ninja. A schoolgirl on the back of a motorcycle smiled.

My mother exhaled loudly, but at least I had gotten Rose to laugh. Meadow slipped her arm through Mom's and patted it consolingly.

—Was I really that bad? she asked, but we were laughing too hard to answer.

My mother later recorded in her journal the only truly unsettling incident that we witnessed during our vacation, which came and went in an instant. On the drive to Port-au-Prince, somewhere in the Artibonite, we had driven past a body in flames. We did not speak of it afterward, that I remember, although my father also mentions it in his journal, so someone must have told him what we saw through the windows of the station wagon.

It had been a momentary glimpse in a crowded open-air market. A tire shoved over the victim's head, arms pinned by the melting rubber. Thick smoke billowed. Spectators had gathered.

We didn't pull over to find out what had happened, so we were left only with speculations. A man or a woman? A thief? A murderer? A scapegoat? Had anyone protested, or were they too afraid that they might be next?

There was a tense silence in the car after we drove past. We turned our attention to the road ahead. Breathed inaudible prayers, or tried to distract ourselves with any other image but that.

We did not mourn, at least not openly; did not light a candle for the life snuffed out. I did not write about the horrific scene in my journal, or in letters to the grandparents, as if my silence could blot out the smoldering, blackened silhouette. I did not know what to say, did not want to accept that life could be reduced by such agony to ashes and bone. This death was sinister and ugly. Uncleansed by grief. Our silence was our complicity.

Perhaps this was why, on our last morning in Port-au-Prince, Milos insisted that we visit the Missionaries of Charity Home for the Dying. He wanted to give massages, as did one of the other nurse volunteers. To be touched is to understand that we are connected, he explained. We followed him into the dim room. Haitian nuns in white and blue moved between creaking metal bed frames. My mother let go of Rose's shoulders and slipped her hand into the outstretched palm of an elderly man. His leg bones stretched gaunt under a white sheet.

—*Bondye beni ou.* God bless you, he murmured.

—*Bondye beni ou,* my mother echoed.

Milos took a dying man's feet in his hands, gently massaging the callused skin. A woman with high cheekbones and a concave chest stared at the opposite wall. I moved toward her, aware of my discomfort.

So much of my time on the compound had been spent avoiding the hospital, but perhaps this was what I had come to Haiti to learn: that my well-being was inextricably linked to the lives of every other person in this room. We belonged to the same earth. Our lives were of equal significance.

—*Bonjou,* I whispered. I placed one hand in hers. Her skin was cool against the frayed sheets: the taut muscles, the fragile bone structure.

My sisters and I didn't try to hide our disappointment when we said goodbye to Milos. He and his more adventurous entourage had decided to take a *kamyon* back to Limbé so they could have one more full day in the capital, whereas we'd already promised to meet Dad in Gonaïves. If we'd been able to call and change our plans, I'd have jumped at the chance.

The long, hot drive to visit Cherylene was demoralizing. My mother seemed to grow increasingly irritable as the day wore on. She insisted that I change out of my jeans—which not a single person in Port-au-Prince had found objectionable—and put on a more culturally appropriate skirt before we met my father.

—But *why*? I argued.

She sucked in her breath and stopped the car abruptly, dust swirling over the cactus. —I'm going to take a walk while you get changed! she announced, her voice high with forced cheerfulness.

Rose stuck her feet out the car window. —Apricot, come on, you're just making it take longer!

—It's hot, Meadow mumbled.

—You know she's only doing this because of Dad, I pointed out. My attempts to inspire mutiny were futile.

—Well, that's better! Mom said briskly when she sat down again behind the wheel.

I ignored her. I had slammed down the gates of the fortress, untouchable.

Cherylene's relatives, as usual, hadn't known to expect us, so our hosts spent the better part of two hours getting dressed so that we could take their photographs. *Why are we here again?* I muttered under my breath.

It had only been a few months since our last visit, so when Cherylene stepped into the room, my father leaned forward, I thought, far too eagerly. His laugh seemed unnecessarily loud. The whole act rang false to me. He hadn't seemed particularly glad to see us after three days away—if anything, he seemed even more disappointed in us than usual—but he was stumbling all over himself to demonstrate his devotion to Cherylene. Whom exactly was he trying to convince?

As soon as we got back in the car, conversation quickly ground to a halt. He wasn't interested in our stories from Port-au-Prince, and we were equally bored with his updates about the ant infestations in the vegetable gardens. I did ask about my puppy, and he said it was doing fine. He'd had to get up one night to throw a cup of water on it because it wouldn't stop whining, but it had toughened up since then. He glanced in the rearview mirror, hoping for a reaction, but I refused to give him the satisfaction.

When one of our tires blew out just over the pass of Pilboro, he knelt by the side of the road and strained against the lug nuts, which had rusted in the humidity. The muscles in his back twitched and he grunted with frustration. A crowd gathered to watch. One woman held a baby with rheumy eyes and a wet slick of mucus running down her nose.

—Take her, the woman insisted, attempting to push the sick child into my mother's arms.

My mother stepped back, flustered. —No, *madame,* thank you. I don't want your child.

—She's sick. You take care of her. Take her.

The crowd studied us. I couldn't tell what to make of their laughter.

The interaction felt theatrical, staged to draw attention to the gaping inequity between us; a farce. I couldn't figure out what they wanted from us.

Milos, I felt sure, would have known what to do and risen to the crowd's energy. Perhaps he'd have pretended to steal the baby and called the mother's bluff.

Then I thought of Olynda. Her mother had given her away. What would I have done in her place? How angry would I feel if I could not protect my own child from harm yet had to watch others sail past, blithely shielded by resources I could never dream of possessing? No wonder the resentment ran so deep; no wonder Aristide's campaign promises had resonated so powerfully, why uprooting the old order might have seemed like the only option.

My father wiped his hands on a rag and slammed the flat tire into the hatchback, then yelled at Rose for accidentally spilling water on the seeds in his backpack. My mother rubbed her temples. Was he always this angry? His hands gripped the wheel as he steered us down the darkening mountain. We sank deeper into the strained silence.

Love in a Time of Dechoukaj

Limbé, 1991

WHEN WE AWOKE the next morning, thick black smoke curled over the barbed wire into the compound. I could hear angry voices, the sound of running feet. My father had already been over to the Doctor's study to hear the news for himself. While we slept, Roger Lafontant—the man who had commanded the Tonton Macoutes terror squad during the Duvalier years—had taken over the National Palace. To prevent the newly elected Aristide from taking office, the provisional president, Ertha Pascal-Trouillot, had been forced at gunpoint to read a televised resignation speech. Lafontant had declared himself the new head of the republic. Aristide urged his followers to protest.

Milos and the other volunteers had escaped Port-au-Prince just before businesses seen as Duvalierist sympathizers roared into flames. Looters ducked in to salvage what could be pulled from the wreckage. Torched car frames and tree branches barricaded the national highway. In the north, houses of both Lafontant supporters and his rival, Marc Bazin, were *dechouked*.

Jericho School continued as normal, though Meadow's middle school teacher, Mary Hays, arrived windblown on the back of Manno's motorcycle; they'd had to talk their way through the barricades. I realized belatedly that what I had mistaken for bravado in Manno was, in fact, courage.

My father, rather than risk the streets on his bicycle, and risk repercussions to friends in the countryside, spent the morning with

Dr. Hodges in the clinic, helping to translate for a group of visiting medical students, until protestors gathered to hurl rocks at a house across the street while neighbors shouted at them from behind closed doors. Rumor had it that both the house and a nearby school belonged to a Lafontant supporter, who was said to have been in Port-au-Prince at the time of the coup.

Rocks still in hand, the protestors turned toward the missionary hospital. For a moment, it looked as if they were about to storm the clinic, until some in the group joined hands and formed a human barrier. My father watched, his body tense with adrenaline, as the young men changed course and continued down the road, a sign shattering behind them in a rain of glass.

By nightfall, the military coup was over. Roger Lafontant, though he'd claimed to have the support of the army, had been arrested, along with his co-conspirators. News reports announced that seventy-five people had been killed in clashes across the country.

My father informed us over dinner that some of the places we had just visited in Port-au-Prince had been burned to the ground.

—It sure sounds like Aristide is inciting his followers to continue the *dechoukaj* and then denying it all in the same breath, he told us.

—I'm so glad we're not still driving back and forth from Haut-Limbé, my mother said, rubbing Meadow's knotted shoulders.

Meadow had been able to eat only a few bites of dinner. Her breathing was shallow and uneven. Steve James had listened with his stethoscope but hadn't been able to detect anything amiss. He'd suggested gently that it could be anxiety.

—Who knows what's next, my father said as he pushed back his chair to join the other men in Dr. Hodges's study. —The Doctor used to say that things are getting worse all over. Now he just says it's all disgusting.

That night, my mother curled up next to Meadow on her narrow twin bed, the frame creaking beneath them every time my sister tried to take a deep breath, but it was eleven-thirty before she was able to fall asleep.

My mother stayed late at the school the following afternoon, absorbed in third-grade math problems and misspelled essays, until the sound of rocks smashing against the wall snapped her back to the present. One of the kindergartners was trying his hand at *dechoukaj*. She sent him home, then realized that her own daughters must still be processing the coup. She found Rose and Meadow both in tears. Rose had been told by the other little girls on the compound that she was too bossy; Meadow was having trouble breathing.

That night even my mother agreed that the puppy should be allowed to sleep inside, for comfort. It seemed to help—that is, until Rose woke at midnight to something warm and wet seeping into the mattress and started crying all over again.

—Flip, I told you this was a bad idea! my father yelled as my mother and I got up to change the sheets. —That puppy is spoiled rotten!

My mother wasn't there the next morning to witness my father's rage (she'd slipped out of the house at six a.m. to finish lesson plans) but Rose came running over to the school in tears to tell her what had just happened.

How should we deal with his uncontrolled anger? my mother wrote in her journal. *I feel like there's nothing that can be done.*

My father, furious that the puppy had interrupted his sleep, had hurled our schoolbooks off the table and torn up Rose and Meadow's homework folders.

—Dad, stop it! Just stop! I had screamed as he aimed a kick under the mattress. Meadow held open the screen door, and the puppy darted out with a yelp.

Meadow hid in my arms, shaking, as our father kicked the bicycles into a clattering heap on his way out. The puppy slunk back eventually and I knelt and stroked her soft belly and oversize paws while she gobbled up her breakfast. —I'm sorry he scared you, I whispered.

My father spent the rest of that morning helping Ron plant seedlings in the hospital tree nursery. —*Pa fè sa!* Stop that! he roared when kids on the other side of the barbed-wire fence whizzed rocks at his head.

It was as if he sensed that our privilege was at the root of their anger, but he understood it only in the form of shame. He had already uprooted us from our country and it occurs to me now that if it had been within his power, he might have gone even further and *dechouked* the American greed and comfort that tainted us: our preference for puppies and movies in the lounge, our disinterest in learning Kreyòl. We were the ball and chain that tied him to the compound. He couldn't figure out how to escape.

My father, although he may have appeared to the kids who hurled rocks at his head to have everything, couldn't achieve the one thing he wanted most: to belong to Haiti.

My first priority, as soon as school let out, was to find my puppy, but though I clapped and called, I couldn't find her anywhere. She didn't come running, not even when I filled her bowl with boiled bulgur and tiny silver *ti yaya* fish and walked all the way back to the highway behind the Jameses' house and around the fishpond, calling her name into the shadows.

My father said she must have gotten too close to the hospital and been stolen, but I blamed him. The next day, as if in penance, he took my mother and sisters on a foray through the nearby streets to ask if anyone had seen a small gray puppy. I didn't bother to join them. I knew that she was never coming back.

I climbed onto the roof of the school and shredded a dried leaf between my fingernails. There was no point in loving a creature like that anyway. I was going to have to say goodbye sooner or later; it wasn't like my father would let us bring a dog back to the States from Haiti. Life was full of losses. I should have figured this out by now. And how did I have any right to complain when people were dying in hospital beds and houses were being set on fire?

By the end of the week, *kamyons* were once again blaring past on the highway, and the burned tires and garbage had been shoved into the gutters. Port-au-Prince and Limbé seemed to have reached a holding pattern, but my father assured us that Cap-Haïtien was still explosive. No one on the compound had driven that far, but the rumor was that the Esso gas station had been burned to the ground, along with the only store that sold propane.

My mother sat down with Rose on our small brick patio and lifted up her mug of tea. —A toast to the cookies! To the bananas! To the Nutella! she proposed. Rose smiled reluctantly. Meadow, her lip quivering, admitted that she was lonely.

—You know, I'm lonely, too, my mother agreed, and marched both of my sisters upstairs after dinner to watch *The Sound of Music*. She couldn't resist singing along when indomitable, flibbertigibbet Maria clasped the hands of her frightened children and led them to safety across the mountaintops, fields of wildflowers fluttering in the breeze.

I stayed behind to clang around the kitchen, skimming the fat off a jug of fresh milk to make whipped cream while my father camped out at the dining room table with a stack of letters to answer. He seemed to have forgotten entirely that tomorrow was Mom's birthday.

Today marks our one-year anniversary in Limbé, he wrote in a long, frustrated missive to Grandma Lois. *We arrived so hopeful. At this point I'm ready to write the place off. It feels as though these people are intent on self-destruction and that there is no purpose in knocking on their hard heads. I hope I don't get swallowed by a whale.*

Drowning in his Jonah the prophet role, he did not notice the telltale warning signs: his reduction of an entire country to "those people," as if each individual mother, daughter, grandfather, farmer, schoolgirl, *kamyon* driver, or nurse could be lumped into one dismissive category, their stories erased.

On my mother's thirty-eighth birthday, Nancy James brought over a vase of roses clipped from her garden, and even my father sat outside under the trees to savor forkfuls of gingerbread cake, whipped cream, and one carefully hoarded can of peaches.

It was Saturday, and when the mail arrived, I pulled a thin envelope from the pile, addressed to me. It was from *Youthwalk* magazine.

Remembering that I had sent in a submission six months earlier, I hid the envelope at the bottom of the stack and ducked into my closet. I opened every other letter first, a vain attempt to slow time down while my heart tap-danced double time.

I was braced for the inevitable rejection, but there it was—completely implausible but printed in stark black ink for anyone to see—they wanted to publish what I had written! Or at least they would consider including my essay in their next devotional if I could add a few more lines and send in a photo.

I burst into the dining room and handed the letter to my mother. She shrieked and hugged me, then blurted out the news before I had a chance to shush her.

—I'm not published yet, I insisted, suddenly feeling shy.

Two days later, when I disappeared out of the back gate of the compound with my mother's Nikon camera thumping against my chest, I still couldn't believe my good fortune.

My mother, completely out of character, had agreed to let me go on a walk—alone—as long as I promised to be gone no longer than forty-five minutes. It helped that she was relaxed from birthday celebrations and that the *Youthwalk* editor had asked for a photo. Also, my father hadn't been there to veto the idea.

It had felt strange to read my essay again, so many months later. I felt ambivalent about leaving the puppies in the story, since they hadn't survived: *The God of the storm is the same as that of the snuggly, furry puppy . . . How lucky we are!*

We had lost all three in just six months, though it seemed petty to complain; others had lost much more.

Theologically, I wasn't quite sure what to do with the problem of pain. Joanna's newsletters about the hospital always seemed suspiciously cheerful, but it didn't feel right to just ignore the heartache. Or was that the point: that life was full of pain, but God was fierce and wild and unpredictable—and able to hold on to us even in the midst of loss.

I paused, heart pounding, on a dirt path at the top of a ridgeline and studied the Limbé valley through the viewfinder. So much history had played out in this one valley alone: Taínos, conquistadores, slaveholders, missionaries, revolutionaries. What were we to do with all of that grief?

I had used up almost a whole roll of film (my mother was going to kill me) and had promised to head straight back, but I wasn't ready, just yet, to return to the compound. I needed a little more time to think— about my *Youthwalk* submission, about Peter. I sat down and pulled on a tuft of grass.

Peter would be heading back to college soon, and while he hadn't said anything definitive, when I sat next to him in Kreyòl church, I could feel his skin brush against mine every time he adjusted his posture. Olynda raised her eyebrows disapprovingly every time she caught me looking at him, as if to say *My brother, really?*, but I couldn't help imagining how easy it would be to just lean over and rest my cheek against his shoulder. Was I, as Olynda warned, a hopeless flirt?

I brushed off my skirt and stood. One last look before I reentered the claustrophobia.

The hovering iridescent wingbeat of a dragonfly. A cricket clicking in the dry grass. A mango tree framed against a distant ridge. And then I saw them—two sparrow hawks, wingtips lifted as they circled the sky.

Beauty, it seemed, had been here all along: a wild summons, a name for God that did not stick in my throat. It felt suddenly absurd that as missionaries we had come to teach Haitians about God. God was already here. Maybe our only job was to bear witness to the beauty—and the sorrow. Without denying either one.

When I slipped back inside our volunteer cottage as quietly as I could, my mother and Milos were at the kitchen table with cups of tea and a devotional on suffering. I was only fifteen minutes late—I'd been gone barely an hour—but Milos, whose joyful disregard for protocol I had always assumed to be boundless, frowned into his beard and told us that he'd been jogging along the highway earlier that afternoon when a crowd blocked his path. They weren't laughing. Some had grabbed rocks to throw at him. My mother gasped. —Oh, Milos! That's awful!

—Well, I stayed off the highway, I said.

—Still, Apricot, you could have been hurt!

—It's probably unwise, given the current political climate, Milos began.

—But I'm here! I came back. I'm fine, I said, closing the bedroom door firmly behind me.

My father was equally exasperated when he found out that my mother had let me go. Apparently, the American Baptist mission board representative from Cap-Haïtien had driven out earlier that afternoon to talk with the missionaries about emergency evacuation plans, should they prove necessary.

My parents sat up late at the kitchen table after my sisters and I had been sent to bed, to debate where we would go if—as it now seemed possible—we had to leave Haiti early. My mother was adamant that we would *not* be moving back into the one-room cabin in Idyllwild with the pit toilet. My father wasn't so sure. What was wrong with living simply?

—But I thought that was the deal, my mother argued. —We'd go to Haiti, and then you'd get a real job with benefits! She pounded the table with her fist. —I thought that this poor living was finally supposed to be over!

He lowered his head like a man in the stocks. He didn't want to sell his soul just to pay a mortgage. He wanted his life to count for something significant.

My mother groaned. —But Jon, we've done our time!

When my sisters and I got in on the conversation, my father did, at least, agree to a two-week train trip across the U.S., coach class, from Florida to California. My mother, realizing that it would be one of our last family trips before I left for college, and that we could stop through Oregon on the way, clasped her hands across her chest and sighed: Oh, Oregon!

She described the mint fields and picking wild blackberries straight off the vine. We teased her, but she closed her eyes and shook her head as if she couldn't hear us, her mouth easing into a tired grin.

I was rather elated myself, as Peter had made the bold move of sitting down next to me at the picnic table—in broad daylight, not caring who might be watching—for no apparent reason except to be near me. I had been practicing Kreyòl with Annalise, one of the women who worked on the compound, while she kept an eye on her two- and three-year-old missionary kid charges. Peter did not laugh at my stumbling Kreyòl, and Annalise teased me only a little. By the time I raced over to help Olynda tally the pharmacy charts (late as usual), I was practically skipping.

Olynda refused to say a single word to me during the entire twenty minutes that it took us to flip each stained yellow chart to the correct page and tap the numbers into the ten-key calculator, but the angry whir as the receipt spat out its curled tongue seemed only to repeat the magic words: *He cares! HE CARES!*

It had been weeks since my father had hiked up to visit the gardens in Rey—he'd barely left the compound since the attempted coup—and he stalked between the clinic and the tree nursery like a caged beast.

He helped a visiting surgeon remove a farmer's anthrax-ridden, gangrenous leg with a saw, the gory scene unlike anything that he had ever witnessed. The farmer was so terrified that the doctors feared he would die of shock mid-operation. He survived but would never be able to farm again.

Everywhere my father looked, he found reasons to despair. Grandma Lois mailed a newspaper clipping about four hundred houses that had been burned to the ground outside of Gonaïves. Cherylene, who lived near the bus station, should have been fine, but it was impossible to know for sure. When my father drove a group of hospital volunteers to the airport, the uprooted gardens along the highway made him sick to his stomach. He grumbled that if my mother hadn't been teaching at Jericho School, we might have just packed our bags and left.

He was even more dismayed when he found out that Cleanne, the frail single mother whom he'd befriended, had walked six miles from Garde Cognac with her nine-year-old daughter, worried that she would be late for her follow-up consultation in the missionary clinic the next morning. They had slept beside the river, two thin bodies curled up against the night, because she hadn't been able to afford the twenty-cent *tap tap* fare. He would have given them a ride if he had known.

Even worse, when Cleanne showed my father her hospital chart after the consultation, he realized what she did not. She had tested positive for HIV. Her immune system had already been destroyed, and there was nothing more the hospital could do for her. My father explained what this meant. She would die soon.

He urged her to find a home for her daughter before it was too late, so the girl would have a future. But Cleanne had already placed a daughter as a live-in servant in someone else's house and could not bear the thought of losing the only child she had left. She could not face death alone.

My father asked if he could pray with her, and Cleanne nodded. She explained that she didn't attend church because she didn't have the right clothes to wear, but she did trust in God.

—God doesn't care about what kind of clothes we wear, my father insisted.

He gave her what she needed to pay her hospital bill, plus extra for *tap tap* fare and food, but was haunted by the realization that she did not have the support of an extended family. Had she been given a bed at the hospital, she could have at least spent her final days in the care of nurses who could offer some relief from the pain. But the beds were reserved only for those who had some hope of recovery. And every bed was full.

Love in a Time of Dechoukaj, Kontinye

Limbé, 1991

AFTER MY SISTERS fell asleep, I creaked open the screen door and sat on the steps, unwilling to leave such beauty unwitnessed. I pulled out my journal.

> *This is another world, sitting here beneath the moon. It seems so distant from time and everyday worries. It's so bright! Almost as if it were full day, but softer, kinder, and more mysterious. And she sees my dearest tonight.*

The night before Peter left for college, in the companionable half-darkness of the swing set, he had confessed that we had a very special relationship. He didn't try to hold my hand, but he did say that he would miss me. It was enough to set my heart soaring.

I kept thinking of him, settling back into his dorm room, as the missionaries gathered around a bonfire at the Jameses' house. Hot dogs had sizzled and marshmallows had puffed into toasty, sticky perfection over bright red coals—all that remained of our spindly Christmas trees from Morne Bois Pin. The moon had been almost full through the silhouetted trees. I turned back to my journal:

> *I wonder if he's thinking about me? Not half as much as I'm thinking of him, surely. Five months is too long. Half a day is too long! I want to see him, and talk with him, and tell him I'll die if he*

leaves me again (which I won't, of course, but it sounds much more tragic than something like, "If you leave me again I'll have a sullen fit and mope around the house for a few days").

The next morning we woke once again to burning tires and angry voices in the streets. Although the Haitian military denied it, rumors of a failed plot to free Lafontant from prison had touched off new protests. The house of an alleged Lafontant supporter in Limbé was firebombed. David Hodges roared off on his red motor scooter only to watch the home of the local Bazin representative burst into flames. Gunshots ricocheted across the marketplace. Dr. Hodges spent the evening removing a bullet from the leg of a young girl who had been caught in the cross fire.

That week, five houses in Limbé were *dechouked*. The tribunal office was ransacked and its archives burned. The ex–police captain's truck was set on fire and his Uzi and revolver stolen. When a group of young men attacked houses directly across from the hospital during the night, no one stopped them. Even the police seemed increasingly reluctant to intervene.

My father was dumbfounded. Enough is enough. *Ase se kont*, he said to anyone who would listen.

My father left as soon as it was light to work with Ron at the tree nursery or translate at the hospital. My mother holed up at Jericho School for up to ten hours a day to grade papers. Rose and I distracted ourselves with friends.

Meadow, alone at the dining room table in our volunteer cottage, slid an X-Acto blade along a length of red paper, the knife's edge slicing a thin ribbon. Red and gold curls from a fading perm brushed against her shoulders. She pushed them away from her face. Her lips pursed as she wound the curled paper tight around a pencil and tugged it loose, one edge crimped into a crease—the whorled petal of a quilled flower. Her forehead wrinkled as she eased the petal into a pearled dot of glue.

Crack.

At the sound of the explosion, her hand jerked. Glue smeared. The paper gummed into a tangle.

In that first startled split second, the brain cannot distinguish between the sound of a gunshot and the sound of a rock hurled against a tin roof. Both explode with the same sharp noise, which triggers the amygdala to flood the brain with adrenaline. The heart pounds. Lungs suck in air.

Meadow heard the rock clatter and bounce off the tin roof and fall into the garden. She processed it all in seconds. It was not gunshots, not this time. But her face was already flushed, her heart hammering.

She squeezed her shaking hands and reminded herself. *It's just a rock, just a stone skittering across tin. The door to the bedroom is closed. You can't be hit if you're sitting at the table. It's probably just some kids at the water fountain trying to see what will happen if they hit one of the missionary houses.*

She stretched her neck, eased out the kinks. Twelve years old. Coiled so tight. She picked up the ruined flower and tried to smooth out the paper, then set it down. Picked up the knife, held it between her fingers. A deep rattling breath. Slowly, everything became quiet again. Her fingers cut, curled, folded, glued, created. A stillness she could climb down into, hide in its ordered depths. This insignificant small loveliness, a paper-thin barrier of beauty to hold out the fear.

When the hospital itself was threatened with *dechoukaj* the following day, Dr. Hodges made the unprecedented decision to drive into Cap-Haïtien and phone the American ambassador. For weeks, he had been weighing the possibility that the upsurge in violence might indicate the beginning of a religious war, a modern-day Catholic crusade against Protestantism.

—I'm going to go in and try to pull the plug, he announced soberly to the missionaries who congregated outside the hospital office.

My father offered to go with him, but the Doctor cleared his throat and told him that he was needed to stay behind and hold things to-

gether. Barbara and Paul piled into the waiting vehicle to escort their
father through the roadblocks while their brother David yelled after
the retreating station wagon: How dare you call yourselves Christians
when you turn to worldly authorities at times like these! You should be
praying to God for protection!

Dr. Hodges lowered his chin. It was the first time in over thirty years
that he had left the hospital during clinic hours.

In Vaudreuil, just outside of Cap-Haïtien, one of our friends, a
missionary nurse, was in the midst of consulting with a patient when
her Haitian colleagues ran over to alert her that Dr. Hodges had just
driven past on a clinic day. Something awful must have happened in
Limbé.

A hostile crowd had gathered in front of Belle and Paul's house across
the highway from the compound, and Belle placed an urgent phone
call over the missionary party line to ask for prayer. My father, watching
from the back gate of the compound, suspected that the local gangs
weren't quite bold enough to *dechouke* the home of a missionary, until
pickup trucks started to arrive full of young men he didn't recognize,
who jumped down to swell the ranks. My father wanted to intervene,
but David Hodges ordered caution.

My father returned home to eat lunch, but he couldn't help feeling
that perhaps he could forestall the attack. He talked his plans over with
our cook, Anna Rose, who was washing dishes at the sink. When he
marched out the screen door moments later, she threw down the dish
towel and ran over to the school to tell my mother.

Inside the whitewashed walls of the missionary school, unaware of the
tensions outside, our pencils ticked through world geography work-
sheets, geometry, social studies. If I had known that at that very moment
my father was entertaining notions of heroism, I might have worried
about him, but only my mother received the bulletin, and she promptly
persuaded an entire classroom of nine- and ten-year-olds to get down
on their knees and pray.

—God especially listens to the prayers of children, she explained, —so you need to pray extra hard.

My father, striding resolutely toward the back gate of the compound, did not know that Ron Smith, at the hospital tree nursery, had also reached the end of his patience. Each man decided alone to confront the growing crowd. Their paths converged as if led by unseen hands.

The Haitian yard workers had already gathered to watch the disturbance through the gate, and when they realized what my father and Ron had in mind, they tried to block their path. Drawn by the raised voices, Nancy and Steve James emerged from their quiet house to join the heated debate.

Steve was wary of being drawn into violence, even in self-defense. When an unseen assailant had slit the screen in his daughter's bedroom and grabbed her leg, causing her to jolt awake with a scream, Steve had sat up for several sleepless nights in the vain hope of talking with the *volè* should he return. But neither Steve nor Nancy could deter my father or Ron.

The two nurserymen pushed open the gate and entered the highway. As soon as they reached the crowd, they were surrounded.

—We have no problem with you, *Agwonòm* Jon, a voice called from the back of the crowd. —Go home. This has nothing to do with you.

—What do you mean this has nothing to do with me? my father argued as the crowd pressed in around them. —These are my friends. These are good people. Why are you doing this?

Pushing through the crowd to reach Belle and Paul's gate, he felt a prick of metal against his neck. Knives flashed in raised fists. Then he heard someone say: *Sonje sa yo te di nou.* Remember what they told us.

The knife eased away from his throat. He tried to decipher what it might mean. Was someone else giving orders, stirring up the violence from afar?

Once the threats had been made, the collective appeared undecided about what to do next. There was no leader. The young men, teenagers half of them, seemed to be united only by their formless discontent.

Their frustrations were not unreasonable. The world they had inherited was far from just. Parents with subsistence incomes had made harrowing sacrifices to put their children through school, but still there were no jobs. Opportunities seemed to be given only to other people, in other countries, or to the privileged few, funded by foreign income, who hid in the mansions of Pétionville or behind walled compounds. Scarcity was a coiled snake that lunged at their heels. There seemed to be no future unless they could yank it out of someone else's hands.

My father had little patience for this logic. If the protestors wanted a more just world, then they should do something about it, not just tear down the few people who were making a difference. They could always plant trees if they couldn't think of anything better to do. But as the crowd pressed in around him, he paraphrased a line from Gandhi, frequently quoted by Steve James: If everyone demands an eye for an eye, where does that get us? We'd all be blind. We have to find a better way to solve our disagreements.

A few of the teenagers seemed to listen. My father wondered if their show of strength had more to do with some trumped-up political disagreement than a vendetta against Belle and Paul. The young men seemed less malicious than resentful, and my father was just beginning to hope that the standoff would deescalate when two new *blan* burst out of the back gate of the compound.

Ron's sixteen-year-old son strode up onto the highway with a stony look on his face, prickly for a fight, followed closely by David Hodges, who was yelling that my father and Ron shouldn't have gotten involved in the first place. The two nurserymen exchanged glances. There was no point in trying to push their luck.

As they made their way back toward the compound, more people began to gather around the perimeter, curious about this noisy street theater—*blan* against *blan*. In all the commotion, none of the agitators seemed to notice when Belle and Paul slipped out their front gate together, stepped away from each other, and walked separately along the outside edge of the crowd, to meet on the other side of the highway.

Only as the back gate to the compound opened and Belle and Paul made it safely inside did someone in the crowd point at them and yell: That was Paul! Didn't you see Paul, why didn't you get him?

Belle wondered afterward if the Lord hadn't just closed their eyes (a miracle for which my mother's class would have gladly taken credit).

Belatedly, the young men seemed to remember their lost purpose. A few grabbed rocks to hurl at someone or something. Others rolled a few small boulders onto the highway, but the energy had dissipated. The *tap taps* laid on their horns and swerved around the dispirited barricade.

Dr. Hodges's trip to Cap-Haïtien to phone the Ambassador proved ineffectual. Belle and Paul spent the night on the missionary compound. While we slept, their house across the highway was broken into but not *dechouked*—nothing was broken or set on fire.

Dr. Hodges drove to Cap-Haïtien for the second day in a row, as the American ambassador had failed to take seriously his warnings about an impending religious war.

This time, two embassy representatives returned with him to assess the situation. My parents, along with the rest of the missionary adults, squeezed between the desks and chairs of the hospital office with their arms folded across their chests (we children were forcibly distracted at Jericho School).

The embassy men, clipped and professional, were blunt. —What if my superiors should decide that the best course of action is to evacuate all American citizens?

Paul Hodges spoke for everyone in the room. His usually confident voice seemed to crack with emotion. —We won't leave. Too many people's lives depend on us, and we couldn't carry the guilt.

The embassy representatives reminded the missionaries that they could not guarantee the protection of any American citizens who chose to stay.

No one volunteered to leave.

The missionaries lingered outside the pharmacy to rehash the conversation. The missionary kids, finally released from mandatory distractions, tried to figure out what was happening.

I overheard the Doctor announce that *never*, in over thirty years, had it felt so dangerous to live in Haiti.

My mother came out of the meeting in surprisingly good spirits, all things considered. There seemed to be something exhilarating about having taken such a courageous stance—setting aside thoughts of personal safety for the betterment of others. When my father and Herb Rogers decided to sleep at Belle and Paul's house to try to prevent another break-in, my mother encouraged him to go. Meadow demanded: But how do we *know* that we will be safe?

—That's just what the embassy people asked! my mother laughed, surprised. —But Meadow, God is watching over us! He has his angels protecting us right now!

She drew her daughter into the curve of her shoulder. Meadow did not relax.

I couldn't work out whether the threat was real or imagined. I had long ago dismissed the Hodges family as histrionic, though I was beginning to second-guess myself; my parents, on the other hand, seemed to have the remarkable ability to stare danger straight in the eyes and not even recognize it.

I took a deep breath and glanced at Rose. Whatever fear we felt, we had learned to tamp down tight.

Just after midnight, with my father across the highway at Belle and Paul's house, my mother's confidence began to waver. My sisters and I had finally fallen asleep, but a barking dog had jolted her awake. She got up to write in her journal at the dining room table, her bare feet on the concrete floor. *Jon told me more gory details of things that are taking place in Limbé. Supposedly Haitians like empty houses to destroy.*

She described the meeting in the crowded office and a Bible study that Milos had led several nights earlier.

> *We often cause ourselves more pain by trying to avoid suffering than if we accepted the suffering itself. I fancied we couldn't label anything as "suffering" because we were to consider it all joy when we faced trials. It's given me words to understand myself better.*
> *I just heard a gunshot. It's hard being away from Jon.*

No attack was made on Belle and Paul's house during the night, although my father and Herb got up every time they heard a noise to check the windows and doors. Paul called at eleven p.m. to say that he had just seen fifteen men wearing the red armbands of the Duvalier secret police destroy a house with machetes, but the only thing my father saw was the full moon cutting long shadows across the deserted streets.

The following morning, as implausible as it might seem, having been awake half the night to prevent a friend's house from being *dechouked*, my father took a trip to the beach. It was not exactly an impulsive decision, though perhaps it lacked foresight. For months, he had been corresponding with a forester friend in the States with whom he had worked in the early 1980s, though they had not seen each other in years. The Webbs had left Cap-Haïtien abruptly during the post-Duvalier upheaval (they had lived with their children in a lovely but isolated home at the top of a long winding road without a good escape route), and after their sudden departure they had never returned, although they had remained in touch with friends in Limbé.

When the Webbs booked a Caribbean cruise that would stop for one afternoon in the north of Haiti, a flurry of letter writing ensued. Once the plan had been set in motion, even after weeks of political upheaval and *dechoukaj*, my parents didn't know how to call off the reunion. Also, my parents were optimists.

The morning the cruise ship was due to arrive, the day after the visit from the embassy personnel, my mother taught school as usual and lined up a substitute for the afternoon so she could have lunch with her friends. My father drove to an implausibly serene white-sand beach called Labadie.

With its nonnative palm trees and orderly blue and white deck chairs, Labadie is a meticulous fabrication. The cruise ships that docked in Cap-Haïtien in the early 1980s had rerouted their itineraries after Haiti became unfavorably linked with the AIDS epidemic, but to this day, regardless of political upheavals, epidemics, and earthquakes, cruise ships drop anchor at Labadie because armed guards ensure that the artificial paradise remains inaccessible from the Haitian side. Attractions have grown to include a 2,600-foot zip line and a roller coaster, and tourists are discouraged from wondering exactly where they are in the Caribbean. The official website lists the peninsula only as *Royal Caribbean's private destination: Labadee, Hispaniola*—a misnomer as old as Columbus. Haitian artist friends who sold handcrafted wares at the "native market" were advised not to advertise that Labadie was, in fact, on Haitian soil, as its disease-ridden, dirt-poor reputation was not considered conducive to the shopping experience.

My father, as planned, met the Webbs at the beach. Leaving behind the gated paradise for Limbé was, predictably, a jarring reminder of the economic uncertainties that still gripped Haiti, but the reunion was nevertheless a fond one. On the compound, hugs were exchanged and children exclaimed over. We had just sat down to lunch around the Jameses' dining room table when gunshots erupted. The Webbs blanched. They had already lived through more violence than they cared to remember.

My mother felt sure they were overreacting but didn't know what to do. She sent my sisters and me back to our classrooms at Jericho School; my father put the Webbs in the back seat of the car; and away my parents raced in the direction of the cruise ship.

I do not remember if I felt afraid. There had been so many gunshots already. But I did understand that it would take them several hours to return from Labadie. And I had not forgotten the warning from the embassy personnel.

My father, behind the wheel of the station wagon, took note of a group of young men who seemed to be gathering by the water fountain as he drove out of the hospital gate. He glanced back at them in the rearview mirror; there seemed to be something disorganized but troubling in their manner. It wasn't until after my father had turned right onto the highway that a whistle blew and the men began to hurl rocks and bottles at the hospital walls.

My parents and the Webbs, en route to Labadie, passed an embassy vehicle full of what they assumed must be representatives from the American consul, followed soon thereafter by a truck full of Haitian soldiers in riot gear barreling toward Limbé. My father pointed out thick black smoke from what appeared to be burning houses when they crossed the bridge over the Limbé River. They did not turn around to figure out the nature of the disturbance.

From the windows of Jericho School, it was hard to tell exactly what was happening. We learned later that the embassy men had arrived to a barrage of broken glass. Soldiers succeeded in dragging several of the agitators to the Limbé prison only to find that the prison itself was under attack. The crowd refused to disperse even after warning shots were fired. Threats reached Dr. Hodges that the hospital would be *dechouked* by nightfall.

This time, when embassy personnel strongly encouraged the voluntary evacuation of all American citizens, the Doctor agreed that it was time to send out the women and children.

With our parents gone, my sisters and I were ushered down the narrow sidewalk to our volunteer cottage by chipper, dependable Mary Hays, Meadow's middle school teacher—she of the curly bob and the determined dimples, which she still managed to coax out, for our benefit, even as she sat at our dining room table to write a note to our parents:

4:30 pm Friday
   Jon & Flip—Due to rumored trouble, women and children are leaving the compound. We have taken Apricot, Meadow & Rose

*with us to the Seminary. You are more than welcome to join them
there. We, in the meantime, will do our best to keep them safe &
occupied. Hold firm! Mary*

We were instructed to fill an overnight bag. My hands shook as I
peeled photographs from the wall. *What would you save if you had five
minutes before your house burned to the ground?* It sounded like an ice-
breaker question from youth group. I took my journals (of course);
makeup; a few favorite items of clothing; a photograph of Peter on top
of Dancor, one of me and Olly sticking out our tongues at the camera,
and one of my sisters leaping off a waterfall; my Bible.

I kept my voice deliberately calm, like the grown-ups', when
Meadow asked: But what if they don't make it back in time?

I answered with undue confidence. —Everything is going to work
out; they will be fine.

Meadow added a postscript to the note that Mary Hays tucked into
the door: *P.S. Mom we have your diary & photo album.*

The other kids were already milling around the front porch of the
Hodges house as we hugged our bags and waited for further instructions.

The rumors were growing: Someone had seen the body of a headless
man being carried through the streets. The phone lines had been cut at
Baptist headquarters in Cap-Haïtien. Pastor Tomas had received death
threats if he showed up to preach at the Limbé Baptist church on Sunday.

Steve and Nancy stood next to each other, as if tethered by an
unspoken question: *Will you still be here tomorrow?* Asia and Andrew
clung to their father, four arms circling his waist, not wanting to let
him go.

The high school boys, both Hodges grandsons, had no intention of
missing the fight if there was to be one. Ryan's jaw was set. His adopted
sister, Angelina, beat her fists and howled, furious that her mother and
brother were not coming with her. Susan had also refused to leave the
hospital, although she, too, was sending her children away.

Cars filled unevenly and bags were shoved onto laps as mothers
made sure they knew exactly where all of their children were.

Manno leaned against Casso's car, the keys clinking in his hands. He had driven over to help talk us through any threats we might encounter along the way. He was risking his life for ours. I felt ashamed that I had misjudged him.

We were the last to leave. Manno took the wheel, next to our fearless youth group leader, Kathy Brawley. Mary Hays, my two sisters and I squeezed into the back. I wondered briefly if we should have grabbed Mom's camera, but it was too late now, the car thumping down the rutted dirt road, past neighbors who leaned back on their porches to watch us leave. My father had already told us some of the accusations being made about the missionaries: We were greedy foreigners who only wanted to steal from Haiti; we had made ourselves rich by their suffering.

I hugged Rose on my lap. I had forgotten how small she was—barely four and a half feet tall, her clear eyes taking it all in. Meadow huddled between us, her hands like ice. Every bounce of the shocks startled her.

And then we saw it—the blue station wagon. We leaned out the windows and waved frantically to flag them down. My mother leaned across my father in the front seat, looking windblown and surprised after their rushed beach trip.

Her smile faded as soon as she heard the news. My father, to no one's surprise, said that he would stay with the men. My mother would hurry home and pack; she'd meet us over at the seminary as soon as she could get there.

—Don't forget the passports! Meadow called after them as the station wagon pulled away.

My mother found herself standing in front of the refrigerator, staring blankly at our carefully stockpiled mozzarella and yogurt. Faced with the possibility that the house and everything in it might be gone before the night was over, her foxhole realization was a defiant commitment to happiness: *We should enjoy life more!*

She caught a ride to the seminary with the last departing vehicle and stayed awake for hours, getting down on her knees throughout the night to pray and beg God to protect those who were still at the hospital. Saturday morning, she dashed off a worried update to Grandma Lois:

I have passports, tickets, money and little else. Last night, Mary,
Laurie and I kept up a prayer vigil, taking turns getting up to pray
by the hour through the night. We haven't heard any news yet.
    There's no trouble in Cap or the seminary so we're safe and well.
We'll keep you posted.
    Can't tell you any news about Jon.

Love, Flip

The letter slipped out on the missionary plane before we learned that everyone was fine—no attack had come in the night.

Bright morning sunlight filtered through the windows of Mary and Kathy's cottage on the seminary campus as I folded my journal open on my knees and tried to write. The crowded living room didn't have the serenity of the roof of the school. There were tea bags drying from a string for reuse, and my sisters were sprawled out on the couch with books—but I was glad for the quiet interval to clear my head.

In Limbé, we had been scared for our lives. Bewilderingly, just four miles away, all was calm, all was bright. The campus we had been so eager to escape only months before was virtually untouched by threats of violence.

My mind kept trying to bend around the apparent contradictions. Was Limbé simply a powder keg, as the Hodges family believed, or was there something about the hospital's relationship with the community that had contributed to the crisis?

Kathy Brawley announced later that afternoon that she was going to drive into Cap-Haïtien to make sure all the other missionary evacuees had heard the good news that everyone on the compound was safe. It didn't take much persuasion to agree to join her.

The Mont Joli Hotel had donated a dozen free rooms to the missionary families, so we swam and drank Cokes and made a holiday of it. What I remember most about the evacuation is the *konpa* band that played beside the pool on Saturday evening, and how eleven-year-old Fabienne, whose father had left her in Susan Smith's care, shimmied and twirled and was scolded by the missionary wives. I tried to convince the other teenagers to go swimming at midnight, but my mother said she was too tired to supervise.

The attack on the hospital never came. Pastor Tomas preached on Sunday to an overflowing crowd at the Limbé Baptist church. The threats evaporated with as little warning as they had arrived. Perhaps the prayers had worked their magic, or—as my father wanted to believe—the silent majority in Limbé had decided that enough was enough.

My father spent one more night at Belle and Paul's house, then came to look for us at the seminary only to discover that we'd left to join the pool party at the Mont Joli. Exasperated at our self-indulgence, he drove back to the compound and left us to figure out our own way home.

When we finally returned to the compound after two nights away, it felt like waking from a dream. We did not know how to speak of the evacuation, even among ourselves. We had been baptized into the same fear as our neighbors, the ones who had no option to leave, and there was something in those murky depths that we were eager to forget. Whatever fear or grief we felt, we buried deep.

I berated myself for having been so foolish as to believe that we were really in danger. Despite our assumptions, it seemed increasingly clear that the story did not really revolve around us. We had leaped so quickly into that old, tired role: the beleaguered whites surrounded by a rioting black mob. But we had misread the cues. Our need to see ourselves as benefactors—without whom the Haitians, impoverished and hopeless, were doomed to live in darkness—was outdated at best. Why would Haitian visionaries and entrepreneurs settle for menial entry-level jobs in a missionary hierarchy that would never let them rise to the level of their giftedness? We, too, were responsible for this unraveling.

We had all participated. Aristide, proclaiming the gospel of justice and the gospel of dechoukaj at the same time. My father with his gospel of trees. The Hodges family's unswerving allegiance to the hospital. So many saviors ready to die for their causes.

Always it was the same: We placed ourselves, like heroes, at the center of the story. As if it was our destiny to save Haiti. What we couldn't seem to understand was that Haiti needed our respect, not another failed rescue mission.

I taped my pictures back up on the wall of the bedroom, then sat down at the table in the corner and tried to write.

My mother, disappointed that we had not been evacuated all the way to Idyllwild, had already grabbed her lesson plans and headed for the school. Meadow found a book. Rose pedaled off on her bicycle. My father disappeared to the Doctor's study to talk politics.

I tried to explain in a letter to Peter that it all felt rather like a strange dream: *half a nightmare and half a normal afternoon; "on vacation," I suppose.*

Hearing a knock at the door, I set down my teal green fountain pen to answer it. A woman holding a bundle of cloth stood next to her husband. They were looking for my father. I couldn't understand everything they were saying—they wanted money?—so the woman pulled aside the fabric to show me. In her arms she held a dead baby.

I understand now that she must have been in shock, just as I was still in shock, but we had no words between us to express this. I stood frozen on the patio. Even in English I wouldn't have known what to say. A child had just died. What words, in any language, could be offered?

I fumbled an apology and ran to find my father. I wished later that I had given them my favorite black scarf, the one with the silver and gold threads, to wrap the child's body.

My father, once he realized what had happened, grabbed the car keys and drove the family back to the seminary to spare them a crowded *tap tap* ride. He explained to me that the baby had died of dehydration from diarrhea before they even arrived at the hospital.

I sat back down at the desk feeling suddenly shaky; my own fears overshadowed by this far more staggering loss.

Oh Peter, isn't anyone going to cry for that baby? Can anyone die unnoticed? It's not right! I'm so sick of this stupid, heartless world! What is the point in it all?

When the U.S. State Department issued a travel warning against Haiti, shortly thereafter, the Missions Committee at the Idyllwild Bible Church wrote to assure us that if we wanted to leave early, they would support whatever decision we made. *We know this must be a hard time now and very scary. You are in our hearts and prayers.*

My father's summary was terse: *Things have been a little quieter. The hospital continues to function as usual. We're fine.*

After the evacuation, life on the compound resumed as if the evacuation had never taken place. My mother taught third-grade math and spelling; my sisters and I bent over our homework. My father took us on evening walks through Limbé, which had been transformed, in our absence, into a parade route.

For Aristide's upcoming inauguration, light poles and fences had been swirled in flowers and streamers. Tables and chairs were set up to welcome the new president. Pebbles, limes, rice hulls, flowers, and soil had been artfully arranged in front of the houses. Women swept their dirt courtyards into billowing clouds of dust. Even the tree trunks had been stripped of their branches—*butchered,* my father noted scornfully in his journal—and dressed in festive whitewash. Kids with drums and shakers sashayed down the newly level streets, paved with load after load of donated gravel (the owner of the gravel pit being careful not to protest).

The neighbors seemed to have forgotten their former animosity toward us—or had I only ever imagined it? Perhaps even during the evacuation there had been those who were worried on our behalf. The world was full of kindness and beauty; it was also full of hurt and anger and revenge. I couldn't make assumptions. I would have to figure out how to read each person's eyes and gestures to decide when it was safe to trust. Life was even more complicated than I had realized.

On the long-awaited day of Aristide's inauguration, my father was one of the few from the missionary compound to attend the official ceremonies in Limbé's town square; the rest of us celebrated with an all-compound wiener roast.

My mother led everyone in singing praise songs on her autoharp, then sat under the trees with Milos, Steve, and Nancy to talk about the importance of prayer during these hard times.

My father explained in a letter to the grandparents that Aristide had announced in a press release that he had conducted a wedding between the army and the people, and no more blood should be shed. *It all sounds wonderful,* my father noted dryly, *but there are some real skeptics among us.*

There wasn't much to be done besides put one foot in front of the other. There were still trees to plant, patients to treat, lesson plans to organize. My mother spent most of February distracting her students with Valentine's Day activities. Her class decorated cards for sick families in the hospital, complete with cookies that she and Rose got up at six a.m. to bake and decorate, each heart frosted with pink lemon icing. (Rose and I also left anonymous secret-pals gifts for a few of the volunteer nurses, but when they heard rocks hitting the walls and the sound of running feet, they were too terrified to open the door; my father had to go over and explain that it was just us.)

When the big day arrived, I was over the moon when Agape Flights delivered a big red envelope addressed to me from Peter. Olynda followed me home to watch me open it.

> *Valentine's Day is the perfect time for people to express their feelings and not be shy. So here goes . . .*
>   *I L . . .*
>   *I LO . . .*
>   *I LOV . . .*
>   *I'm very fond of you.*

Isn't it perfect? I gushed to my journal. *He cares!*

In a rare show of emotion, even my father wrote an extra nice Valentine's Day poem for my mother that year.

Love was a powerful barricade against despair.

A Medieval Feast in the New World

Limbé, 1991

SIX WEEKS AFTER the evacuation, we still jumped whenever we heard rocks hit the roof. The Hodges family decided that it was necessary to improve the hospital's defenses.

In the beginning, the compound had been demarcated from the town of Limbé by only a low hedge of *rakèt* cactus and a colonial dike designed to hold back the river in the event of a flood. Over time, the *rakèt* had been replaced by barbed wire, across which the local women hung their laundry. Following the evacuation, two tall metal gates went up, attended by guards. David Hodges ordered his men to construct a concrete wall around the perimeter.

I was not a fan of the new fortifications, though the high school boys put me in my place whenever I tried to argue. *I keep wondering what we are doing here if the compound is so locked up and isolated,* I wrote in my journal. *We on the inside are locked in, and those on the outside are being blatantly kept out. If we really are here as missionaries, to help the people, why are we devoting so much time and energy to keeping them out and making the hospital "safe," or "defensible"? It's like something is eating away at the heart, changing and distorting so that instead of helping we are isolating ourselves.*

Dr. Steve James, whose house faced the highway, directly across from Belle and Paul's—and was therefore the most vulnerable to attack—was by far the most vocal opponent of the wall. He argued that the missionaries would send a troubling message to the people of Limbé if they built a wall to keep Haitians out. Steve advocated strongly that if a wall must be built, then at least the section behind his house should remain unfinished. He quoted Robert Frost: *Something there is that doesn't love a wall.*

Good fences make good neighbors, Ron retorted, also quoting Frost.

Eventually, the Hodges family acquiesced; the wall was built, but the Jameses' house was protected only by barbed wire.

On Wednesday and Saturday afternoons, when the clinic was closed, Dr. Steve James would pull out his hand-powered lawn mower with rusty metal blades. He had asked the yard workers at the compound to please allow him to mow his own lawn, which he viewed as a monastic ritual, a practice to anchor him to earth: a concrete reminder that, as a physician, he was still capable of humble physical labor. He felt almost at peace as he pushed the querulous machine over the uneven ground, stooping to free a tuft of wiry Saint Augustine grass when it jammed in the blades.

Sometimes, however, through the barbed-wire fence, strangers on the road cursed and spat, accusing him of deliberately hoarding his money because he refused to pay someone to do his yard work for him. Steve accepted the insults as an act of solidarity with his hero, Jesus the Man of Sorrows. Occasionally, strangers threw stones. His children, avoiding the drama in the backyard, stayed inside.

The missionaries, parents and children alike, were all teetering on the thin edge of exhaustion. High time, my mother decided, for a party. She had not forgotten her promise to herself during the evacuation: to enjoy life more.

St. Patrick's Day was a holiday not often celebrated in Haiti, but my mother has never been one to be deterred by lack of precedent. She had read about a St. Patrick's Day–themed medieval feast in a *Focus on the Family* magazine (a tenuous connection, granted, but it sounded fun). My mother took the bare bones of an idea and breathed life into it—or rather, she was trying.

Well past midnight on a school night, she leaned over our kitchen table to roll flatbread trenchers to use as plates and illustrated a long, winding scroll with the story of Saint Patrick, that famous long-dead missionary who had converted an entire island with a fistful of sham-rocks. My mother's enthusiasm, once aroused, was as irresistible as the Pied Piper's flute, at least as far as children were concerned.

All of the guests at the Medieval Feast, my mother explained to her class of nine- and ten-year-olds, needed to come prepared with a song, a story, or a joke to amuse the King or Queen—an honorary title that would be bestowed upon whomsoever bit in to the winning hors d'oeuvre that contained a single uncooked bean.

Rose and her classmates immediately started daydreaming about whom they would choose if they should pick the lucky cheese and cracker; the older kids professed disinterest. My mother just revved up her starry-eyed sales pitch.

No New World foods would be allowed at the feast: no tomatoes, no corn, no *militon,* no mangoes (never mind that the compound was about thirty miles from the ruins of the first official outpost of the so-called New World). We would eat with our hands from bread trenchers, and toast their royal majesties with goblets of powdered pink lemonade. There would even be a gingerbread castle.

But the castle, as it turned out, was only the first disappointment. In the tropics, bread does not grow stale; it molds. Gingerbread—even elaborately sketched out and executed gingerbread castles with stained-glass windows made of melted lollipops that, when lit from behind, emit a hazy, romantic glow—has a tendency to go limp in the humidity.

To make matters worse, my mother realized mid-project that she didn't have quite enough candy for the stained-glass windows, so she and my two sisters hopped on their bikes to ride to the Limbé market. On the way home, clutching sticky red, gold, blue, and green lollipops like banners flying, they rode headlong into a gang of teenage boys who suddenly closed in around them, bringing their bicycles skidding to a halt.

Meadow and Rose were frightened, but my mother was still try-ing to figure out what the surly boys wanted. She spoke just enough Kreyòl to understand that they were flinging curse words. She thought she heard them say "your mother is a stinging wasp"—*gèp manman ou*—because the phrase *gèt manman ou*—"your mother's clitoris"—was unfamiliar to her.

Unsure how best to protect her daughters, my mother was relieved when a Haitian man that she recognized from Kreyòl Sunday school came to their rescue. He shouted and ran toward them, whipping his belt out of his pant loops. My sisters cowered as he swung the leather whip through the air. A buckle landed on bare flesh, and the boys scattered, cursing.

This knight at arms my mother rewarded with flustered thanks before retreating into the missionary fortress.

Safe at home, she dismissed the trauma—a skill essential to survival—and focused her attention on assembling the gingerbread castle. But sugar-crusted icing could not hold the weight of the listing structure, so we had to resort to cans of tuna fish and peaches to prop up the teetering walls.

By the night of the Feast, only the little girls seemed to register enthusiasm. They clustered around the sagging gingerbread castle and squabbled over whose turn it was to try on the tarnished sequin crown.

I felt deflated. My mother was trying to yank us out of our lethargy, but even her stubborn strength was no match for the heaviness that hung over the compound.

The evacuation had torn a hole in the narrative. The missionary confidence that we were hope-bearers, shining with Christ's love had been replaced with a fundamental uncertainty: Were we even wanted? There was a palpable sense of failure in the room.

Most of the missionaries dragged in at least twenty minutes after the Feast was supposed to begin, sinking reluctantly into folding chairs in the chapel. Steve James was on call at the hospital, just one floor beneath us, but he didn't even bother to make an appearance for the introductory remarks, although his four daughters kept glancing over their shoulders for his arrival. He was still missing when my mother passed out the hors d'oeuvres. At her joyful command, a gaggle of girls bit gingerly into their cheese and crackers, eager for the prize.

Steve's golden-haired daughter Carrie squealed with excitement—

she had found the hidden bean! The other third-grade girls pouted with envy.

—All hail the Queen! my mother sang as she placed the sequined crown on the nervous but excited royal brow. Her Highness must now choose a King!

At that moment, Steve pushed open the screen door. Carrie saw him first. Her father, whom she loved best in all the world, had arrived just when she wanted him most.

—I choose Papa! she announced, her face radiant.

Steve looked startled as all eyes in the room turned to him. My mother danced toward the doorway holding the King's crown.

We wanted him to make us laugh; we wanted him to push the pain aside for a night, to help us forget the torn world outside the chapel.

Steve froze, then turned abruptly on his heels and vanished.

The screen door banged shut behind him, the spring buzzing like a startled cicada.

The nine-year-old Queen didn't crumple under the shock. Her eyes welled briefly, but she blinked the tears away. My mother flailed around like a singed butterfly as the Queen chose a runner-up and we raised our glasses to toast Their Majesties' good health.

As the party limped on, I studied the Queen under her lopsided tiara. Her tawny eyes flickered as she readjusted her slipping crown. Something in her had snapped shut. She was more self-possessed than I had been at nine years old. Her smile was fixed and impenetrable. But I remembered my own jealousy when my father brought Ti Marcel home from the hospital. Nothing I could do could win back his attention. I had lost him to her—to Haiti. We couldn't compete with such single-minded devotion.

————————

Twenty years after that ill-fated night, when I asked Steve James what he remembered about the Medieval Feast, he confessed that walking out on his daughter was one of his deepest regrets as a father.

He and his wife, Nancy, still lived in the Limbé Valley, although they had left the missionary compound. His eyes were lined with wrinkles. After years of meditation, he had the quiet poise of a monk. He flattened his gray hair against his skull as he spoke.

Steve explained to me how conflicted he had felt on the night of the Feast between his daughters and the promise he had made to God. He had vowed that, as a medical doctor to the poorest of the poor, he would do everything in his power to heal those who came to him in need.

On duty one floor below the chapel on the night of the Feast, the emergencies just kept coming. A limp and dehydrated child. A probable malaria case. A near-comatose woman carried in with a decomposing fetus in her womb.

This last case was critical, for if Steve did not work quickly, infection would set in. While his own children prepared for the celebration upstairs, Steve dropped to his knees before the birthing table. He knew that if he did not remove every fragment of the dead fetus, the mother would die. Conditions were miserable in the hot, airless room. There were no fans to stir the wet air, and the woman was clearly suffering as the doctor labored with her, up to his elbow in her clenched uterus.

He didn't have much time. His gloved hand tugged loose tissue, putrid with decay. As he gently extracted the tiny body, he felt his head swim with nausea, but he centered himself, determined to wrest life from death.

Finally, after two excruciating hours, it was finished. The mother would live. The child's body was taken away to be buried.

Steve washed his hands and tried to pray a blessing on the woman, on the dead child, on the missionary hospital, on the anguish that sat on his shoulders like death itself, a burden he could find no words for. The smell would linger in his nostrils for days.

He wanted to go home and shower, to sit in silence and let the pain slowly ebb from his shoulders. Lay to rest the memory of the child's torn body, the woman's moans. He craved the stillness of his study, his Bible open on his desk. Instead, he bowed to familial obligation and climbed the stairs to the chapel.

On the landing, he paused to prepare himself for the weary disillusionment of the parents; the eager, oblivious energy of the children. His daughters had been talking about this Feast all week.

He opened the door, hoping to find a quiet seat in the back, but instead, he felt all eyes turn hungrily toward him. He froze, taking it all in—his daughter with the crown on her golden head; the sagging gingerbread castle; our strained, hopeful smiles.

We wanted him to set it all aside. To laugh with us. To forget.

He was so tired. He couldn't shoulder the weight of our expectations.

Steve's daughter Carrie, now a nurse in the U.S., had long ago forgiven her father.

—She is so loving every time we talk about it, Steve admitted, then paused, his voice breaking. His voice trembled, then trailed off. —That guy who walked out on his daughter . . .

—And yet, he added with a wry smile, —I am still learning to love myself. He sighed, then laughed.

—We can't change the past, he admitted finally, as if extending the only benediction he had to offer. —But we can work on the present.

He let silence fill the space between us as parrots and cicadas took up the chorus outside.

Desire, betrayal, forgiveness. The only story we have to tell.

———————

The ill-fated Medieval Feast in the chapel was not, in the end, a complete debacle—thanks in no small part to my mother's relentless cheerleading. There were still juggling acts, poetry readings, the requisite number of knock-knock jokes.

The walls of the gingerbread castle, despite our efforts, collapsed before we had time to light the candles, but the ruins tasted of buttery molasses and sugar frosting and left our hands sticky with crushed lollipops.

On Beauty and Sorrow

Limbé, 1991

B Y APRIL 1991, with only four months to go before our agreed-upon year and a half of missionary service was complete, my father's letters to his parents were increasingly exasperated. Someone in Limbé had been sneaking a goat through the barbed-wire fence behind the Jameses' house to graze. Even after repeated warnings to the goat's owners to cease and desist, it had chewed a grotesque ring of bark off a fruit-bearing citrus, almost killing the tree. When my father found the marauding beast in the process of munching its way through the seedlings in the nursery, he took his pocketknife and slit its throat, then threw the still-bleeding animal into the street.

I've been threatening to do it for some time, he explained to the grandparents, with more than a little bravado. *We did have a lot of little rocks thrown at our house yesterday afternoon and evening. Such is life in paradise.*

And yet, despite this unrepentant foray into *dechoukaj*—the very opposite of what he'd preached with a knife held to his throat—my father realized that to leave, as planned, and give up on Haiti was the most bitter prospect of all. His second-to-last newsletter was notable chiefly for its thinly veiled undercurrent of hopelessness: *Sometimes I wonder how I will fit back into the States after our exposure here. I expect I will squirm under the theme of hope and joy, remembering people here.*

I, too, was increasingly nervous about our return to the U.S.

Haiti had opened my eyes to both beauty and suffering, but it was the beauty that blinded me, that made me reach for my pen to write it all down—the storms that lashed the mango trees; the awkward dance of the fiddler crabs at the beach; the moonlit mountains, each receding ridge a deeper shade of gray, like a sketch outlined in charcoal.

Ever since Peter had left for his second term of college, I had been dashing off eight-page epistles, chock-full of passionate meditations. On Saturdays, when the mail arrived, I made excuses to linger by the kitchen table in the Hodges house, waiting for a reply. He wrote to his cousins. He wrote to his papa, the Doctor. But he did not write to me.

Finally, after aching weeks of silence, he wrote to say: *I'm going to put this as blunt as possible. Good friends never break up, but lovers sometimes do. We won't have much time together, so to start something would be crazy. Besides, we'd like to be able to see each other in the future without having any uncomfortable feelings about the past.*

I stumbled through the week in a daze.

Craving solitude, I slipped out of the hospital gates and found myself on the road in Limbé. Children held up their palms: *Blan, ban mwen yon ti bagay; ban m mont lan.* I shook my head and smiled, trying to evade the demands: *Blan,* give me a little something; give me your watch. After all these years, I still didn't know how to escape that hated role.

Outside of Limbé, the dirt road stretched out against the hills. Women dipped their clothes in the muddy river and conversed in loud voices. I wanted to sit down next to them but was afraid that I would interrupt the banter. Instead, I sat on a rock at the edge of the sand and wrote: *If only this place wasn't so beautiful! You want to love it, to make it your own, but it won't take you. It only looks at you strange, then laughs behind your back. Rather humbling, you know? But it's good for us tèt cho Americans to know we can't have everything.*

My father, sensing weakness, angled for an ally. *Another long talk with A,* he noted in his journal. *Might be willing to stay in Haiti.*

He spent his last few months preaching the good news about *ramp vivan* terraces, by which he hoped—his final, last-ditch effort—to save the world through trees. Living terraces had already been employed elsewhere in Haiti, often with grass to hold the soil in place, but as soon as the heavy rains came, the barricades broke apart; when the organic matter decomposed, the work was lost. Trees, on the other hand, were an investment in the future.

Zo, in Camp Coq, was a natural ally in this new undertaking. Using a rough, improvised level made of two poles and a wooden crossbar from which hung a string tied around a rock, they swiveled their way across the slope of the mountain, creating a low-tech contour map. It was crucial that the line be perfectly level, without any low spots to weaken the dam, and along this they buried seeds. As the seeds grew, the roots wove a thick mesh to hold the soil in place. Eventually, the pocked and ruined garden would be transformed into a miracle of stairstep terraces neatly stacked against the side of the mountain. In theory, it was brilliant. Implausibly, this time the theory worked.

Planting individual trees was too time-consuming and promised only limited results. *Ramp vivan,* my father was convinced, might be the only hope to save what little soil was left on the mountains.

He poured his energy into a fevered attempt to persuade as many farmers as he could to install living terraces. Leucaena branches, rich in nutrients, could be cut and carried for animal feed, and the larger trunks could be cut for charcoal without damaging the resilient mesh of roots.

A few farmers listened. Most didn't have time for the latest big idea of the *blan.*

If, like my father, you suffer from a savior complex, Haiti is a bleak assignment, but if you are able to enter it unguarded, shielded only by curiosity, you will find the sorrows entangled with a defiant joy.

Olynda and I, invited to the wedding of her aunt's cook, were supposed to attend only under the watchful eye of Barbara, but when she hadn't made it home from the pharmacy by the time the wedding was supposed to start, we slipped out unchaperoned, giddy at our own daring.

The wedding was supposed to start at six p.m., but the bride and groom were taking showers when we arrived at six-twenty, feeling a bit foolish for our overeagerness. An hour later, we all piled into borrowed cars and drove the long way through the streets of Limbé, honking and waving. We passed the church three times before we went inside.

Only the bride and groom were allowed into the pastor's living room, where the service was held. I wished that I had the guts to stand on tiptoe like the people from the market and stare through the open windows—there were no secrets in Haiti.

Afterward, we made another noisy procession, this time all the way down to the Limbé River and back. I sat on Olynda's lap because there were so many other people in the car, but the honking and shouting had worked its magic: a huge crowd was waiting in the street to cheer as the bride and groom walked through their front door.

We followed them inside, where streamers and bright plastic flowers hung from the ceiling. The table was piled high with rice, chicken, beets, and crabs in their shells. Melons and fat pineapples were studded with toothpicks and decorated with a green maraschino cherry or a cheese curl. The wedding cake was dense and gritty, as if it had been baked over charcoal. Popcorn neatly wrapped in paper napkins was passed through the open windows to the voyeurs outside.

When the lights flicked on and off, signaling that it was time for the dance party, Olynda and I sashayed onto the living room floor. We twirled our skirts to Kreyòl pop music, and I swung a little girl in a pink dress around and around in a dizzy circle until we both fell down laughing. Well past curfew, Olynda's cousins walked us home in the dark.

Kerosene lanterns threw shadows across the dirt road and voices called *bòn nwit*. At the entrance, the watchmen turned back our escorts and we continued inside alone, the electric lights glaring over our scuffed shoes and tousled hair as the gate slammed shut behind us.

I felt a bittersweet sense of impending loss as our final months in Haiti skittered past. Meadow turned thirteen and taller than me. Her surprise party ended in tears. My father wanted to read her birthday letters out loud, and I argued that they were private; we all ended up shouting at each other.

On Mother's Day, having planned ahead this time, we strolled bare-foot along the high-tide line at Plage Saint Michel. Jericho School's jovial white-haired kindergarten teacher, Ms. Whitt, regaled us with stories. Left to fend for herself after her husband died, she had climbed down an empty swimming pool ladder to stalk a particularly aggressive woodchuck, then killed it with one shot. *Makes you realize life is NOT over at 40!* I scribed with admiration in my journal.

Low, crumbling walls of coral blocked the waves, and when we ventured out into the quiet pools, bright fish blurred the rippled sand. Meadow, lost in thought, felt an awareness of a larger shift within her: standing at the edge of the land and the sea, she understood, deeper than argument or observation, that the earth's resources were limited; our collective consumption, left unchecked, would outstrip our ability to care for this planet. The realization awoke in her a worried kinship with the earth and its creatures.

Even Rose, at ten years old, had been changed by our brief stay in Haiti. Her dimpled smile was more guarded, braced for arguments with friends or a stinging insult. She, too, had been slapped, though by one of the other missionary girls. I seethed and promised retribution, but my mother talked me out of it.

Too young to join Meadow and me for youth group on Wednesday nights, Rose wandered around the compound alone until her Sunday school teacher, a volunteer nurse named Sonya, invited her over for tea—every week, a standing invitation. To be seen as unique on the compound, with singular sorrows and idiosyncrasies, was a rare gift. Sonya was beloved not only by my sister, and by the other missionary girls in her Sunday school class, but also in the hospital pediatric ward, where her laughter rang down the corridors when she played with orphans and teased her Haitian coworkers.

On an ordinary Friday afternoon, having carefully addressed her letters to fly out on the missionary plane, Sonya was in a car full of friends from the hospital, on the way to Port-au-Prince for the weekend, when a *kamyon* slammed into the vehicle and snapped her neck, killing her instantly. She was the only fatality.

When the news reached the compound, all the little girls who loved Sonya best were at a birthday party for Laura Rose at the seminary, so a driver was sent over to bring them home. Nothing was explained about why the birthday party had ended so abruptly. When the girls tumbled out of the car, they guessed only that something terrible had happened. The missionaries on the compound were blank with loss.

Parental arms pulled them in for hugs, but it was assumed that they had already been told. Rose learned the truth hours later, by eavesdropping. Having observed that no one else was crying, she, too, was silent. Another grief, buried.

Sonya's last words, already stamped and sealed, flew out on the missionary plane, though she herself was beyond the reach of language.

Sonya was remembered and eulogized by the missionaries and their children, as well as by her Haitian coworkers, but there was no one to mourn the death of Cleanne, the young woman dying of AIDS.

Neighbors had heard Cleanne moaning, begging God to deliver her from the pain. By the time my father heard the news, the nine-year-old daughter who had slept with her beside the river had disappeared.

Grieved, my father sat down on the front steps of our house with his head in his hands and did not try to hide the tears that streamed down his face.

He was found in this pose by another missionary agronomist, who had learned to disguise his broken heart behind cynicism. —Do you really think your wandering the hills has done any good? the man asked. —It's just another Haitian tragedy, they're everywhere.

My father was too numb to reply.

The End in Sight

Limbé, 1991

I SPENT ALL morning trying in vain to steady myself the Saturday that Peter was due home from college. I would have given anything to be able to convey disinterest, or at least self-contained poise, but my emotions were about as subtle as a neon sign: *Scared! Excited! Embarrassed! Wildly happy!*

When Rose rode her bike over to tell me that they'd arrived, I bolted up from my desk and raced toward the front steps of the Hodges house before I could stop myself. I at least had the presence of mind to stop and breathe before I burst out from behind the bamboo. His back was turned.

I stumbled twice trying to climb three stairs, then put one hand on his arm and waited for what felt a tortured eternity until he looked down at me, smiled, and put a long, stiff arm around my shoulders—a safe "brothers and sisters in Christ" kind of hug; no more body contact than was absolutely necessary. My heart plunged. He really had decided that it was over.

Why did I do that? I berated myself afterward in my journal. *Maybe it would have been different if I could have stood there just a little longer and said two words to him.*

Peter did not come with us when we puttered one last time in the hospital motorboat out to Île-la-Rat, though I thought of him when I put on a snorkel and drifted over the coral alone. My sisters collected brittle stars and dove off the boat into warm, perfectly clear water.

Oh help, I wrote when I sat down in the sand with my journal. *I just want to forget, at least for today. It's too lovely to spoil with could-have-beens.*

Had I been given the option to stay in Haiti, I was no longer sure what I would say. I hated the thought of leaving Olynda (and never seeing Peter again) and was worried about starting over at a new school in the fall, a nondescript American high school.

My father wanted to move back to the cabin in Idyllwild, but we'd heard that the prep school had closed abruptly due to bankruptcy. My mother planned to look for work in Nebraska when we stopped to visit the Divine grandparents during our cross-country train trip, but to my ears, small-town America sounded almost as claustrophobic as the missionary compound. My mother no longer cared where we landed so long as it wasn't Haiti. For her, the end was in sight. Under a month and Limbé would be a distant memory.

Meadow was having recurring nightmares, and Rose's jaw was swollen with an abscess that ached whenever she tried to speak. Dr. Hodges had been unable to determine a cause.

My mother, struggling with depression and overwhelmed by the needs of her daughters and students, confided to her journal: *I was never convinced God "sent" us this time. The other times, yes, but surely this trip was to appease Jon. How can I choose to keep loving unconditionally when I have feelings of not being loved by my husband?*

He would spend long hours in conversation with our cook, Anna Rose, or others on the compound, but he barely acknowledged my mother if they were in the same room. Most mornings he was out the door by six a.m. School kids along the road from Limbé to Garde Cognac recognized the blue station wagon when they saw him coming, and had learned to flag him down for a ride, but by the time he kicked off his shoes after a long day of preaching reforestation and planting living terraces, he had nothing left to say to his wife.

My mother's empathy was depleted. Haiti was little more than a competing lover who had stolen her husband.

She did manage to secure one last-minute, errand-packed night alone with him before we left the country—a quick overnight trip to Port-au-Prince so that they could pick up exit visas for the U.S.

My sisters stayed with friends. I, for once, had the house to myself. The sovereignty was glorious. I ate dinner with Olynda at the long table at the Hodges house, and we raised our eyebrows and gave each other sidelong glances when the Doctor cleared his throat and pontificated. Afterward, we sat cross-legged on the hood of one of the compound vehicles and talked about everything and nothing.

At midnight, I baked brownies, then sneaked over to Olynda and Tamara's room with a warm, gooey plate of chocolaty goodness, scraping on the screen window to get their attention.

—Psst! *Blan yo!* Psst! I whispered.

The response from inside was everything I had hoped for. Olynda leaped off her bed, fumbled to stop the music, then stood frozen until she recognized my laugh.

We played Skip-Bo until two-thirty a.m., when she yawned and announced: Go home and get your stuff. And hurry up already.

The next day, having the volunteer cottage to ourselves, we baked pizza and watched a storm lash the breadfruit trees while we did the dishes.

> First the sky got all dark and gray and the wind started blowing, very rough and strong, and in a few moments, everything was being mercilessly pelted by a thousand drops of water. And the thunder! (I so love thunder) was beautiful—so loud and deep. I wished we could have gone out and stood in it, but (sigh) you know these domestic duties.

We were just sitting down to lunch when my parents returned, windblown but relieved to have successfully completed all of their errands. I couldn't remember the last time I had seen my mother so relaxed.

Dieulila

Limbé, 1991

WHEN I WAS in my late twenties and read through my father's journals for the first time, I was startled when I came across his final entry, after which the journal abruptly ended. The cramped note, scrawled in pencil, was the size of a postage stamp:

> *Monday, June 24, 1991*
> *Did mango grafts at Dieulila's. Heard more of her life history.*
> *Hugged her in a way I shouldn't have. Told Flip.*

While the rest of the family had spent the day packing, I'd noted irritably in my journal that my father was nowhere to be found.

We left Haiti exactly one week later. Dieulila was never mentioned again.

More than a decade after we'd left Haiti, at a family Christmas gathering, my father told my sisters and me the rest of the story, adding: Here's something else for your book, Apricot.

My sisters were devastated. I wasn't sure what to feel.

There is, in colonial literature, a recurring image: a foreign man, emboldened by his authority and by the lack of accountability, takes on a native mistress as a token of both his unquestioned power and his affection (if such a word may be used) for his adopted country.

It was like this and not at all like this with my own father.

During our final few months in Haiti, Dieulila, her husband, and their three small children lived across the river from Zo's village, in a mud-walled house surrounded by a grove of young mango trees. Their land was too flat to benefit from living terraces, but my father nevertheless felt free to offer unsolicited advice. Noticing a mound covered in dirt and banana leaves, left to slowly smolder into charcoal, he told the family that they needed to replant the trees that they had cut down.

Dieulila's husband seemed disinterested, but she asked questions. Her curiosity took on a more urgent nature when her husband died unexpectedly a few months later.

It was a season of anarchy and his death came without warning. He had been swept up in a revenge plot, leaving Dieulila at home with the children as he grabbed his machete. Only when he reached the home of his enemy, miles upriver, did he realize, too late, that he was the intended target. He was high in a coconut tree, hacking off the dry fronds so that they could set fire to the house, when the group turned on him.

When Dieulila heard the news, she packed up her three small children and her cooking pots, and abandoned the solitary house by the river. She moved into the village of Camp Coq, where even if she was surrounded by her husband's murderers there were at least others nearby to hear her screams.

She still tended her gardens along the river, as she had no other income. And it was in those fields, alone with her work, that my father's notice of Dieulila began to take on a different hue.

She was not afraid of hard work, and for this he admired her. Her body was slim, but she hefted and sank her hoe into the uneven soil with a furious determination. She did not ask for pity. When he chided her for her hand-rolled cigarette, saying that it would destroy her lungs, she replied shortly: I smoke so that I do not feel hungry.

Once, she asked him for advice. A friend in Jamaica had promised her easy work that paid good money if she left her children behind. My father could only imagine what Dieulila was hinting at—there were few options available to a beautiful woman, far from her children, among men who did not speak her language.

My father was tormented. For all her confidence, there was a fragility about her that he longed to rescue. She had no one to fight for her or offer comfort. Once, he found her limping back from her fields because a fungus had cracked and split the skin between her toes. He drove her home, then begged a prescription from one of the missionary nurses. Dieulila thanked him with a thick baton of roughly processed chocolate from her trees, which my father brought home as a gift for my mother.

For my father's fortieth birthday (that famed and fabled celebration of the midlife crisis), we tried to persuade him to let us plan a birthday bash—all the missionaries dressed in mock mourning, perhaps a skit—but he wasn't interested. He didn't have time for parties. Instead, he spent his birthday among Haitian farmers, one of whom chided: What are you doing here? You shouldn't be working, you should be with your family!

My father knew that most farmers in Haiti didn't celebrate or even know the date of their own birthdays. He smiled, enjoying the attention, then announced: When I was nine years old, I drove the tractor all day on my birthday. I was angry and didn't think that I should have to work, but I'm thankful now that I had a father who expected a lot from me.

If my sisters and I had been there, we would have rolled our eyes. (Grandpa Lee himself later admitted that it was a memory he regretted.)

Although my father didn't confess it until years later, he had hoped to spend his fortieth birthday with Dieulila. He was disappointed when we insisted that he at least join us for dinner so we could sing him happy birthday. We promised there would be no streamers.

Even if my father did not spend his birthday with Dieulila, as he had hoped, he let himself imagine how the evening would have gone—the joke he would have told when he showed up at her door, the meal she would have prepared for him.

For he had begun to notice that whenever he stopped by her garden to check on her, she seemed as glad to see him as he was to see her. He wondered what it would feel like to put his arms around her waist. There was not much time left.

He had second thoughts, plenty of them. Invited to speak at a church along the River of Suffering, he was too distracted with thoughts of Dieulila to prepare a proper sermon. He looked for a shade tree to collapse against, ignoring the repeated warnings not to sit under the mango tree, which could—and did—drop a ripe mango heavy enough to dent a man's skull. But instead of hitting my father, and possibly knocking some sense into him, the mango merely tumbled onto his Bible, which was sitting beside him in the open *makouti*.

A near miss. He had come so close.

If it was a warning, he didn't listen.

Exactly one week before we were to leave Haiti, my father made an official note in his day planner to visit Dieulila's gardens. Because her fields weren't steep enough for terracing, he had decided to introduce her to the potent miracle of grafting.

He had already given a rudimentary lesson on grafting in Garde Cognac, which Dieulila had watched. Grafting, he knew, could improve the yield of fruit trees regardless of rainfall, so whenever he visited a cluster of houses, he'd ask around to find out who had the best-tasting mangoes. Beckoning to his audience to gather round, he'd flip open his handmade grafting knife (an invention he was proud of: a single rotating scalpel blade attached with a screw and wing nut to a piece of Haitian oak). Instead of using expensive imported grafting tape, he cut strips of discarded plastic bags, which he'd picked up along the highway, hoping that his innovations could be easily replicated once he was gone. Then, under the watchful gaze of his audience, he'd cut—with the owner's permission—a fertile length of scion wood from the favorite tree, no wider than a pencil. This scrappy green branch he'd wrap in a wet washcloth and carry to a nearby sapling—an unspectacular garden-variety mango, with stringy pulp and unremarkable flavor.

It wasn't a complicated process, but he hoped that the value of the graft, once executed, would be self-evident. For although they dangled like cheap green baubles when in season—falling to the ground with such force that the rinds, like a parable, split open to reveal the gold within—not all mangoes were created equal.

The stringy, oblong *fil blan* mango, ubiquitous in the Limbé Valley, came into season all at once, with such glut and abundance that the rank and rotting excess was kicked aside for pig food. My father knew men who had eaten as many as forty mangoes in a single day, their cramping guts so taut with hunger that even the illusion of satiety was worth the agony that followed.

But the *fil blan* mangoes, plain-flavored, with strands that stuck in the teeth, were not those for which one's mouth watered. That honor went to the mangoes of Passe-Reine and the Central Plateau: Mango Batis, Fransik, Wozali, Mango Dous Dous. These luxuries, brought over the mountains on the back of straining *kamyon* trucks, the burlap sacks full to bursting, were stacked like prize jewels at the open-air markets by women who leaned back haughtily, pipes in hand, to wait for the best offer; these were the mangoes for which one hoarded and haggled. Whenever possible, my father used scion wood from these coveted varieties, but he knew that even better-than-average mangoes could fetch a decent price at the local markets, especially if they bore out of season.

Having thus secured his audience's attention, he showed them how it was done: First, remove the extra leaves from the scion and cut a gently sloping angle, roughly three inches in length. Cut an identical angle into the severed tip of the rootstock. Match the two cambium layers together so that the flowing sap would make, of the two, one new tree, then tightly bind the wound with strips of a plastic bag.

Voilà, he revealed: a new and improved mango, capable of bearing coveted fruit years ahead of its peers.

The temptation, of course, was to greedily push the grafted tree beyond what its tender limbs could carry. For with wood from a mature tree bound to such young rootstock, the sap throbbed and pulsed through the old veins like a miracle of gestation; like grizzled Sarah giving birth to laughing Isaac. Years before the sapling would have been capable of it—had it been left unmolested—the branch would swell with a sweet round globe of fruit. The risk was that the weight could splinter the young branches.

On the day my father planned to meet Dieulila in her mango grove by the river, to teach her grafting while the rest of us stayed home to pack, he was exasperated when another missionary threw a kink into his plans by asking to tour one of his *ramp vivan* projects. My father agreed, careful to hide his reluctance, and led the missionary agronomist, plus a visiting volunteer, up a steep footpath to a mountain ridge high above Camp Coq.

The living terraces, several months old, were already springing up green behind the mounds of dirt, leaves flared open to catch the sun's heat and transform it into energy, the tangle of roots a promise of things to come. But as mesmerizing as the project was to my father, the sun was hot, and it made the volunteer's head ache. To the untrained eye, the entire project could appear to be little more than rough trenches stretched across a bare hillside, from which a few scattered leaves sprouted on withered stalks.

My father noted with exasperation that the volunteer appeared on the verge of heatstroke and promptly turned her back down the mountain.

Back at the compound, he dropped off the expats and made dutiful small talk. He spoke briefly with a Haitian friend who had hiked down from another village to tell him about a feud brewing between neighbors.

Jealousy is such a problem here, he noted irritably in his journal. He took a shower. And then, his heart warring with mingled desire and dread, he drove back to Garde Cognac to meet Dieulila.

She had been expecting him since that morning and had set aside a cold malted drink, wrapped in leaves. —They told me to give this to you, she said, her fingers grazing his as she pressed it into his hands.

My father paused for a moment and wondered fleetingly if he was about to come under the influence of a *batri,* a love potion heavy with the dark magic of Erzulie, the goddess of desire.

Despite Dieulila's attempts to keep it cool, the bottle had been sitting unrefrigerated in a plastic container since morning. It was warm. He drank.

They left her children at the edge of the river and hiked alone into the mango grove. The sun was low in the sky, and the light filtered green and gold through the leaves.

He asked how she had been given her name, and she told him that her given name was Woslyn, but she had nearly died at birth. Her father, cradling her tiny body in his arms, watched her fight to breathe and announced: There is a God! *Dye li la.*

All around them, in the music of the hidden birds, in the sap flowing soundlessly through the trees, was the pregnant possibility of new life about to begin.

They found a young mango tree, and my father pulled out the donor wood from his bag. Dieulila placed her hand around the trunk and gripped the blade, severing the branch neatly. My father placed his hand on her shoulder, aware of her warmth.

While he watched, she inserted the scion wood into the gash and deftly wound the tattered strips of plastic around the wound like a cast; like a wedding knot. Her hands were confident. She smiled up at him. She had been paying attention.

She led him to the house where she had lived with her husband before the *dechoukaj.* It was dark inside, after the warm green light of the mango orchard.

Dieulila reached on tiptoe into the rafters, her fingers searching for a lost ring or a bracelet that she had left behind when she fled. Her fingertips brushed against cobwebs and loose splinters of wood, but her treasure was gone—knocked down by rats or pocketed by a stranger who had entered in her absence. A furrow of disappointment lined her face, but she pushed the loss aside and turned toward my father, pressing against him in the shadows.

He put his arms around her, circling her waist. He bent toward her and kissed her open mouth. Her lips were unmoving. He leaned back to study her, ran his fingers across her strong back and shoulders, touched her breasts.

The room was threaded with light, where the sun slanted in through broken chinks in the mud walls. The floor was uneven. Animal droppings had been kicked among the ashes of a cooking fire.

These details he noted only in passing, but what he sensed even more viscerally was that they were not alone in the room.

He felt the arrival of unbidden guests crowding in from every side, invisibly. He could not be sure if the spirits were *lwa* who had come to goad him with lust and hunger, or if they were the tormented ghosts of men like himself, mercenaries and missionaries who had broken trust, who had pressed their bodies in furious desire against women to whom they had made no promises; men who, even in death, were weighed down by violation.

The hairs pricked at the back of his neck as the unseen spirits curled around them in the dark. Disembodied words from the book of Proverbs, words he had read aloud from his Bible, began to sound in his head—

> *May you rejoice in the wife of your youth*
> *May her breasts satisfy you always, may you ever be captivated by*
> *her love*

Dieulila, wrapped in my father's arms, breathless in the hope that she had found a man to shelter her, murmured something about the children they would make together. Her words reached him through the din. He stepped back from her and shook his head.

—It won't work, I've had an operation, he explained, his voice stiff. His desire for her was undiminished, but he could not silence the voices in his head: *Drink water from your own cistern, running water from your own well.*

He pulled Dieulila toward him, felt her heart hammer against his own like a caught wild bird.

He let go of her and stumbled out into the sunlight. The voices disappeared.

That night, on the missionary compound, after my sisters and I were in bed, he led my mother by the hand over to the swing set under the *zanmann* tree. There, while they rocked over the scraped and battered dirt, my father told her what he had done—and what he had almost done—with Dieulila in the abandoned house by the river.

My mother cried into her hands.

Thursday, June 27, 1991

It is 3:30 a.m. There is too much anguish to feign sleep. Three days ago Jon took my hand and led me with him to the swing set to be by ourselves. It was the first time he had been romantic toward me in so long I'd forgotten how fun it was. That very day he had found himself hugging and fondling a Haitian woman out near her garden. There was another love in his life. It was the crowning slap on what was already the worst year of my life. No emotional support after the evacuation, all the times he would literally ignore me and walk out the door preoccupied and on his way to visit others on the compound. I had been so faithful to him. No wonder I feel so shriveled inside.

My mother did not give me her journals to read until years after I'd finally worked up the courage to ask my father for the rest of the story. It was past midnight. I had driven down to my parents' farmhouse, surrounded by open fields, for the night. My mother had already gone to bed, not wanting to relive the memory yet again.

As my father told me the story in all its excruciating detail, I, too, was surprised at the image of him holding my mother by the hand and leading her over to the swings. The tenderness felt out of character. He had given us so little during those years.

—Had you ever sat with Mom on the swings before that night? I asked.

—No, my father said, looking down at his dirt-stained hands, —I hadn't. He paused, then continued. —But I knew I had to tell her. She was my best friend. I didn't know what else to do.

I kept my eyes down, following the lines of ink as my pen scratched across the page taking notes. —I think this is one of the most awkward conversations I've ever had, I finally admitted with a strained laugh.

My father exhaled loudly. —Yeah, me, too.

When the silence became unbearable, we watched two mice scurry across the kitchen floor to pillage the cupboards for stray crumbs. In a hundred-year-old farmhouse, keeping them out was all but impossible, no matter how hard my mother tried. I paused, then broached the question I was afraid to have answered. —Dad, we used to joke, although to be honest, it never felt like much of a joke, that you loved Haiti more than you loved us.

I let my voice trail off.

—It was a hard time for me, he admitted. —For years after we left, I thought of Dieulila every time I blew out my birthday candles. I always made a wish that I'd be able to see her again.

His nonanswer did nothing to alleviate the hurt. I wondered, not for the first time, why my mother had stayed.

He said that he had tried to take a photograph of Dieulila but couldn't get the camera to work. She was gone by the next time he returned to Haiti. She had moved to Port-au-Prince to find work and to escape her husband's enemies, and while she was there, she either became very sick with tuberculosis or was pushed into a vat of boiling chocolate and died from the burns. The stories her relatives tell are inconsistent.

As I gathered up my notes after our late-night conversation, my father set out a live trap to try to catch the scavenging mice in the kitchen.

The next morning, he carried the trapped creatures down the long hill to the creek, where he dumped the tiny, frightened mice into an empty five-gallon bucket, then flung them across the water, as far as he could hurl them.

The mice swam, their tails like rudders, their paws like paddles, until they reached the opposite bank and scurried under fallen logs. Exposed, vulnerable, no longer sheltered by the bounty of my mother's kitchen. At the mercy of owls and snakes.

Oregon, Ho!

1991

OUR LAST WEEK in Haiti—for me, at least, if not for my miserable parents—was a contented blur of goodbye parties and farewell trips to the beach. The day after my father led my mother by the hand to the swing set to confess his betrayal, my sisters and I, little imagining the conversations that must have been going on at home, spent the night with missionary friends in a house that overlooked the blue, glittering Baie de L'Acul.

Kirsti was to perform a piano recital at the seminary that afternoon, so my sisters and I hiked over the ridge to hear her play, the Limbé Valley stretched out cool and green beneath us. The trail took us past the yellow concrete house where my father had hoped we would make Haitian friends. *You miss a lot shut up on the compound,* I noted with regret. I sat up to watch the moonlight glimmer on the water. I had arrived with my fists clenched, determined to let nothing touch me, but I left with my arms full of glory. A cloak pulled around me to heal the hurt.

My father, who had arrived with so much hope that he had extra to give away—advice, hope, courage, all tucked away like seeds into his *makouti*—was now the one with clenched fists. His shoulders were bent under the weight of his disappointment: in Haiti, in us, in himself. His failure felt mountainous.

At Zo's going-away party for my father, we were the only *blan* in attendance, sitting politely on wooden benches under the trees while a live band made a tremendous racket on improvised electric guitars, powered by our car battery: bare wires dropped into battery acid, translated into music.

Drawn by the commotion, more people had gathered in the dirt clearing than my father had anticipated. Zo introduced him, and thanked him for the long hours he had spent in the gardens around Camp Coq, and my father reminded the hundred or so neighbors and local farmers how important it was for them to carry on the work of grafting, and to take care of their trees. Voices shouted: *Amèn!* But when my father held up a box of rare red coconut seedlings to give away, the decorum shifted to chaos.

I had not yet witnessed how Haitian community groups distributed resources—profoundly aware that an unequal distribution of resources could have dire consequences in a community struggling for survival. These events were politic and methodical, so that no one would be left out. Our haphazard benevolence upset the balance.

Elbows dug into ribs, fingernails pinched, voices shouted. Hands grabbed for the trees, ripping delicate leaves. There wasn't enough to go around.

My discomfort only felt amplified when Zo called us inside his mud and wattle house after the party had broken up. He had butchered three rabbits, and his wife had spent all afternoon preparing a feast: tender rice, slow-cooked meat, and an entire regime of plantains soaked in salt and fried in hot oil for a heaped platter of *banann peze*. There were only five chairs at the table.

Not even Zo would sit down to eat with us, although he and his family stood around us and watched with approval as we raised our forks and lifted the bounty self-consciously to our lips. It was painful to receive a gift that left us so aware of our inadequacy: We, the privileged, had been reminded of our poverty. We possessed more than we could ever consume and yet we could not match this generosity. We left humbled, yet again, by a rabbit banquet.

Our last night on the missionary compound, I finally worked up the courage to write Peter one more heart-on-my-sleeve letter, having decided that I would rather know the truth—no matter how bitter—than wonder forever if I had misjudged his feelings. I left the note on his pillow and slipped down the hallway with my heart racing, terrified that someone might see me ducking out of his empty room.

He joined me on the swing set half an hour later. In the shadowed lamplight, I could tell that he was smiling.

We did not hold hands as we crossed the dark playground to find a place where we could be alone. We sat down on the back steps of an empty volunteer cottage, and Peter asked if he could put his arms around me. I leaned back until I could feel the tremor of his heartbeat. He held my waist as if I were made of spun glass.

—I don't know how long I've wanted to hold you like this, he confessed as the bamboo rustled and swayed over our heads. —And I can't think of a single good reason why I had to wait so long to find out.

I snuggled up against him. I would not have been surprised if the cicadas had burst into hallelujahs and fireworks had shot out from my fingertips.

He rested his chin against my neck and asked: Is this as good as picking avocados in the moonlight?

I laughed.

He did not kiss me, but it was enough to know that he'd always wanted to. When we hugged each other good night I slipped home through the trees determined that we would find a way to see each other again. Perhaps he could visit me on a break from college. Now that I knew that he loved me, nothing could stand in our way.

As the bus pulled away from the compound the next morning I pressed my face to the glass. Olynda and I had both been crying. Tamara leaned on her crutch and waved. Peter held my gaze with a secret smile only for me. *I thought this was going to be the longest, most horrible experience of my life,* I wrote to my journal. *And here it's been the best thing that ever happened to me.*

I took blurry photographs out of the windows on the long drive to Port-au-Prince of women threshing rice, donkeys laden with bags of charcoal, schoolgirls in gingham uniforms with matching ribbons in their hair. I did not want to forget anything.

On a trash heap outside of the capital, I thought that I glimpsed a dead body, but though I craned my neck back for a second look, I could not be sure. Perhaps I had been mistaken. I wanted to believe that it was only a trick of the light. A life lost, no matter what the circumstances, deserved to be put to rest with dignity.

When we reached the airport and learned that our return tickets had expired, my parents had to slap down most of the money they had squirreled away after selling the station wagon, which spiraled into a familiar parental argument. Our secondhand clothes and *abitan* luggage—ragged cardboard boxes stuffed with all of our earthly possessions—marked us as hicks, come to visit the *Gran Peyi*. We even spoke Kreyòl with a thick peasant accent. When I tried to take a sip of water from a drinking fountain at the Port-au-Prince airport, my mother yelled out: Apricot, no! My father held out a battered honey jar with a peeling label, full of well water from Limbé. I refused. Even in Haiti we stood out like yokels.

As the plane lifted above the slums of Port-au-Prince, tin-roofed houses pressed against the hills as if clinging to the earth itself. I had fantasized for so long about escaping Haiti. Now, I realized, I wasn't ready to leave.

Miami felt dispiriting even from the air: the orderly streets; the drab, predictable subdivisions. *Everything is just so planned-out and all the same,* I wrote as I sat outside the terminal, waiting for a shuttle bus to take us to the train station. The streets were empty, the only sounds the noise of the endless cars—brakes squeaking, engines grinding, the splash of rainwater as they hurtled through the puddles.

I think I miss Haiti, I confided to my journal. That splendid, complicated, troubling, maddening, beautiful country that I would have been proud to call home.

———————

It took us three weeks to ramble across North America by train, stopping to watch fireworks explode above the Lincoln Memorial in Washington, D.C., and to shuck corn and watch Laurel and Hardy videos with the Nebraska relatives (I was relieved when my mother couldn't find any jobs she was qualified for in the local newspaper).

On the morning our train finally rolled across the Idaho/Oregon border, my mother was awake at five a.m., her eyes glued to the scenery.

—I already saw six deer! she announced triumphantly as we stretched stiff necks and rubbed the sleep from our eyes. Steep, angled cliffs loomed above a broad, clear river. Through gaps in the trees, waterfalls plunged through ferns.

From Portland, we drove to a converted schoolhouse owned by friends, which was surrounded by flower beds and apple trees heavy with fruit. We wandered through the garden as if in a dream and plucked handfuls of ripe blueberries and raspberries. When we lifted the sun-kissed sweetness into our mouths, the juice stained our fingers. Finally, we understood our mother's love affair with Oregon.

A few days later, my father was offered a job as the manager of a native plant nursery. The owner, a plant pathology professor he'd worked for in ag school, had not forgotten his legendary work ethic. My mother couldn't believe our good fortune.

Our rental house was ten miles outside of town, across the highway from a wildlife refuge. The asphalt paths were overgrown with wild blackberry vines. Thistles glistened in the rain. When the school bus set me free, I'd drop my backpack and walk for miles, hearing only the high *scree* of hawks. The silence was as vast and gray-toned as the sky. I spoke to no one on these walks except sometimes the beauty itself. I returned with flushed cheeks and windblown hair, more grateful than I could put into words for that bracing solitude.

I missed friends in Haiti, but I didn't know what to say if my father happened to casually bring up in conversation that we had just moved back from a year and a half of volunteer missionary service. After this, the conversations usually foundered, then fell flat. No one seemed to know what follow-up questions to ask. I began to realize how very absurd it was for us—a white family with something of a savior complex—to claim a connection to Haiti, however tenuous. Nor could I figure out how to describe the missionary compound in a way that would sound believable.

My parents, caught up in their own crises, gave me no more curfews. The hovering claustrophobia of the compound was gone. There were no more family game nights.

No longer required to play the part of the missionary's daughter, I could disclose only what I wished. In Oregon, my pale skin rendered me invisible. No one asked for my earrings, for the watch on my wrist, or for food because they had not eaten in three days. The anguish that such inequities existed had not disappeared—the sorrow surfaced most often as guilt—but I was no longer the *blan,* staring across a fixed boundary.

I tried out for the school play and landed the part of Ariel in Shakespeare's *The Tempest*—never once guessing that a renowned poet from the Caribbean, Aimé Césaire, had adapted a version of the play, set in Haiti, with Ariel as the accommodating mulatto and Caliban as the revolutionary slave. I memorized my part while walking alone through the wildlife refuge across from our house, a Penguin paperback tucked under my arm, shouting lines to the sky: *All hail, great master, grave sir, hail! I come to answer thy best pleasure; be't to fly, to swim, to dive into the fire, the ride on the curled clouds . . .*

Only in dreams did I return to Haiti. I slid down a steep bank, my shins bloody, as Olynda, Ana, and Peter disappeared down the road ahead of me. I couldn't keep up. Drowning in a waterfall, I reached for an overhanging branch, and the slivers in my hand turned into tiny silver *ti yaya* fish, their eyes like bright moons. I watched, helpless, as they burrowed into my hand, swimming into the bloodstream.

I wrote to Olynda so she'd have letters to open when the mail arrived on Saturdays, but gently sodden Oregon felt increasingly disconnected from the tightly wound drama of the compound. I didn't know how to describe the life we had stumbled into, and I was ashamed by how easy it had been to disown Haiti.

For the first few months, I wrote long-winded letters to Peter, though his replies came less and less often. My final missive—a particularly impulsive one, plagued with self-doubt—fluttered out of the car window on the drive to school. I ran back to search for it in the weeds along the highway (mortified that someone else might read it), but I never found it or found the courage to write another. Our brief long-distance romance was over.

My father, pining for Haiti's eroded hillsides, corresponded far more diligently with friends in Limbé, expat as well as Haitian. The political violence had returned, and letters once again described factories, businesses, and elegant walled-off homes that were being attacked, purportedly by Aristide supporters. My father had nightmares about Belle and Paul's house going up in flames.

U.S. newspapers, by contrast, pointed out with admiration that in just seven months in office, Aristide had succeeded, for the first time in almost two hundred years of independence, in passing legislation that recognized Kreyòl as a national language equal to French. Aristide also continued to insist that the future of Haiti rested on the shoulders of the poor—the ones too often left out of the political process.

My father interpreted this to mean that Aristide was tacitly encouraging his supporters to seize what was rightfully theirs, hiding artfully behind metaphor when he urged them to uproot the rotten trees from the land. For it proved far easier to *dechouke* than to replant.

By late September 1991, a military junta had elbowed its way into the fray. Aristide's democratically elected idealism came to an abrupt and untimely end.

In Limbé, agitators once again hurled rocks at the hospital gate. Joanna wrote to say that the windshield of Barbara's car had been smashed by a flying bottle while she was running errands in Cap-Haïtien. A crowd was said to have torched the Haitian Baptist headquarters, presumably because of the pastors' vocal opposition to communism. This time, perhaps luckily, my father wasn't there to confront the protestors who gathered in front of Belle and Paul's home. Paul Romeus was alone in the house when his car, parked in the front yard, exploded into flames. He escaped through an opening in the back wall and hid in the home of a neighbor. Their dogs were killed. The carpentry shop burned to the ground.

Even at the height of the terror, Hôpital le Bon Samaritain continued to function, although one afternoon, instead of seeing the usual four hundred patients, the doctors saw only twelve. Driven by desperation, a pregnant woman was carried inside the clinic in the process of giving birth, the hand of her baby thrust like a revolutionary fist from the birth canal. Dr. Hodges and the new missionary surgeon quickly rolled the woman into the surgery wing and delivered the baby successfully by C-section. As the doctors lifted the baby into its mother's arms, the Haitian nurses burst into a hymn, their voices weaving a tent of song.

The U.S. Embassy, just as it had done during the Duvalier regime, urged all nonessential American citizens to flee the country. Dr. Hodges and Joanna, along with their four grown children, refused to leave, as did Herb Rogers and the new missionary surgeon, but this time, thirty-six women, children, and missionary spouses boarded emergency flights out of Cap-Haïtien.

I called Olynda in Nebraska, where she and Tamara were staying with Bernice Rogers and keeping in touch with the compound via ham radio. Olynda told me that she had been so scared when they left. She didn't know when, or if, she would see everyone again. The Jameses were in Pennsylvania. The Smiths were in Florida. My family had been lucky to leave when we did; everyone else had been able to take only twenty pounds each of carry-on luggage.

Now that we were both enrolled in American high schools, Olynda and I swapped stories. Our six-person classroom at Jericho School felt laughably small.

—Most people here are friendly, Olynda hedged circumspectly. —But it's a little strange to be the only black student in the entire school.

Already she'd had to negotiate questions I had never been asked: *Where are you from? Why are you here? You don't look Haitian.*

My anonymity in Oregon was a privilege I hadn't recognized. I was accepted implicitly as a member of the dominant culture. I was not perceived as a threat, even if I felt out of place at odd moments. Olynda's was a dilemma I would never have to face. Into that loneliness, I could not follow her.

My father, three thousand miles away from the trauma that was unfolding in Limbé, was tormented that he was too far away to help. He had arrived in Oregon as I had arrived in Haiti—with bitter fists. The thick blankets of winter fog plagued him. He refused to eat at restaurants or to shop anywhere but Goodwill, out of solidarity with Haitian friends trapped in poverty. Nor would he let my mother buy new furniture, arguing that it was a waste of money; we could find what we needed at yard sales.

When eleven-year-old Rose asked him to buy me a single red rose for the closing night of *The Tempest,* my father dropped the flower on the table with disgust and asked: Do you know how much this cost? Don't *ever* ask me to spend that kind of money again.

He yelled if we turned on the baseboard heaters at our rental house. In the mornings, our breath made white clouds above our lips. We stayed under the covers as long as possible, then huddled by the crackling woodstove.

Eventually, my parents sold the cabin in Idyllwild to make a down payment on the native plant nursery. They now owned land in Oregon, just as my mother had always dreamed. But there wasn't much to spare after the mortgage was paid. My father dug trees in the rain and my mother got a second and then a third part-time job, driving a school bus and potting transplants at another nursery. She was livid when she discovered that my father had written a check for eight hundred dollars, depleting half of their savings account, and had sent the money to friends in Haiti without even consulting her.

—Everyone else is more important to you than we are! she sobbed, hiding her face in her arms while my sisters crept over to bury their faces in her neck. By the time she turned forty, every last one of her jaunty curls had faded to gray.

My father slammed the door and stalked off to cut more firewood.

My father hacked at the encroaching blackberry vines around our rental house as if trying to escape, then handed my sisters and me sawed-off milk jugs with the handle left intact so we could hook them through our belts—an innovation he took some pride in—and sent us out to pick a gallon of blackberries per person, per day. It pained him to see God-given fruit go to waste.

Eventually, he discovered an apple tree under the two-story tangle and spent every spare evening thereafter locked in a battle with the blackberries that left his arms scratched and bleeding. The apple tree was starved for sunlight, but he patiently mounded compost around its roots, and by the following year, there were translucent yellow apples to pick along with the obligatory gallon of blackberries.

In the evenings, when it grew too dark to work outside, he sat at the kitchen table to slice watery half-moons for the food dryer, so that when we woke, the house smelled of warm apples—unless, that is, the evening news had featured some grim update on Haiti that portrayed Aristide as a deposed hero, in which case he sat up late at the dining room table to write indignant letters to the editor.

My parents' marriage felt tenuous in those years. Haiti was the unnamed presence that stood between them: the deforestation, the embargo, the skeletal children, the widows waiting to be saved.

My father couldn't seem to forgive us for having trapped him in Oregon. Growing trees for commercial properties was no consolation when topsoil was washing away in Haiti. It was as if his obligations to our family had steered him away from some dramatic destiny he had been meant to fulfill.

When friends at church asked, innocently enough, how my parents had met and if there was a romantic proposal story, my father informed them that, actually, my mother had proposed to him. My mother pressed her lips together and declined to comment.

—I wasn't ready to be tied down, he told me once as he gazed wistfully over our back pasture, just before I graduated from high school.

I was seventeen when I left for college. I had learned that it was best to avoid my father when I was at home. If he saw me with a book in hand, he assigned me another chore. We rarely talked. But once I moved away, I found a new letter waiting for me every week in my campus mailbox.

He updated me about the garden, the weather, the pheasant they found in the chicken coop. The old white rooster had died. Mom had canned thirty-eight quarts of grape juice. He had planted thirty-nine maple trees to eventually cut for firewood. Would be time to start up the woodstove soon.

When he took a short-term job shoveling pumpkin seeds at a local factory to bring in extra income, he wrote to me from the night shift. The wisps of translucent pumpkin-seed husk that floated up in the fans, eerily lit by the drying lights, reminded him of moths on a summer night.

He admitted that he had been much happier as a ranger, as a farmer, or when we lived in Haiti; when he had been able to devote himself to work that satisfied, and didn't care whether he got paid or not.

Over time, his confessions began to feel no longer like a weight but like kindness; a shared stumbling forward into the dark. It was easier for both of us to find our way toward each other through words on a page than to be in each other's presence, but it was at least a beginning. I finally understood what must have been so obvious to others—it was his way of saying that he loved me.

He Who Dies, That's His Affair

Limbé, 1991–1995

M Y FATHER, WHO supported the hospital whenever possible with proceeds from the native plant nursery, received regular updates from Joanna in embattled Limbé. The American Baptist Board of International Ministries had continued to pressure the Hodges family to join the other evacuated missionaries but Dr. Hodges had refused, arguing that more than 100 Haitians would die within the first few weeks, including 20 handicapped children, 30 abandoned babies, and 90 diabetic youths who relied upon the clinic's free insulin. If he and his family were to leave Limbé, he argued, the hospital would be looted and destroyed.

John Sundquist, the head of the Board of International Ministries, did not agree with this assessment, and as the conflict became more heated, Joanna photocopied both his and the Doctor's letters and sent them on to loyal supporters.

We will not let thirty years of work be devastated, Dr. Hodges wrote from Limbé. *Our presence signifies a commitment to Haiti, no matter what the political situation.*

Sundquist pointed out that the Hodges family had isolated themselves in an unhealthy situation. Exasperated with their stiff-necked insubordination—after all, the Board of International Ministries would be responsible should anything happen to one of their missionaries—Sundquist was of the opinion that the Hodges family exaggerated their own importance; no one was irreplaceable. From Sundquist's perspective, Dr. Hodges simply didn't want to let go of the dynasty that he had created.

Dr. Hodges put his chin down and marched through his rounds, his head throbbing with arguments. His sixty-seven-year-old body was amped up and edgy from holding it all together in a prolonged state of mental and physical alertness. He pronounced a diagnosis on his exhausted body: vertigo. When he moved his head, the world turned sideways.

The American Baptist Board of International Ministries had every right to shut the hospital down if they saw fit, yet Dr. Hodges refused to acknowledge their authority. It was intolerable. It was flagrant insubordination. It was, in a way, so very Haitian.

Ayiti Cheri, land of the untamed spirit, home of the free and the proud. So deceptively acquiescent to foreign aid, so resistant to foreign rule. Beloved Haiti: reformer's paradise; colonist's bane.

For it was not the Hodges family alone who flaunted their noncompliance. The military generals who had deposed Aristide felt the same self-evident right to rule. Asserting that they alone understood what was best for their people, they had disregarded protocol to accomplish their purpose.

But if the Board of International Ministries took offense at the Hodges family, that was nothing compared to what the U.S. and the United Nations felt about the military junta in Haiti. And there is no enemy quite so formidable or self-righteous as the U.S. government when it believes that the reputation of Democracy is at stake.

The Organization of American States, under pressure from the U.S., leveled an economic embargo against Haiti. Dr. Hodges wrote outraged newsletters arguing that economic sanctions against the poorest country in the western hemisphere were ludicrous. Those with money and power would find ways of getting around the restrictions—there was a centuries-old tradition of smuggling on the island, after all—but the embargo would only devastate the rural farmers, who relied on public transportation to sell their harvest. "Embargo," in Kreyòl, became a twisted, mocking play on words: *anba gwo*, squashed beneath the powerful. "Democracy" was ridiculed as *demokrache* (to spit) or *demokraze* (to destroy).

The only diesel available, on the black market, sold for twenty-eight dollars a gallon, and the price of kerosene rose to twelve dollars a gallon in Limbé. There was no electricity or running water in Cap-Haïtien. Dr. Hodges warned that the country was doomed to return to the age of pirates. Without kerosene, farmers and day laborers reverted to Paleolithic technology: a smoky wick dipped in cooking oil. These plucky embargo lamps the Doctor championed in his newsletters as symbols of human ingenuity and obstinacy: U.S. meddling hadn't crushed Haiti yet.

Joanna mailed out support letters titled "EMERGENCY ENERGY CRISIS FUND FOR LIMBÉ" and recruited funds for solar power so the hospital could continue to supply twenty-four-hour-a-day electricity for the lab, the surgical wing, and the five public water fountains. In subsequent updates she added, *You can also send us care packages: candies, chocolate, chocolate chips, soups, sprinkles for Christmas cookies for the kids in the hospital, tea bags and cereal. I like Frosted Flakes and the kids like Honey Roasted Cheerios.*

For those without access to missionary support planes, life was considerably more difficult. Overcrowded fishing boats crammed with refugees fled the country in droves. Île-la-Rat, our picnic spot at the edge of Baie de L'Acul—the tranquil bay into which Columbus had sailed with such ardent anticipation—was one of the staging grounds. There, on the pristine white-sand beaches where we had flopped down after a day of snorkeling, refugees were loaded like ballast and sent out to sea.

For this privilege—a perilous trip across the ocean to Miami in an unreliable boat, with no guarantee of survival, much less a warm reception if one did make it onto U.S. soil—three hundred dollars was demanded of each would-be illegal immigrant, even though the holding pens at Guantánamo were the most likely end to the journey, followed by a humiliating return to Haiti.

In the end, the United States sank more than a hundred small wooden boats in an attempt to keep the Haitians out of Florida. Racketeers stole the hospital's wooden rowboat and demanded three hundred dollars for its return. Dr. Hodges announced that he didn't have the time or the men to go battle for it. Without the rowboat, the Hodges family finally lost their foothold on the Morne Bois Pin peninsula. The trees on that famously reforested peninsula were soon to follow, pillaged for housing projects or sold on the black market. Within a year, Pine Tree Mountain was as barren as when Dr. Hodges first set foot on its ruined soil. The small rock outcropping carved with a crusader cross—perhaps notched by Columbus himself, the Doctor had conjectured—was no longer shaded by leafy branches. Eden had been plundered. History on repeat.

Even as the political situation imploded around him, Dr. Hodges remained a man who felt most at home in the past. The five hundredth anniversary of Columbus's arrival in the New World was an event about which he had dreamed for decades, and he was unswerving in his allegiance to the Admiral of the Ocean Seas, even after scholars began to accuse the great man of genocide (Dr. Hodges admitted ruefully in a letter to a friend that his loyalty might be construed as *an isolated relic of earlier times*).

When filmmakers from WGBH in Boston arrived in the Caribbean to make a documentary about the upcoming quincentenary anniversary, and invited Dr. Hodges to participate, he was eager to set the record straight. But when the program aired in the midst of the U.S.-backed embargo, he clicked off the VCR and never watched the tape again.

———————

A decade after the documentary aired, I hunted down a copy of *Columbus and the Age of Discovery* and found myself on the floor beside a stack of videocassettes, fast-forwarding through the slow parts. I was surprised that it had warranted such a violent reaction from the Doctor. There were positive things mentioned about Columbus's skills as a navigator, for example, and his perseverance in spite of the odds. But it no longer seemed possible to pretend that Columbus hadn't participated in the destruction of the Taínos.

As the WGBH-sponsored sailboat *The Westward* rocked at anchor in the glittering blue Baie de L'Acul, a handful of Haitian fishing boats drifted in loose companionship around the stern. The camera pulled back through the boughs of a ragged Caribbean pine to follow a worn straw hat in the corner of the frame. Dr. Hodges emerged, carrying under his arm a thick black doctor's valise.

It felt strange to see him again after so many years. He seemed more vulnerable than I had remembered. His high-waisted gray cotton pants were held in place by a pair of red suspenders, and his right foot slipped slightly on the loose soil, though he quickly rebalanced without losing his dignity and glanced at the camera at the appropriate moment. He smiled faintly, an indulgence that none of the other experts had allowed themselves. He looked like a boy who hoped to be recognized for his discoveries.

The copper mine on Morne Bois Pin, which Dr. Hodges had discovered shortly after he arrived in Haiti, was little more than a rough depression in the soil. With the red earth cut open at his feet, the Doctor announced to the camera with the confident authority of one accustomed to pronouncing diagnoses: If my interpretation is correct, and I believe it is, why, this is one of the first pits or hard-rock mines dug in the New World.

He smiled, a collection of loose pens crowded into his breast pocket, a living artifact from a more idealistic age. I was surprised that he seemed so oblivious to the implications of his statement. The mines had been excavated by slave labor and had touched off widespread deforestation; Columbus's arrival in the New World had precipitated genocide.

The copper mine slowly faded from view, but the narrator's voice-over continued, qualifying Dr. Hodges's enthusiasm with the more wry observation: *Greed and the promise of gold changed Hispaniola forever.*

The Doctor's final appearance in the documentary took place in the consulting room at Hôpital le Bon Samaritain, where he explained the exchange of diseases during Columbus's first voyage, although, to judge from his flat, disinterested expression, he would have preferred a less contentious subject.

The historical evidence pointed to the transmission of syphilis from the Taínos to the Spaniards; the Spaniards, for their part, inflicted small-pox and a host of other diseases. For a moment, between questions, the Doctor's professional confidence faltered. I had never seen him in this light; he looked like a man tired of contemplating contradictions.

Dr. Hodges's dispiriting voice-over continued as the camera showed him scratching notes on flimsy triage tickets on the porch of the hospital, a solitary figure engaged in a Sisyphean struggle.

And then the hospital disappeared altogether, fading into a dusky blue oceanscape as *The Westward* raced on to more compelling historical events. Coming up next: the *Santa María* runs aground on a submerged reef outside Cap-Haïtien!

I turned the tape off. I already knew how the story ended.

In 1992, while the rest of the world chose to ignore the holiday, Dr. Hodges held a defiant, sparsely attended five hundredth anniversary celebration to honor Columbus's ill-fated inaugural city, La Navidad. He was aware that his hero's legacy was now in question, and that he, too, was considered a controversial figure by the Board of International Ministries for refusing to submit to their orders. In the commemorative photographs that Joanna mailed to us, along with a snappy write-up of the event, her gray hair tumbled over her ears. The Doctor's thin-lipped smile was etched with wrinkles.

There were no TV cameras or foreign dignitaries in attendance, but the embargo would have deterred them even if they had wanted to come. It was a bittersweet ceremony, although there was something fitting about the way that the gathering was in itself a statement of opposition—*in the world, but not of the world*, as if it were a verse lifted out of context from the King James Bible.

After the second missionary evacuation, it took almost a year before any of the doctors and nurses who had fled to the U.S. felt safe enough to move back to Haiti. Some never returned. The imported fruit trees at the Ag Center in Cap-Haïtien died, and Ken Heneise visited only long enough to close down his remaining projects.

My parents, like the Board of International Ministries, did not learn the full story until after the paperwork had already been signed, but as the embargo wore on, making it all but impossible to buy fuel for the hospital generators without documented not-for-profit status—a legal technicality that Dr. Hodges had never bothered to obtain—the family took matters into their own hands.

With the help of a Haitian lawyer, the hospital was registered as a not-for-profit foundation in Port-au-Prince. The name Hôpital le Bon Samaritain, however, had already been taken, so the family came up with an alternative for the official documents—Havre de Bonne Santé, the Harbor of Good Health—thereby preserving the "HBS" initials and allowing the hospital to maintain the illusion that nothing had changed.

The Hodges family also, unbeknownst to the Board of International Ministries, set up a board of directors to oversee the hospital. But the clause that sparked the greatest controversy—when it was discovered—was the one stating that the board must include two members of the Hodges family, both of whom would have veto power over the remaining board members.

It was an unprecedented exploit in the history of American Baptist International Ministries. Sundquist flew down for a tense conference during which he accused Bill and Joanna Hodges of violating a sacred trust.

—People stood up and actually swore, Joanna recalled with a prim flutter of indignation. —In a missionary meeting.

The Hodges family, from her perspective, had willingly sacrificed their personal ambitions for over thirty-six years to keep Hôpital le Bon Samaritain afloat, with very little help from the mission board. She did not see any harm in wanting to preserve an institution they had paid for with their own sweat and blood.

Sundquist, responsible for missionaries in almost ninety countries, found it incredible that the Hodges family alone believed that they did not have to defer to the indigenous church.

It feels to me like you have confused yourself with the hospital God has created, he wrote to Dr. Hodges. *I do not like unilateral decision-making, ultimatums, or threats. They have no place between Christians, but Bill I am soon going to be forced to act. Our understanding of missions is that no matter where we serve, no matter who we serve, our missionaries work alongside of the people of the country, preparing them to assume responsibility and ownership of all ministries. A family-controlled institution is in direct conflict with the very core of our Missiology.*

Dr. Hodges tapped an indignant rebuttal: *If placing two family members on a board of five, in a land that is melting away under our feet . . . is an attempt to gain personal advantage from a dilapidated medical service in Limbé . . . then I must either be demented or deluded . . . Who would <u>want</u> to own an unstable, run-down, crowded medical service in a small tropical town, where charity considerations alone demand an infusion of at least $10,000 a month?*

The possibility that the Doctor, like Columbus, had mismanaged the mission that he had been entrusted with was a verdict he could not bear to accept.

My father, reading Joanna's dramatic updates, felt his loyalty torn. He wrote a long letter to Dr. Hodges and confided his own tangled family history regarding the date business that hadn't survived the transition from one generation to the next. He felt a deep loyalty to the Doctor but he worried that the family's reactionary strategy didn't seem viable long-term.

The Hodges children, as to be expected, voiced strong opinions. Susan had moved to Florida to be reunited with her children and husband after a year apart, but wrote to say: *I want to tell you both how <u>proud</u> I am of you. I'm <u>so glad</u> you are both "grenadier" and not on the <u>retirement list!</u>: playing golf or growing roses, flying to Hawaii . . .* Joanna and Bill had taught their children the lyrics to "Grenadiers à L'assaut" when they first moved to Haiti in the 1950s, a fighting song from the Haitian revolution: *Grenadiers, to the assault! He who dies, that's his affair!*

David Hodges, who had kept his wife and children in Limbé throughout the chaos of the military coup and the subsequent embargo, stormed and shouted, convinced that the mission board was waiting to kick the Hodges family off the compound as soon as they had the chance. Barbara and her brother Paul weighed in as well.

Dr. Hodges briefly considered walking away and letting the board of International Ministries have Hôpital le Bon Samaritain. He could finally devote himself to his archaeology and historical writings; he could even open a small clinic if he so desired—his children assured him that half of the staff from Limbé would probably follow him.

But he couldn't let go of what he had built. He claimed that he was too old to start over. If he had been ten or twenty years younger, he might have attempted it, but he had just turned seventy. He had spent too many years trying to force the unwieldy institution to resemble the ideal he carried in his imagination: a sanctuary of hope in the midst of suffering.

Joanna urged him to hold his ground. And in truth, no one really believed that the Board of International Ministries would follow through with their threats. Dr. Hodges and Joanna had been loyal, productive missionaries for almost four decades: Why would the mission board turn its back on them now, over something so small as veto power?

Outside the compound walls, Haiti was in full-scale meltdown. Aristide supporters had convinced the U.S. government to reinstate the deposed president using Special Forces commandos (a betrayal by his own countrymen that the Doctor felt keenly). During Operation Uphold Democracy, Green Berets took over the Limbé police station and blared psych-ops rock music as a warning to anti-Aristide rebels. Helicopters thundered over the valley. Anti-American sentiment skyrocketed.

Dr. Hodges holed up in his study after long hours in the clinic, numbing himself with American movies. He was haunted by *At Play in the Fields of the Lord,* about missionaries in South America who destroyed the very community they had come to save. *Pretty Woman* entranced and confused him. It was an artifact from a civilization he no longer recognized as his own.

He informed the Board of International Ministries that it was a bad time to press the issue of leadership and asked for a year's reprieve.

The Board of International Ministries refused.

In March 1995, Sundquist flew to Haiti for one final negotiation. Bill and Joanna met him at the Hotel Roi Christophe in Cap-Haïtien. The encounter was, in one sense, a wry fulfillment of the old witticism that Baptists can't stand authority and no authority can stand them. Neither side was willing to surrender.

Sundquist, a confident, broad-chested man who had made it his business to stay abreast of the latest missiological debates, insisted that it was long past time for the Hodges family to defer to local leadership; the White Man's Burden was no longer a defensible strategy.

Dr. Hodges, quick to dismiss the insights of a man who spoke no additional languages and who had never lived outside the U.S., concluded that Sundquist simply didn't understand the harsh reality of Haiti. If the hospital were surrendered to the Haitian Baptist Convention, funds would be swiftly redirected to local pastors' pet projects, and the hospital would cease to function.

In the end, Dr. Hodges and Joanna were informed that if they refused to relinquish veto power, HBS would be cut off from financial support by the American Baptist Board of International Ministries as of July 1, 1995. All missionaries who remained on the compound after that date would be fired.

It is hard not to be bitter, Joanna wrote to her supporters. *I guess you might say Bill gave it a "gung-ho" but we struck out. And life goes on. The tickets have to be given out in triage this a.m. Breakfast must be prepared, letters written, and problems solved. The sick people must still have care and so life goes on . . . with chin up . . . Joanna.*

Two days later, John Sundquist drafted an official statement on International Ministries letterhead:

> *Dear Colleagues in Christ,*
>
> *It is with real sadness that I write to inform you that Dr. William and Joanna Hodges have legally made the Good Samaritain Hospital in Limbé, Haiti, a family-controlled institution.*

HBS continued to function after the Board of International Ministries cut off support, thanks in no small part to Joanna's relentless fund-raising, but the conflict splintered the missionary community. Loyal friends who had spent twenty years at the hospital packed their bags, convinced that God was calling them to move on to other work. Steve and Nancy James were the only ones who defied orders.

—You can fire us, they told Sundquist, —but we feel that Jesus is asking us to stay in the midst of this difficult situation.

Dr. Hodges had little strength to continue the work. His one pleasure was the class he called HHGG: Haitian History, Geography, and Geology, which he taught to his grandchildren and the few remaining missionary kids at Jericho School. He had discovered a Taíno settlement behind his retirement house at Chateau Neuf, and on Saturday afternoons he took the children foraging through the dried grass stalks to search for fragments of broken pottery.

In the two weeks before his death, the Doctor finished several historical newsletters. One was on the ruined palace of Sans Souci, the elegant throne room of Haiti's first king. He had obtained a coin engraved with the figure of a rising phoenix, alongside Roi Henri Christophe's motto: *Je renais de mes cendres*. I am reborn from my ashes.

He never finished his last newsletter. On Wednesday, when the clinic closed early, he invited Steve James to accompany him on a hike. He intended to photograph Vodou flags for an upcoming newsletter—a historical explanation of how the flags corresponded with African tribal identities. At Christophe's inauguration, the newly freed slaves had marched under the flags of Africa, announcing to the world that they had not been broken by slavery. Despite their suffering, they had not lost their identity.

Steve carried his one-year-old son, Micah, in a backpack as the two doctors forded a stream and climbed the narrow footpaths to the top of a nearby mountain. The embargo had forced Dr. Hodges to change his blood pressure medication (the pills he usually took were unavailable), and he had to stop occasionally to catch his breath as it was a two-hour hike to the summit, but Steve noted that he was in reasonably good shape for a seventy-one-year-old.

When they reached their destination, a Vodou priest and his wife were sitting in their front yard with their children. Dr. Hodges greeted them cordially. Over the years, he had treated almost everyone in the Limbé watershed, and *bòkò* often referred patients to him. He had a reputation among Vodouisants as a man who worked with two hands— one hand blessed by God, the other by magic—though he himself scoffed at this analysis. He was a rationalist; he had little patience with the supernatural.

While Dr. Hodges made polite small talk, the *bòkò's* wife disappeared inside the house and returned with a sick child. She requested a triage ticket, and Dr. Hodges obliged. He advised her to bring the ticket to the clinic the following day, or on Friday, adding: If I'm still alive.

—No, Dr. Hodges! You're not going to die, the woman said, readjusting the sick child on her hip. —You'll live forever.

Dr. Hodges cleared his throat. He snapped the photos he had come to find, then hiked back down the mountain.

The following day, September 15, 1995, Dr. William Herman Hodges worked a full day in the clinic, drove to his home at Chateau Neuf, and collapsed of a heart attack. His son Paul wanted to summon a U.S. Army helicopter to airlift his father to a military base—he'd made the necessary phone calls and was assured that a helicopter could be there in twenty minutes—but the Doctor refused.

—We'll sweat it out right here, he announced. He had always insisted that when it was time for him to go, he didn't want to drag out the inevitable.

As his strength ebbed, his wife, his daughters, his sons, and their wives gathered around him. He was lucid to the end, administering orders to Steve James and to the nurses who attended him. His final words were: Tell everyone that I forgive them.

At the funeral service the following day, the pastor of the Limbé Baptist church gave an emotional eulogy, chastising the congregation for ever having complained when the hospital was too full to admit any but the sickest patients.

—He planted trees when he saw our mountains were bare. He's American, but he's being buried here. And what is he being buried in? He's being buried in the very trees that he planted on our hillsides to give us life.

Joanna was moved when two thousand mourners burst into wailing.

—Dr. Hodges died because he burned his heart out for you and me. Now he's gone, and you won't have to complain anymore! the pastor berated the packed room. —But I have talked to the Hodges family! he said, holding up his hand. —The clinic will still open on Monday morning.

The room erupted into a chorus of fervent *Amèns!*

Joanna thought the oration was marvelous and wished the mission board had been there to hear it.

The graveside ceremony, later that afternoon, was a simple affair. As he had wished, Dr. Hodges was buried in an unadorned pine box behind his home at Chateau Neuf, within sight of the two-headed mountain that Columbus had beheld on his first voyage to the New World. Barbara painted Henri Christophe's rising phoenix and a verse from the Book of Ruth on a hand-drawn plaque: *Where you go I will go and where you stay I will stay. Your people will be my people and your God my God. Where you die, I will die, and there I will be buried.*

Above his coffin Joanna placed a simple wooden cross that the termites later destroyed.

Dr. Hodges was eulogized as a Haitian patriot in the French-language daily newspaper *Le Nouvelliste* for his refusal to abandon Haiti during the U.S. embargo and invasion: *Le Dr. Hodges a eu la position d'un patriote Haitien.*

My father heard about his death from a friend in Port-au-Prince, who had heard it announced on the radio, and he made the impetuous decision to attend the Doctor's memorial service the following weekend. I called home, worried about his safety. It had been four years since we left, but I had visceral memories of roadblocks and burning tires.

My father scoffed at my concern. The news reports had exaggerated the dangers of the American invasion, he assured me—we'd lived through worse.

When my father hung up, I was surprised to realize that at some level, I was still afraid of losing him to Haiti; afraid that he might never come back. I was also irritated. To my eyes, Dr. Hodges was a stubborn old man who had brought his own doom down upon his shoulders. Unlike my father, I felt no allegiance to the compound. If anything, I felt grateful to have escaped when we did.

Haiti was a riddle that I could not solve, and it was simpler to not think about it. I didn't yet know about my father's near-betrayal, or understand why my mother seemed so resentful of his continued interest in Haiti. Unless my father brought it up, we seldom spoke of the years we had spent as missionaries. Haiti had shifted from a place that I had loved to a country that I was relieved to have left behind. I had all but lost touch with Olynda.

I had not yet figured out who I was or where I belonged, but the world was vast, and I was determined to find my place in it. On a scholarship semester abroad in Edinburgh and London, I wrapped a blue cape around my shoulders and memorized T. S. Eliot (no surprise: I had trouble relating to people my own age), then took a year off to teach Shakespeare to six-year-olds at a home for at-risk youth in Tennessee, reenacting sword fights in the kitchen with butter knives, and practicing backflips from boulders into the Little Pigeon River.

The closest I came to reawakening trauma was when, in a sexual abuse training session at the children's home in Tennessee, I realized that I myself had been molested at fourteen by the nineteen-year-old on the scuba diving trip. I sobbed when I told the story for the first time. The shame was no longer mine to carry. But it hurt to reawaken the past.

Dr. Hodges's memorial service in Limbé was scheduled to take place one week after his death, and when my father's connection through Dallas was delayed, he had to scramble to catch an earlier flight out of Portland. He had sliced open the side of his wrist on a cardboard box (a delivery for a Haitian friend of a friend in the capital), and was in too much of a rush to wait for the shuttle bus from the long-term parking lot, but he had a devil of a time flagging down a ride to the terminal with a thick welt of dried blood congealing down his arm.

In Port-au-Prince, he caught a *kamyon* to Limbé. Was it this trip or another when the bus was oversold and he had to climb on top with the burlap sacks full of charcoal and mangoes? The other passengers scooted over, and my father settled down with his worn blue backpack between his knees. Goats and chickens, their legs tied in stiff knots, dangled from the brightly painted roof.

The conversation turned, inevitably, to politics. A well-dressed Haitian man who had emigrated to the U.S. and was therefore regarded with both envy and contempt as a member of the *Dyaspora* announced with disdain that Titid (Aristide's diminutive new nickname) was no friend of Haiti. His reputation as the people's savior had been tarnished now that he was so chummy with the U.S.

The road was gouged with potholes from years of neglect, and the *kamyon* tilted dangerously as it crept along the shoulder. Pushing to make up for lost time, the driver floored the gas when he hit the flat open fields of the Artibonite. Sacks of mangoes and charcoal battered the legs of the passengers on the roof. The young *Dyaspora* with the expensive shoes began to look queasy and leaned over the edge of the roof. When he vomited, the wind flung it upward, directly into my father's face.

A thin, wiry man seated next to them leaped to his feet and yelled: *Dyaspora kaka sou blan! Dyaspora kaka sou blan!*, the roof shifting and bumping beneath him as he shook his fist into the wind. He shouted as if his anonymity had been avenged; a lifetime of powerlessness vindicated by this one reversal: The *Dyaspora* smeared shit on the *blan!*

No one offered my father anything to clean his face, but he laughed it off as best he could. He had nothing in his backpack but a camera, his wallet, and his passport. It was an hour before the *kamyon* made its next stop and he could climb down and scrub his face in a muddy rivulet by the side of the road. He left his backpack on the roof while he washed, calculating that his humiliation had earned him a measure of respect. When he returned, his passport, camera, and wallet were untouched.

On the second leg of the journey, my father found a seat inside the *kamyon,* beside a woman who said that she remembered Dr. Hodges with great respect and was sorry to hear that he had died. She and her son would have died in labor were it not for the doctors at Hôpital le Bon Samaritain.

When my father finally arrived at Steve and Nancy James's house late that evening, he was welcomed as if he were a long-lost member of the family. He was given a towel and was able to shower. One of the nurses bandaged his bloody hand and warmed leftovers for dinner. He listened and chimed in as the missionaries retold favorite stories about Dr. Hodges: his trombone playing, the trademark red suspenders, his gentleness with his patients, the parrot that echoed his dinner whistle, his gift for languages and archaeology, his relentless historical curiosity. He had died as he'd wanted: with his boots on.

The following afternoon, an elaborate memorial service was held at the Guahaba Museum. The grass had been carefully cut and the reflecting pool was full of water lilies. Mournful oboe music from *The Mission* drifted over the heads of the mourners, Haitian and foreigner alike, who had come to pay their respects to the Doctor.

When the rain began to fall, no one moved.

BOOK THREE

Do not be daunted by the enormity of the world's grief.
Do justly, now.
Love mercy, now.
Walk humbly, now.
You are not obligated to complete the work,
But neither are you free to abandon it.

TALMUD
MISHNAH, *AVOT* 2:21

At least there is hope for a tree: If it is cut down,
it will sprout again, and its new shoots will not fail.
Its roots may grow old in the ground and its stump die in
* the soil,*
yet at the scent of water it will bud and put forth shoots
* like a plant.*

JOB 14:7–9

Peregrinati

Oregon, 2001

WHEN I WAS in my twenties, Haiti was a country I confessed to only when cornered: *You're not American, are you? Where are you from?* The questions arrived at odd moments: over a drink; in grocery store checkout aisles. My ridiculous chameleon voice gave me away.

Geography slipped out in unguarded syllables: the raised lilt at the end of the sentence (London); the sun-bleached tic when I talked too fast: You know, like? (adolescent vestige of California girl); the reflexive: Yes, sir; yes, ma'am, when pulled over by the cops (Tennessee); my slow, careful overenunciation. I was like the caddis fly larvae that my sisters and I used to poke at in the creek in Idyllwild, their shells stitched together from shards of mica and Styrofoam, sand and bone, buffeted by the moving water. My wanderlust was my robe, my petty splendor.

The simplest answer—which left out nearly everything—was that I was born and had graduated from high school in Oregon. The real story took too long to tell, and I had learned to brace myself for the moment when their eyes glazed over. I had done the math once, out of curiosity: seventeen different addresses and ten schools, and that was before I left home at seventeen. Sometimes I quoted Steinbeck: *I have lost all sense of home, having moved about so much. It means to me now—only that place where the books are kept.*

The rest of the family had put down roots in Oregon, but after a year and a half of college in Santa Barbara, and a semester abroad in the

UK, I'd moved to Tennessee, where at nineteen I had fallen briefly, tempestuously in love with a fellow missionary kid from Nicaragua—the grandson, as it so happened, of sweet, meddlesome Ivah, who had convinced both the Hodges family and my parents to change their plans and move to Haiti. Even in retirement in Florida, Ivah had not lost her busybody flair. She later confessed in a letter to my mother that even when I was a child, she had been impressed by how responsible I was, keeping my little sisters in line, so she sent her grandson to visit me in a snowstorm, all of his earthly belongings crammed into a pickup truck with engine problems. She thought I might be just the one to come to the rescue.

Having seldom been asked on dates, I was flattered by the attention. Even though he'd grown up in Nicaragua and my family had lived in Haiti, we shared a vague sense of displacement. We felt out of step with Americans our own age. Three months later, we were engaged. My mother worried that I was too quiet and constrained in my fiancé's presence. I felt that the brokenness of her own marriage hardly gave her room to criticize. It took me almost two years to realize that proving my mother wrong was a terrible basis for a marriage. I swallowed my pride and gave back the ring. We only knew how to hurt each other.

At twenty-one, I waited tables in Knoxville, squirreling away my tips to pay for my English lit degree, then moved back to Oregon for a year, where I poured coffee to pay the rent and wrote poetry in a tiny apartment above a garage that I shared with my sister Meadow. At twenty-three, I landed a job teaching Shakespeare and the Ramayana at an international school in the highlands of Java. Muslim neighbors invited me in to sip tea, and I learned to ride a motorcycle (badly) and to talk my way onto crowded trains, staying up half the night to hear the stories of strangers. My students were from Taiwan, the UK, Japan, Australia, Korea, the U.S., and Indonesia, and spoke a minimum of two languages. Their identities were hybrid, suspended between worlds. They asked beautiful questions.

For the most part, I had made peace with the God of my childhood, though we still got into shouting matches from time to time (I did most of the shouting). Sometimes I offered very practical advice on how to run the universe more justly, though I seldom saw my suggestions put into action. I hadn't told my father, but I had come to the radical conclusion that God was not nearly so prudish as the churches that claimed to speak on Her behalf. I clung to Irenaeus's centuries-old observation: *The glory of God is a human being fully alive* and to George MacDonald's quip: *It is the heart that is not yet sure of its God that is afraid to laugh in his presence.*

But my father's voice was still loud in my ears. When I finished my two-year teaching contract, I realized that I was tired of flitting from one adventure to the next in the hope of trying to evade the one story that I didn't know how to tell: my own missionary childhood.

I thought of Suzette, who had first assured me that I was a writer. Perhaps it was finally time to face what I did not understand.

So I moved to Seattle—close enough to family but not too close—joined an Irish band, and found a job waiting tables at a French restaurant.

I would have loved to give the impression that I was world-weary and sophisticated, with a dozen stamps in my passport and a stack of cardboard boxes filled with books in several languages, elephant statues made of melted-down alarm-clock bells, and an icon from Jerusalem, but I was still unmistakably a missionary's daughter. The guilt was stamped like Cain's on my forehead when I counted up all that I possessed: a roof over my head, a warm bed, food and wine, what passed for freedom. Opportunities denied far too many young women my age, born into different circumstances.

In my swallow's-nest apartment above the thunderous roar of the highway, I sat down at my rickety garage-sale table and began to write:

Here's to a place that I've never met but long for. Here's to home. Here's to my beginning.

Petrichor

Oregon, 2002

M Y FATHER WAS suspicious and critical when, shortly after I moved to Seattle, I fell in love with a high school friend who had first fallen in love with me a decade earlier, when we, the hapless ex-missionary family, stumbled into a home and a job in Oregon.

David was an irreverent, peaceable man who had taken a boat from Denmark to meet me in London when we were both in college, though we just missed each other (the world before cell phones). Once, on a misty drive together to the Oregon coast when we were in our twenties, I had told him that we were going different directions in life: ergo, this could never work. Still, he had written to me when I moved to Tennessee, and he had told me, while I was engaged, that he would always regret me.

I had a tendency to fall for drifters and idealists—the ones my father liked. David had a degree in accounting, and his family had lived in Oregon for six generations. He had spent his entire childhood in the same house on a quiet cul-de-sac. (He was the one about whom my mother sometimes asked: What about David? He's such a nice boy. To which I invariably replied: Mom, *please*.)

It took me a decade to understand that kindness was exactly what I was looking for in a companion. He made me laugh. He asked good questions. If I ran away this time, I would always regret it.

My mother couldn't stop smiling when I admitted that finally, after ten years, I had fallen in love with my good friend David. My father stomped off, disgusted, to fix the clogged water pump at the native plant nursery.

—People have to work around here! It's time to quit this nonsense and get to bed! he shouted, storming into the living room when we were on the couch laughing at midnight.

My mother's lips tightened. —Jon, we'll go to bed when we're ready.

He picked up the fireplace tongs and hurled them against the wood-stove. The metal clattered and rang against the stone.

—Jon Anderson! she shouted.

The bedroom door slammed shut. The conversation was over.

—He doesn't share our family's love for a flexible lifestyle, my father explained to me a few months later, on the night when—unbeknownst to me—David had called to ask for my parents' blessing. (My mother was out of town, so my father laughed and said: Well, we'll have to talk it over. I'll get back to you.)

It was just before Christmas, and my father and I were alone on the farm in Oregon. I sat down by the woodstove, wary of his sudden interest in my affairs. He chose his words carefully, trying not to set me off.

—David seems weighed down by material possessions, he warned, eyes averted as he warmed his callused, dirt-stained fingers by the fire.

—You don't have to live in poverty to love the Kingdom of God, I shot back.

The following summer, Olynda flew up from Florida, and a few former students from Indonesia came to help us celebrate. At our rehearsal dinner, David played the song "Hard-Headed Woman," and meant it favorably.

I walked alone down the aisle on our wedding day. I did not lean on my father's arm. He had raised me to be self-sufficient, and I had learned his bitter lesson. I was not going to repeat any of his mistakes.

So precarious was my parents' marriage, in the years after we left Haiti, that I had braced myself for divorce when my sister Rose left for college. But once they were alone with each other, my mother's emails described canoe trips along the creek behind their house, or seed-collecting expeditions to the coast and the mountains. Just as they had done in their college years, they pulled off the highway after a day in the wilderness and slept under the stars.

My father returned from these forays with five-gallon buckets full of native seeds that he cleaned while watching foreign films checked out from the library, his berry-stained fingers rustling through the husks, his work forever unfinished. He covered the dining room table with fine-mesh screens that he used to separate the seeds from the chaff.

My mother scolded him for the spiders that spun dusty webs inside the car windows, and for stealing her measuring cups, her sieve, and her blender, but there was a tenderness in her voice that I hadn't remembered.

For years, they led parallel lives. My mother led the church youth group on canoeing expeditions and joined the board of various evangelical not-for-profits, filling her passport with trips to Indonesia, Italy, China, and Mali—trips that my father was usually too busy to join. He put in long hours in the garden and at the nursery, counting down the months until he could go back to Haiti. The proceeds from their u-pick blueberry stand paid the salary of a Haitian *agwonòm* named Edner, who hiked through the villages around Limbé and taught farmers how to build living terraces and graft fruit trees, since my father was no longer there to insist on it.

My father lived for the weeks when he bumped along dirt roads on the back of Edner's motorcycle, visiting Zo and checking on the gardens. When he returned from these adventures, he offered everyone who stopped by the house a hunk of dry, chewy *kasav* and answered the phone in Kreyòl.

David was with me when I traveled with my parents to Limbé for the first time in a decade. We visited trees that my father had helped to plant in the village of Rey and spent a day with Zo. Joanna regaled me with stories.

—You smile more here, David told me on our last night in Cap-Haïtien. —Maybe it's the sun on your skin and the extra color in your cheeks. You seem very comfortable here, almost more comfortable than you are back in the States.

I had told David only the painful stories, where the trauma eclipsed the beauty. I had forgotten so much.

My relationship with my father, even after our trip to Limbé, remained tempestuous. I realized that I was like him in the ways that Haiti had gotten under my skin. Just as my sisters and I were once forced to sit, motionless in the heat, and listen to a three-hour service in Kreyòl, I now cornered my parents and insisted that they recount the intimate details of our lives there—our arguments, our adventures, our betrayals. My mother squirmed, wishing for any other topic of conversation. My father rose to the occasion, using the opportunity to preach, once again, the gospel of trees.

He was still far more liable to express his disappointment in me than offer a compliment, and more than once he hung up on me or told me via email that I was clueless. But as I pored over his journals and struggled to evoke him on the page, he became, for the first time, a character with whom I could empathize. I had been marked by his anger and high expectations, but I hadn't understood his buried fears or his unswerving devotion to his calling. As my mother explained, when the topsoil in Haiti washed away, part of my father went with it. Even after so many years away, he had not managed to uproot himself from that fertile, devastated soil.

When I first began to write about Haiti, before my sons were born, I did not yet imagine that those first resentful drafts would become a meditation on love, in all its complexity. Or that what I had to learn from that troubling, joyful, infuriating missionary compound would become an inheritance that I would one day want to pass on to my own children.

When David placed their first grandson in my parents' arms, my mother rocked him for long minutes, singing and crying as she welcomed him into this world. My father recited the Latin names of trees over his pink, scowling face—and then spoke to him in Kreyòl.

Tranbleman de Tè

Oregon, 2010

ON JANUARY 12, 2010, my sister Rose was about to call and wish our mother happy birthday when she saw a news headline flash across her computer screen. A 7.0 earthquake had struck Port-au-Prince.

My mother had planned to celebrate with a long walk and dinner in town but after Rose's phone call, she fell face first onto her bed to sob and pray. My father spent hours on email, trying to contact everyone he knew from Haiti.

My sisters and I stumbled through the week in a daze. Friends from the missionary compound, loosely reconnected on Facebook, posted images of dust-covered survivors emerging from collapsed buildings as the death toll climbed: 200,000; 230,000. An estimated 1.5 million people had lost their homes.

My father called Portland every few days to update us on the latest news. I juggled the phone, tripping over LEGOs on the kitchen floor as my youngest son grabbed the receiver to say hello to Grandpa Jonny.

Limbé, a hundred miles north of the epicenter, hadn't experienced any significant damage, but as refugees straggled out from the capital, even Cap-Haïtien was running low on supplies. Dr. Steve James, who had left Hôpital le Bon Samaritain to support several small rural clinics around Haut-Limbé, drove down to the epicenter with his colleagues to help however they could.

Dr. Manno, the Haitian director of Ebenezer Clinic, filled the pickup with as many refugees as he could bring back to the Limbé Valley. As aftershocks shook the ground, Steve James and others set up an emergency response center under the trees in Gressier, just outside of Léogâne, one of the hardest-hit slums in Port-au-Prince. For two weeks, they slept in tents and improvised splints from cardboard and duct tape. Faced with the magnitude of the devastation, their meager supplies were quickly depleted. Nancy James leveraged contacts in the U.S. to send bandages, Tylenol, and gauze for expedited delivery on the missionary plane.

A week after the earthquake, I strapped the boys in their car seats and drove down to my parents' farm for the afternoon, just to be around others who had loved Haiti. I could hardly concentrate. The country had already survived so much, how could it be asked to endure one more round of devastation?

My mother poured cups of tea while the boys played at our feet. The earthquake was all we could talk about. Cell phone towers were down in the capital, and the infrastructure had collapsed, which meant that it had taken hours—sometimes days—for people in the north to realize what had happened. Laurie and Casso's son Tony, who had been Meadow's classmate at Jericho School, had been among the first to drive down from Cap-Haïtien after the earthquake. His wife's family lived in Port-au-Prince, as well as his cousins on his father's side, and after seeing the extent of the damage, he returned to install satellite telecommunications systems for the Red Cross.

Lolo, the daughter of Haitian-American artist friends, fluent in at least three languages, had lost her home in Port-au-Prince and was sleeping in her car with her two sons. Olynda, in Florida, was in the process of gathering donations. Anticipating that the foreign news agencies would soon arrive to put their own spin on the earthquake, Lolo met the arriving journalists at the airport, determined that they should have access to accurate translations; we later heard her voice on the BBC.

It was jarring to realize that my parents had originally planned to be in Haiti during the first two weeks of January 2010 for an agricultural seminar. If the conference had not been rescheduled at the last minute, they would have been in Port-au-Prince when the earthquake hit.

—I don't know if I would have been able to come out of the rubble singing, my mother admitted. —I hope that I would be able to do that, but I don't know if I could.

We held the unspoken in silence.

The grandsons, well aware that we were too busy talking to pay them any attention, devolved into anarchy. The younger one threw a wooden block, and the older one howled when his carefully balanced tower clattered to the floor. My mother offered to take a nap with the sobbing four-year-old. My father suggested a walk with the feisty little brother.

It was a cold afternoon in late January, and tiny shoots of winter rye grass glinted in the dark earth. My son, not quite two years old, sat on his grandfather's shoulders as we walked across the fields. He pointed with fat childish fingers at the moon. —Dark! he said, frustrated.

—Moon, dark. He had read *Goodnight Moon;* the moon was supposed to come out at night, not during the day. These things should not be.

As we rounded a copse of trees and the winter fields opened up before us, I asked my father if he knew what had became of Ti Marcel, the little girl he had brought home from the missionary hospital twenty years earlier. Could she have been in Port-au-Prince during the earthquake?

He explained that he had visited the family in Gonaïves a few times after we left Haiti. Once, he had spent the night as a guest of Cherylene's relatives and had taken a bucket bath in the courtyard of their concrete block house just like the rest of the family. A gang of kids had watched, awestruck, as he stripped to his underwear. A little girl shouted with surprise: *Li blan toupatou!* He's white all over!

The following morning, he had gone to see Cherylene. She had moved into a slum at the edge of town, where, at eleven years old, she was responsible for her two younger cousins, whose mother was dying of AIDS. Cherylene was on her way back from the water fountain with a five-gallon bucket balanced on her head when my father caught his first glimpse of her. Her slight body bent and swayed under the sloshing forty-pound load. Her bare feet were caked with mud.

—It was hard to see her like that, my father admitted. —You girls never had to live like that.

I nodded. There was nothing to say. The world's deep inequity was an ache that never healed.

My father explained that when he had returned to the home of Cherylene's wealthier relatives later that afternoon, he met a woman he had never expected to see: Cherylene's mother.

She had a long jagged scar across her forehead.

—I thought you were dead, my father blurted out, then immediately regretted his words, as Cherylene's mother turned on her relatives in a fury: how dare they pretend she was dead, she had never been dead, she had no plans to die. The others shouted back that she was as good as dead, causing a scene like this: *Moun fou,* crazy idiot. Now get out of the house, they commanded.

She left, still shouting. Her milk had dried up before she understood that she had a child. She was equally prone to outrage and careless joy. Occasionally, she threw rocks at strangers. The scar on her forehead was from a rock that had once been hurled at her.

My father never saw Cherylene's mother again. Several times he wrote to the relatives in Gonaïves but received no response. The silence was notable, weighed against the stack of tissue-thin airmail envelopes he received from other Haitian acquaintances—each new letter replete with graceful prose, fervent wishes for our good health, and then, invariably, a request for funds. My father sent money for funerals, for a new house about to be constructed, for school uniforms, and for businesses just about to get off the ground, but he never sent anything to Cherylene. Her family either did not receive his letters, or they did not want his help.

—Do you think she's still alive? I asked my father. She would have been in her mid-twenties, a few years younger than Rose.

—It's hard to know, my father admitted.

We were on our way back across the field, my son asleep in his grandfather's arms, slumped and peaceful against his chest.

The earthquake had been only the most recent catastrophe. In 2004, on the two hundredth anniversary of Haiti's independence, Hurricane Jeanne had torn across the mountains above Gonaïves. The treeless hillsides funneled the rainwater into the ravines, creating a river of mud twenty feet high that all but leveled Haiti's third largest city. It was impossible to know if Cherylene had been one of the survivors.

—I used to think back then that she was better off with her family, and that if she had a family to take care of her, then she should stay with them, my father said.

—You don't think so now? I asked.

—It would have been complicated to adopt her, and it wouldn't have been easy for her, either, growing up a black girl in a white family, he admitted. —If we had adopted her, I probably would have thought by now that it would have been better to let her stay with her own family.

He let out a brief, pained laugh.

No matter what path we could have taken, we would have failed her: love's inevitable sorrow.

My son shifted and breathed a deep sigh.

—It was so amazing that she survived when she was a baby, my father said. —There was one time when we went to Port-au-Prince for a few days, and when we came back, they told us that eight or nine babies had died that weekend. She was still alive.

The blackberry vines tugged at our clothes as we cut through the trees. I followed behind with a fallen kid glove and a rain boot. The evening sun made a halo of my son's curls.

—I used to think that she must have been saved for a reason, he confessed.

—And now? I asked.

—I don't know, he admitted, kicking off his rain boots onto the porch. —Perhaps it's made me more cynical.

We stepped inside, and he gently settled his grandson into the green chair where I had been born. My son stirred. My father rocked him with a callused hand until he fell back to sleep.

Could I have shared him with her? Let him be a grandfather to her children as well as my own? I had been so jealous of her when I was younger, but had we adopted her—if her family had permitted it—she would have become ordinary: a sister to quarrel with and defend, whose faults I could have listed as readily as my own.

Now that I was a mother, I understood my father's impulse. I wondered what I would say to Cherylene were I able to find her again. I wondered what she would say to us.

Mon Blan

Port-au-Prince, 2010

IN THE WEEKS after the earthquake, my father contacted every organization he could think of to offer his services, but it seemed that without medical training, he would be of little help in the recovery efforts; there were more volunteers than flights to carry them, and food and water were in short supply in the capital.

Then, unexpectedly, he received an email from a forester in Port-au-Prince with whom he hadn't spoken in decades: *How soon can you get here?*

The missionary forester had been charged with restoring safe living conditions to two hundred thousand children and families in tent cities under the auspices of an American NGO. My parents were asked to fly down as community liaisons for a four-week assignment. There would be room to set up a tent in a courtyard with the other volunteers. One large meal would be provided each day.

My parents booked tickets for four days out, giving them just enough time to prune the apple trees, find someone to feed the hens, and to pack their suitcases with enough dried fruit and beef jerky that they wouldn't be a burden on the local economy.

I was surprised by how strongly I wished to join them. I hadn't returned to Haiti in years. David's work as a software consultant had moved us to London after our first son was born, and when we returned to Oregon I had been involved in other projects—refugee resettlement in Portland; an Artists-in-the-Schools residency; an oral history of a neighborhood in the midst of gentrification. At fifteen, I had seldom ventured outside the missionary enclave, my understanding of Haiti distorted into a one-sided narrative. But I had learned, through the oral histories that I had helped facilitate in Portland, that the quality with which we listen determines the stories that we will be told. To listen was to bear witness—to enter into another's world. I longed to finally step across that divide.

An hour before my parents left to catch a red-eye to Miami, I learned that I had received an assignment to report on earthquake recovery efforts for the Public Radio International program *This American Life*. I would meet my parents in the north of Haiti one month into their trip, though it would mean leaving my husband alone for ten days with our four- and two-year-old boys, longer than I had ever left them. I didn't even contemplate turning down the assignment, though it startled me to realize how much like my father I had become. It was all too easy to ignore my own children, whose needs suddenly seemed less important, being less urgent. In my husband's exhausted but unflagging support, I glimpsed my mother's old weariness.

My parents, whenever possible, kept in touch with my sisters and me from Haiti via Skype and email (gone were the days of cassette tapes mailed to the grandparents).

Port-au-Prince was still choked with decay when my parents set up their tent in a dusty courtyard above the city, one month after the quake. Volunteers had flown in from Korea, Guatemala, the U.S., and work began at four a.m., when the roosters started crowing and the jangling cell phones in the courtyard began to ring.

My parents were the only married couple on staff. My father, with his gruff smile and corny jokes, made friends quickly with his Haitian coworkers, and as my mother joined in, her Kreyòl began to sound less awkward, more conversational. Men and women who had worked as journalists and teachers before the earthquake confided their frustrations and ambitions and my parents listened and asked questions. My parents were sobered by the obstacles faced by their Haitian colleagues but impressed by their stamina. The Haitian staff arrived for work each morning impeccably dressed in crisp shirts and creased pants, but it wasn't until my father visited the tent cities and saw the sunlight piercing the gaps in the tarp that he realized that his young colleague's carefully ironed clothes were her only possessions.

The president of Haiti, René Préval, declared three days of national prayer and mourning shortly after my parents arrived, and as the sun broke over the mountains my parents joined fervent Haitian Christians to fast and pray for their country. My mother was humbled by the unshakable faith of those around her. She had felt so isolated, living on the compound. This time, the sorrow was just as intense, but it was shared sorrow. It was not her responsibility to save Haiti—it never had been—but she could at least accompany others in their grief.

My father kept watch over a seedling Leucaena tree in the courtyard. The tree species had been one of his standard recommendations for soil conservation projects because the leguminous branches, rich in protein, could be cut and carried for animal fodder, while the roots added nitrogen to the soil. In one month, he watched the tree grow two feet. In a year's time, it would be high enough to offer thin shade. Nothing, it seemed, not drought or deforestation, not even earthquakes, could deplete the vitality buried in Haiti's soil.

And yet, as my parents listened to the stories of their coworkers, they felt increasingly uneasy that Haitians were seldom the first to be promoted to new responsibilities. The foreign staff, who knew how to write grants and present funding packages to donors, seemed disincentivized to work themselves out of a job. It was clear that when this latest crisis was over, the NGO would simply move on to the next disaster. The locals, however qualified, would once again be out of work.

Philanthropic endeavors seen from up close do not always yield a sense of accomplishment. Like countless others, my parents had been eager to rush in and help, but only from a distance does altruism appear entirely noble. My mother's assignment was to plot GPS coordinates into Google Maps to update the shifting locations of tent cities; my father joined a team delivering tarps and supplies—although his first assignment was to listen, for hours at a stretch, to an angry Haitian pastor who was livid at the disrespectful foreign aid workers who, in his estimation, persistently ignored the insights of those they were supposed to help.

My father nodded and asked questions. He did not minimize the pastor's outrage. After they'd spent three hours in plastic chairs in the humid courtyard, the pastor shook my father's hand and invited him over for a meal. I was amazed when I heard the story—my quick-tempered father, a mediator?

He shrugged and grinned sheepishly. —I listened.

My mother, tasked with outfitting a second office to accommodate the growing influx of volunteers, was assigned a leased air-conditioned car and sent to a furniture warehouse in Pétionville, an affluent suburb perched above the chaos of greater Port-au-Prince, with a budget of ten thousand dollars. She was dismayed, however, to discover that only imported desks, chairs, and beds were for sale. My mother argued that it would be far better to support the small-scale local artisans whose hand-hewn furniture, painstakingly carved from Haitian oak and mahogany, lined the highway from Cap-Haïtien to the capital.

The salesman explained, curtly, that the roads were still being cleared; Haitian-made furniture would be impossible to deliver on time. He directed her instead to a shipment that had just arrived from Brazil. My mother was offended. Funds had been donated in good faith by people around the world to help *Haitians* recover from the earthquake; it should be given to *local* woodworkers, not to an export business. How else could the Haitian economy hope to recover? The salesman lifted disinterested eyebrows.

Feeling trapped and irritated, my mother sank into the plush backseat of the SUV as the hired driver navigated the potholes on their way back to the NGO headquarters. She would have preferred to take a *tap tap* or a motorcycle taxi, but it was against the organization's policy for foreign volunteers to use public transportation; too much liability. My mother watched through tinted windows as pedestrians stepped irritably aside to let the relief vehicle bump past in a cloud of dust.

The frustrations felt nearly endless, yet when my father visited the tent cities, he was often struck by the dignity and composure of the community leaders. The displaced refugees had lost almost everything, yet sophisticated systems of self-governance had emerged to ensure that no one was overlooked. Volunteer keepers of the peace patrolled the alleys, and teachers whose schools had been reduced to rubble organized youth activities without books or a classroom.

There were stories of rape and theft as well—the flimsy tarps offered little protection—but my father shook his head at the foreign reporters and medical workers who entered the camps surrounded by heavily armed soldiers, as if braced for riots and looting. It was the standard caricature of Haiti: ungovernable, impoverished, forever poised on the brink of violence.

Perched in the passenger seat of the NGO delivery truck, my father listened as Haitian DJs peppered the airwaves with political commentary. Haiti, with its ten thousand registered aid organizations, was lampooned as the Republic of NGOs. Using the bleak misery of the situation for comic fodder, mock ministers pretended to advise Préval, the president of Haiti, to declare war on the U.S.—for if the Americans invaded, then the earthquake would be their problem. The man pretending to be Préval protested glumly: It will never work; with our luck, we'd win.

This got a laugh from the driver, swerving around the piles of rubble to deliver tarps that could barely keep out the pounding rain.

By the end of my parents' four-week term of service with the NGO, they had begun to chafe against the constraints of bureaucracy. The UN high command had decided that no more tarps would be distributed; it was time to move on to transitional shelters, even though the rainy season was about to start and it would take months before any of the promised shelters were viable, giving the existing tarps plenty of time to fray and deteriorate.

Once the UN shut down the warehouses, it took my father's distribution team an additional ten days to gather the supplies for which they had already handed out color-coded tickets.

On the day of their last delivery, the driver pulled into a dead-end alley and unlatched the back of the truck, but once the load had been distributed and it was explained that no more tarps would be forthcoming, the residents were angry. A local pastor tried to defuse the situation, but the crowd refused to disperse. A commanding young Haitian journalist named Lionne, on staff with the NGO, climbed up on the bumper to plead with the frustrated residents but she, too, was shouted down. The truck was trapped, unable to leave.

My father, asked to intervene, said nothing as he slowly made his way along the line of men with fists folded across their chests. Women cursed and shouted from behind the cable. As he walked, my father stooped and picked up stones from the ground, placing one rock in each angry hand.

Then he stepped back, all eyes on him. With shaggy eyebrows raised, he announced: The pastor already told you that there are no more tarps. Lionne told you that there are no more tarps. Now I, the *blan*, am telling you that if you lost your ticket, you will not get a tarp. If you don't like this news, you have rocks in your hands.

He stretched his empty arms wide. —So go ahead, you're free to stone me.

A thickset man a few rows back pushed his way forward and lunged across the cable. He gripped my father's shoulders in his powerful hands, then laughed and gave him a loud kiss on each cheek.

—*Mon blan!* he shouted, his arm around my father's shoulders. —This *blan* is my man.

My father had trusted himself to the public justice of street theater, in which, for uncounted centuries, conflicts have been aired and grievances tried in Ayiti. The crowd broke apart laughing, the cable was lowered, and the half-empty truck revved its engine and rattled away.

Rebwazman

Gonaïves, 2010

By the time I met up with my parents in the north of Haiti, my mother's voice wavered with weeks of accumulated exhaustion. They'd left Port-au-Prince for Gonaïves, where another old friend, Drew Kutschenreuter, had recruited their help on a soil conservation project coordinated by the U.N.'s Office of International Migration. Post-earthquake, sixty-five thousand refugees had relocated to the Artibonite, more than any other region in Haiti. The refugees were jobless, homeless, and vulnerable to the next hurricane—which might bury Gonaïves once again under a river of mud.

Drew's shoulders were bent under the burden of all that remained to be done. Like my father, he had learned that deforestation was not a problem that could be solved overnight, but he could at least give work to refugees building terraces and replanting trees. Harried by grant deadlines, Drew slept, if he slept at all, on a cot in his office; he gave his room, in a house he shared with Cuban doctors on a humanitarian mission, to my parents. Every possible resource must be leveraged to finish projects while the funding was available. My father, swept up in the cause, slipped back seamlessly into crisis mode.

At Kaz Nav, where hundreds of laborers fanned out across the dry hillsides to build stone terraces that would slow the force of the rainwater, my father reported to Drew that although the craftsmanship of the terraces was impressive—masons with dusty hands and strong shoulders could eye the circumference of a rock and, with the tap of a hammer, set it expertly in place without mortar—even stone walls weakened over time and were costly to repair. Trees, on the other hand, only grew stronger as they spread out their roots.

My father's preferred method for identifying the species most likely to survive in each new microclimate was to ask the eldest person in every village what trees they remembered from childhood. He seemed energized by the long hikes over dry hills to talk with farmers, and Drew, at my father's suggestion, requisitioned vetivè and elephant grass—sourced from Zo's gardens—and *bwa blan* seeds to help brace the stone walls against future collapse. But my father didn't translate when my mother lost the thread of the conversation, and he didn't stop for meals. He didn't have time; there was too much to be done.

—We're not a team as I'd hoped we would be, my mother confided when I flew into Cap-Haïtien to join them.

By four a.m. the next morning, we were up and packed, waiting on a concrete wall in Haut-Limbé for our ride to see the soil conservation projects in Gonaïves.

A farmer walked past singing hymns in the dark. My father explained that we'd be riding with Dr. Manno, who was driving down to Port-au-Prince to care for earthquake victims, but until the headlights swung down the dirt road and the driver turned his head to greet us as we squeezed into the back seat, I did not realize that I already knew Manno.

He nodded curtly. It seemed clear that he had not forgotten how I had tried to humiliate him when I was a teenager. I had not seen him in twenty years, not since he had placed himself at risk to escort my sisters and me from the compound in the midst of an evacuation. We had fled from danger. He was once again driving back to the epicenter of an earthquake.

As the vehicle climbed out of the Limbé Valley, I asked Dr. Manno about the work he was doing in Port-au-Prince. He had been driving down for weeks, sometimes with fellow medical professionals, sometimes with carpenters and masons to help rebuild damaged homes. He said that he had been amazed by the generosity of his neighbors in

Haut-Limbé. Time and again, people with very little to spare had donated the only extra pair of shoes they owned.

He loved his country, he told me, and although he had lived in the
United States for a time, he said that never again would he want to live
in such a place.

—The life I saw was too busy, he diagnosed. —I didn't see any patience. They can't wait.

We rounded a corner and suddenly the mountains opened up beneath us, ringed in clouds. A lone fortress from the age of Henri Christophe rose from a ridgeline. I remembered hiking to the summit when
I was a teenager, stunned into awe by such fierce beauty.

As we descended into the arid rain shadow of the Artibonite, Dr.
Manno turned to the subject that we had both been avoiding.

—Here's something I don't understand, he put forth testily, lifting
one hand from the steering wheel. —In other places, you see missionary kids playing with the nationals, but here, they create this separate
space for themselves. I know missionary kids who separate themselves
so completely that they don't even speak the language.

I shifted uncomfortably.

—The missionaries have their own school, their own church. Sometimes I think, *Why do you come to work here? You come to help the people,
and you love them so much that you won't interact with them.*

He shook his head, his laugh bitter. —It's funny. They love Haiti so
much, but they hate us.

I winced at his words. His anger, though it stung, needed to be
heard. Too often the only stories we told ourselves—as missionaries, aid
workers, philanthropists, and journalists—were the small but significant
ways we had helped a country in need, failing to understand that pity
was corrosive.

—When you face an enemy who is trying to destroy you, if you
laugh, you make him feel bad, Manno explained.

—Who is the enemy now? I asked.

—The earthquake. We have to show the earthquake that it didn't
succeed in destroying us.

By the time he pulled over to let us out at a dusty village above Go-naïves, his frustration seemed to have ebbed. We shook hands. He did not linger; he had lives to save. I told him that I admired his dedication. He nodded with formal dignity and got back behind the wheel of the truck to resume the long, slow work of rebuilding his country, with or without the help of the foreigners whose intentions he had learned early to mistrust.

My mother and I had to walk quickly to keep pace with my father and the three Haitian agronomists who led us up to the soil conservation project at Ravine Zeppelin. At eight-thirty in the morning, the sun was already at its brutal full strength. Pink masses of bougainvillea blazed along the cactus hedges, and goats bleated on dry hills. School kids in green-and-white-checkered uniforms giggled as they fluttered past. —Hello! What ees your name?

As we crossed a wide, flat gully, a Haitian *agwonòm* named Geffrard, one of the leaders on the project, pointed out the foundation of a house that had been swept away in a previous flood. All that remained was an uneven square of pounded earth. Pale green stones, the bones of the mountain, glinted in the morning light.

Our sandals were black with ash as we climbed. A fire attributed to a malevolent spirit, a *dyab,* had blazed across the mountain the week before, destroying a month of work. Viewed from above on Google Earth, the remaining terraces looked like sutures on a wound.

A herd of goats wandered across the hills, kicking aside the loose dirt and trampling the fragile millet stalks. My father's face was grim. Goats functioned as walking bank accounts for subsistence farmers, and my father pointed out with frustration that many of the locals who'd been hired to build the terraces were using their soil conservation income to buy more animals, which only put further strain on the already threat-ened ecosystem. And yet, because of the soil conservation project, farmers whose land was too dry to feed their families had not been forced to seek temporary work across the border in the Dominican Republic. The co-nundrum was an old one: Was the project doing more good than harm?

I asked two of the young Haitian agronomists, Sanon Elioth and Georges Ruysdael, what they thought of their country's future—was it beyond help? The two had been studying agronomy in Port-au-Prince when the earthquake hit, and they had leaped to safety from the second floor of their university, only to watch friends crushed under falling cement blocks. Children at an elementary school across the street, trapped under the debris, had thrown pebbles to let their rescuers know that they were alive. But the university students could not reach them fast enough. They dug frantically with bare hands, but the next aftershock brought only silence.

What Sanon and Georges had lived through was unimaginable, and yet less than two months later, they had signed up to plant trees on a deforested mountain, logging long hours in the heat to prevent yet another catastrophe.

—I have hope for my country, twenty-eight-year-old Sanon insisted. He explained that he believed in reforestation, *rebwazman,* and in the soil that remained. It was for this reason that his life had been spared.

He pointed out tiny green seedlings, no more than two centimeters high, that had already begun to emerge after the first good rain. He assured me that in just one year we could stand in the shade of these same trees. Of course it was possible for the ravines to be restored, for the forests to return.

My father, ever the critic, pointed out that possibility and reality were two very different things. Successful reforestation would require that the goats didn't trample the terraces or eat the tender seedlings, and that the hurricanes held off for another year.

As we hiked back down the mountain, my father admitted: I can't save Haiti. I'm an old man from another country. Maybe they will.

My mother and I grabbed hands to keep from slipping down the eroded trail. My father and the *agwonòms* hurried ahead of us. There was work to be done. It was all I could do to keep up.

———————

When I returned, one year later, Sanon Elioth had already lost his job with the NGO. The funding had run out. But he caught a *tap tap* from Port-au-Prince, and we hiked the sun-scorched trail through the bleached exposed bones of the mountain. We could find only one tree standing on the ridge above Ravine Zeppelin. The goats had eaten the rest.

The *bwa blan* seeds, however, which my father had insisted be planted at the base of the stone terraces in the Kaz Nav watershed, had already grown into saplings with glossy dark green leaves as high as my waist. The branches trembled as a wind blew down the mountains and stirred the dry soil.

Ebenezer Clinic

Haut-Limbé, 2010

Tiny Ebenezer Clinic in Haut-Limbé was already crowded with earthquake victims when Dr. Manno returned from his trip to the epicenter with yet another patient, a three-month-old baby named Kwensykaïra. Dr. Steve James, who had an appointment to see her later that morning, explained how Ebenezer Clinic, already in debt for eight thousand dollars' worth of pharmaceuticals, had volunteered to treat all refugees from the earthquake free of charge—an astonishingly generous undertaking for such a small establishment.

There wasn't much time to linger over breakfast. Steve read aloud from a book of prayers as parrots squawked on the porch. Nancy passed around a bowl of mangoes and homemade yogurt and poured steaming mugs of Haitian coffee, then they excused themselves—there were boxes of donated medicines to sort on the patio and earthquake refugees waiting to be treated.

I found Meadow's old classmate from Jericho School, Tony Casséus, at his parents' home, his six-foot-four frame hunched behind a cluttered desk trying to fix the campus computer network. The small Baptist seminary, under Casso's leadership, had expanded into a university, the Université Chrétienne du Nord, with degrees offered in theology, business, agriculture, and fine arts, and Tony was frequently enlisted to solve networking issues.

Tony had spent the weeks immediately following the earthquake setting up satellite telecommunications systems for the Red Cross and Médicins Sans Frontières. Rescue workers relied on functioning communication systems to coordinate airlifts and distribute supplies, which meant the faster the equipment could be installed, the more lives could be saved. Tony had little time to rest. He smoked cigarettes to mask the scent of the decomposing bodies.

Once, when shoveling aside the concrete and twisted rebar to clear a space to install a satellite dish inside the ruined walls of a former elementary school, he froze when he realized what he had unearthed. A child's arm was trapped beneath the rubble. A blue-and-white notebook lay beside the lifeless fingers. Tony, haunted, brought the notebook home to his mother. The French lessons had been painstakingly traced in a child's deliberate cursive: *My cat is named Mimi. He has a long thick tail. He is very adroit and flexible. He likes to fight with the neighbor's dog.*

Laurie worried over the grief in her son's eyes. When she joined him on one of his trips to the capital, a lifetime in Haiti had not prepared her for the devastation. She had written about it after she returned. Her voice wavered as she recounted the stories. Houses perched on hillsides had slid down the face of the mountains, crushing the homes beneath them, an avalanche of loss. Proud historical landmarks like the Cathédrale Saint Trinité and the Palais National looked as if they had been torn apart by a bomb. But it was the senselessness that broke her: fissured buildings surrounded by untouched buildings.

Above a church, a cross hung limp, its left arm dangling. Gaping cracks split the road where a five-story school once stood. Laurie thought of the children who had sung and laughed and recited their lessons within those walls.

She looked south toward the neighborhood where one of her nieces had been attending university. Her niece's body had been lost under the building's collapsing weight. She lifted one hand toward the darkening skyline and spoke silently: *I know you're not there anymore, but I love you. You were beautiful.*

As Tony inched the vehicle through the crowded streets of Port-au-Prince, Laurie could no longer bear to look only at the destruction. Signs of life demanded her gaze. Vendors peddled their wares through the bogged-down traffic: plantain chips and fritters, spicy *akra,* peanuts, sandals, ribbons, water, flashlight batteries.

A crushed car was being dragged out of the city, with a small boy astride the useless driver's seat, grinning as he pretended to steer the wreck, his hands turning the empty air.

An old man cupped water in his hands to rinse the dust from his tired body. His shelter was a two-foot-wide cardboard lean-to in the median.

A plant in a tin can sat beside a fluttering tarp, dusty green leaves pushing toward the light.

Defiant beauty in the midst of so much chaos.

Laurie longed to write a requiem, to set to music all that had been lost, a tribute to those who must continue: *A woman with only one leg balanced sideways on the back of a motorcycle, a pair of shiny crutches clutched to her breast. Dignity on crutches. Life stumbling on.*

Like most homes in Haut-Limbé, Laurie and Casso's house was crowded with cousins, nieces, and grand-nephews who had fled the ruined capital. Another of Laurie's nieces, Jenni, had been in a university lab class at the time of the earthquake. The ceiling had collapsed above her, and when she regained consciousness, she realized that she was trapped under the fallen masonry. Her head was pinned under a slab of concrete, and cement dust was choking her lungs. Then she heard the sound of someone else coughing and crying and realized that others had also survived. She was not alone. The trapped students stretched their hands out until their fingers touched in the dark. Jenni recited every Scripture she could think of. She told the others: If God wants to take us, let Him take us singing.

They sang every song they could remember, until they heard shouts from outside. Others had heard the singing and had come to pry away the rubble.

An aftershock sent small rocks rattling down onto their heads, and

Jenni imagined that the end had come. But instead of crushing her, the slab that had pinned her head shifted loose, and she was able to wriggle free. Four students emerged alive from the four-story building. The entire structure, folded in on itself like a collapsed accordion, was now no more than five feet high. None of the other nursing students had survived.

—If God saved me for a reason, I want to find out what it is, said Jenni. —There has to be a reason.

Her voice broke when she tried to talk about those who had been lost.

Six-year-old Kiki had stumbled out of the earthquake, along with his brother and mother, carrying only the clothes on their backs, but as they slowly made their way north, Kiki understood that their eventual destination was the U.S., where his grandfather lived. Kiki knew that in America, people spoke English, so when he finally arrived in Haut-Limbé, exhausted and confused, and woke up on a green, peaceful campus surrounded by hibiscus blossoms and fishponds, and heard his aunt and uncle speaking to each other in English, he assumed that they must have arrived at the mythical United States of America.

Within days, Kiki had found the rabbit cages in the field behind the agronomy classrooms, and figured out how to lift the latch to pet the soft downy fur of the baby bunnies. He poked at the fish and checked the back gate by the soccer field to see if it had been left unlocked. He invited a hundred university students to his seventh birthday party one month after the earthquake. But when he opened his presents—Matchbox cars, half a dozen new shirts and pants, books in English to help him practice—he looked up at his mother, stricken, and said: There is too much. I don't need all this stuff. Can't we send some of it back to the poor children in Haiti?

He didn't understand why everyone laughed.

Kiki didn't complain that there were eleven people wedged into three bedrooms at his aunt and uncle's house, but Casso paced the campus with a worried frown. As president of the university, Casso did not

regret his decision to take in 100 new students after the earthquake—
without charge, as an act of faith—though it meant that 450 students
were now crowded onto a campus designed for 350.

To make the situation even more complicated, students who had
survived the *tranbleman de tè* were now crowded forty to a floor in the
multistory dorms, haunted by nightmares of walls and floors collapsing
beneath them. The university did not have the funds to build new dor-
mitories, but Casso did not want his students to sleep in fear.

He was deep in conference with two technicians about the university's electrical supply when Kiki grabbed my hand and led me down
the path to look for the bunnies.

—This place is a paradise for a seven-year-old, I said to Casso as
Kiki skittered ahead of me, glancing over his shoulder to make sure I
was following. He took a running leap over a muddy puddle, glorying
in what his uncle agonized to maintain.

—Not so much for the adults, Casso replied with a dry laugh, his
voice slipping into the worried cadence of an administrator. He shook
his head. —We have all kinds of headaches. It's a day-to-day challenge.

When I followed Dr. Steve James out of the university gates to visit
Ebenezer Clinic with my microphone in hand, on assignment for *This
American Life*, Steve explained with what I suspected was relief: I'm not
a program director, I don't run anything, I just stand by and ask questions and encourage.

For a few years after Dr. Hodges died, Steve had stepped in as the
director of Hôpital le Bon Samaritain, but the experience had nearly
broken him. His return to Haut-Limbé as support staff, rather than as
an administrator, had marked a new beginning.

In the dirt courtyard of the clinic, not far from where my sisters and
I once lived, refugees from the earthquake waited under a mango tree.
Steve paused to greet each of his coworkers with a kiss on each cheek,
a custom I did not remember from the hospital in Limbé.

His eyes twinkled behind his spectacles as he led me upstairs to see
the tiny dental clinic and pointed out the pressurized drill and water

spray operated by a bicycle pump. It was the embodiment of *degaje*: the Haitian principle of using what you have to make what you need.

—It's fascinating technology, Steve explained. —He can do pretty major reconstructive dental work; he's even made dentures. Very high-quality care here.

The dentist glanced up from his patient and nodded hello.

As we stepped behind a thin curtain in the consulting room, Steve saw his first glimpse of the three-month-old baby who had been brought back by Dr. Manno from the epicenter. Kwensykaïra was cradled in the arms of one of her aunts and her chest rose and fell gently. She had been trapped beneath the rubble for two days; her mother, who had been buried with her, had not survived.

The aunts, as bidden, had brought in an X-ray from another rural clinic. Without functioning electricity, Steve had to hold the image against the window to study the bone structure. Kwensykaïra's arm twisted hazardously at the elbow, and Steve thought he detected a bone fragment, although it was difficult to tell; the image was blurrier than it should have been.

When Dr. Manno arrived, Steve asked for his recommendation.

Manno frowned. —We can help her with expenses, he offered. —But it's best to ask the opinion of the orthopedic specialists.

Manno was called out of the consulting room a moment later to solve another emergency, and Steve smiled and shook his head.

—Whoever heard of health care centers giving out money to people? I think most health center administrators would have nightmares over that.

He grinned like a schoolboy who had just gotten away with a prank. —The goal is to try to give to the poorest of the poor what the rich have to pay for, he confided, like Saint Francis giving an altar call.

Hôpital le Bon Samaritain, too, had been founded on these principles, but try as I might, I couldn't imagine Dr. Hodges humbly soliciting the opinion of a Haitian doctor years his junior.

—It's not a great difference, Steve conceded, but there is more participatory decision-making in the small clinics. It used to be more top-down, and decisions were made by a few people, whereas this is more of a dialogue instead of a monologue. It's a lot more fun—and a lot less stress, he added.

Steve explained that what he had come to realize during his years as the medical director in Limbé was that while the institutional model produced efficiency, security, goods, and services, it didn't create community.

—It doesn't allow people to feel empowered. It creates, in a way, a new slave-plantation mentality, where the slaves become dependent on their masters, and in the end, one reaps the fruit of slavery: discontent, anger, violence, joylessness, non-love. The other extreme, to break down the citadel, is to purposefully work hard at not becoming a dictator. But it means that people are going to suffer, people are going to die. Goods will not be provided. There's a terrible choice when one chooses community over the citadel. Both carry a price.

Strengthening the skills and resources of local communities—known as "capacity building" among foreign aid workers—was a slow process. Had Steve still been the director at Hôpital le Bon Samaritain, X-rays, surgery, and an overnight room all could have been provided under one roof. Instead, baby Kwensykaïra had to be sent to three different clinics, over terrible roads. Steve conceded that at times it could look very passive—a pie-in-the-sky, apathetic approach to dire need. The limitations could be hard to accept.

He laughed. —That's probably the height of evil to Americans: when you can see the problem right in front of you and you don't fix it. We're a fix-it culture.

He smiled at me, his gray eyebrows lifted. —But what I'm constantly amazed at is the resources, resiliency, and strength of the Haitian people in solving their own problems. These have been the best years of my life in Haiti, these past five years—not that the other years were not wonderful years, but these have been holy years.

As we walked back along the dirt road toward the university campus, Steve pulled me aside protectively as a motorcycle gunned past, stones scattering in its wake. He meditated on the fading cloud of dust.

—Can you imagine wheelchairs on these bumpy roads? He met my eyes with a weary smile. —Nothing is handicapped-accessible in Haiti.

Kiki was waiting when we returned, chewing on a rubber band and clearly satisfied by the noisy squeaks against his teeth. Steve had work to do, but Kiki asked to wear my sunglasses and sang "We Are the World" into my microphone. I let him put on my earphones so he could hear his own strong, clear voice. Piano notes tumbled over our heads as we descended through pale white orchids to look for shimmering fish in the university ponds. One of the beaux arts students was practicing scales in Laurie and Casso's living room.

At three a.m. the next morning I was awoken by another unseen piano student, the determined notes filling the darkness, a counterpoint to the call-and-response roosters and the shrill buzz of the mosquitoes.

Fireflies for Jesus

Limbé, 2010

WHEN THE METAL gate clanged shut behind me at Hôpital le Bon Samaritain, the silence, save for the generator, was notable. Bamboo brushed against the roofs of the empty volunteer cottages. Most of the Haitian doctors and nurses now took a bus from Cap-Haïtien.

The nursery that my father once managed had reverted to a jungle. Gangly Leucaena trees and a few stray bananas reached for the sun where tens of thousands of seedlings had sprouted in plastic trays, waiting to be transplanted. Weeds had overtaken the bare ground.

The yard workers, whose faces I remembered from childhood but whose names I had forgotten, greeted my father with smiles and handshakes. They told me I looked just like him, then pointed us toward the tiny Rose Cottage in the middle of the compound, where *Ma Doktè*, the Doctor's wife, was waiting. (Most rooms in the Hodges home had been boarded up, although a church from Canada was in the process of converting the Doctor's old study into an improvised orphanage.)

Joanna hobbled to the screen door as I approached. My parents excused themselves to visit a friend in Limbé, a former employee from the compound who had started his own tree nursery.

—You look pretty good, Joanna informed me, her gravelly voice every bit as commanding as I remembered. —I'm getting old. My bones are creaking. I'm going to be eighty-seven next year, and next week it will be fifty-three years that I've lived in Haiti—longer than I've lived in the United States!

She had flirted with the idea of retiring in 2004, when her house at Chateau Neuf was broken into. The men had worn T-shirts over their heads and waved guns. —But they were old guns, she explained. She leaned forward in her chair, warming to the tale. —I told them that if they wanted to kill me, that was okay, because I knew that God would take care of me.

—Do you know about God? she had asked her attackers. —Because I don't think he would want you to be doing what you're doing!

She chuckled at the memory.

Joanna had already fought off cancer, and still kept the keys to the hospital storage depots; once, in a rainstorm, Haitian doctors had carried her over the mud puddles in the middle of the night to obtain supplies for an emergency surgery. It was a story she told with a laugh. She liked to feel useful.

She hoped to be buried alongside her husband in the small graveyard overlooking Mòn De Tèt, so that when the trumpet sounded and the Lord came back to claim them, they could go up together. Her daughters Barbara and Tamara were already buried beside him.

I hadn't been able to say goodbye to Tamara, as she had died of a seizure in her early twenties, when I was still in college. But on a previous trip to Haiti I had seen Barbara. Joni had pushed her gently across the compound in a wheelchair. She was almost unrecognizable. Her long black hair fell loose around her face and her eyes were vacant. She had developed chronic fatigue syndrome, and the medical explanation was that self-prescribed medication from the hospital pharmacy had caused irreversible neurological damage.

Joanna had hired Haitian nurses to care for her daughter round-the-clock and had hung Barbara's oil paintings on the walls of the Rose Cottage. On the afternoon I'd visited, Joanna had leaned over the bed to stroke her daughter's bruised arms and exhorted in a chipper voice: You can do it, Barb, you've got lots of friends here to help you!

One of the Haitian nurses stood behind them in the doorway, her lips tight with worry.

—The sun is shining, it rained last night, Joanna told the unresponsive Barbara, her voice bouyant. —Be happy that you're here in Haiti. You have to get well so that you can help me run the hospital!

Barbara appeared to be the one chink in Joanna's armor of optimism. She had confided to me that some nights she went home so discouraged, she just wanted to cry. But then she'd lifted her chin and smiled at me. She said that to cheer herself up she would pray: Lord, this was a bad day. Help me to remember what the Haitians say—Maybe tomorrow will be a better day.

I learned of Barbara's death in a newsletter from Joanna a few months later, which included an anonymous poem: *When you are lonely and sick of heart . . . bury your sorrows in doing good deeds.*

Barbara's paintings still hung on the wall of the Rose Cottage, graceful silhouettes of Haitian women with baskets balanced effortlessly on their heads. I paused before asking Joanna: Would it have changed your mind if you had known that you would bury two children and a husband here?

—No, Joanna answered firmly. —You have to take life as it comes. I didn't even think about that.

She explained that when she was eight years old, she had told her mother that she wanted to be a sunbeam and light up some dark corner of God's earth. —And now that I am getting older, I tell the Haitians that I am trying to be a *koukouy* for *Jezi.* She grinned impishly.

—A firefly for Jesus?

—Yes. And the Haitians, they like that. You know, we saw fireflies our first night in Haiti. I looked up and I said to Bill: How nice of God to light up the dark corners!

The Doctor, having learned that Bartolomé de las Casas had caught fireflies so he could read his Bible at night, had given it a try. Joanna lowered her voice dramatically, as if telling a story to a grandchild.

—He turned out all the lights . . . and it worked! Her scraggly eyebrows lifted like a flock of wild birds, and her eyes twinkled.

A faded photograph captured Joanna and the Doctor at their stubbornly defiant five-hundredth-anniversary celebration of Columbus's arrival in the New World. But Columbus's empire, like so many of the conquerors who followed, had dissolved beneath him.

—This is one of my favorite pictures of Bill, Joanna confided, noticing my interest. —Do you know that when he died, he had about twenty pairs of suspenders? All the men in the yard asked me if they could have a pair. It was the only thing of his they wanted.

She grinned.

I walked slowly around the compound after I left Joanna. The sidewalk to Jericho School was cracked and buckled by the roots of a towering eucalyptus. Smooth gray bark pulled away from the trunk in tattered strips, blood-bright against the tender, exposed green. The flat roof where I used to climb up and stare at the stars was hidden from view.

It was hard to imagine that Joanna would ever give up on the hospital; she would rather die fighting than admit she had lost. But the irony of the tropics was that all institutions eventually collapsed: termites burrowed into rafters; there were rodents, fires, hurricanes, earthquakes. Things decayed, and as they disintegrated, old stones were taken for new buildings or housed behind glass in a dusty museum. Unless one was ruthlessly and tirelessly engaged in preserving the empire—at all costs—it would return to the jungle from which it was carved.

—I will go this far, Joanna had admitted to me when I was first trying to piece together the history of the hospital and its rupture with the Board of International Ministries. —Maybe we made a mistake. Maybe we shouldn't have done what we did. But we did it. What can you do?

I walked beside Joanna when she hobbled over to the pediatric ward later that afternoon with candy and a bag of plastic toys. She leaned heavily on my arm. She was pleased that people in Limbé now called her *Grann*—Grandmother. She liked to spend an hour each day playing with the orphans, though her own health was increasingly fragile.

As we moved slowly through the hospital, a barefoot woman in a head scarf stopped to thank Joanna for her dedication, the famous wife of a famous doctor who had saved the lives of thousands.

Fewer earthquake victims had come to the hospital than I'd expected, but there were more options for medical care in the Limbé Valley than there used to be, including clinics staffed by Cuban doctors.

The upstairs chapel where we had held our ill-fated medieval feast had years ago been converted into a storage depot, its shelves lined with donated shoes, bed pads, plastic Easter eggs, bathing suits, sweaters, eyeglasses, toothpaste, and a Mexican doll with an oversize sombrero marked "50 cents" in crumbling masking tape—gifts from supporters eager to help the missionary cause. Everything was dirty.

The children in the pediatric ward sat in wooden chairs in a loose semicircle around Joanna as she fumbled with the sticky wrappers of donated candy canes. A blind boy reached into her apron pocket for more candy, and she tickled him under the chin. I remembered how uncomfortable I had felt when I visited the pediatric ward as a teenager, but Joanna seemed utterly at ease.

—I used to just bring them toys, Joanna explained, —then someone sent M&M's and they really liked them, so then I got suckers and cheese bits, and someone suggested that they might like peanut butter, but the cooks scolded me for that in the kitchen, said I was using up what they bought for the doctors.

A boy with emaciated legs jabbed at a wobbling M&M, but he could not make his fingers close around it, so he slid off his chair and lay on the floor to lick at it.

—What do you enjoy about this? I asked Joanna, still trying to understand why she kept coming back year after year to dispense such meager kindness.

—I think it's nice to see them happy. She squinted up at me, her wrinkled face beaming.

Toys spilled across the table, and children grabbed favorites. A boy squeezed a toy monkey, which thrust out its tongue. A red plastic car raced across the cement floor until it bumped against my foot and rolled over.

Joanna seemed happy dispensing treats to adoring children. At almost ninety, she was still chipping away at her life's work. If any of her nine hundred–plus supporters complained of toothaches or swollen knees, Joanna replied with a poem: *Oh, a trouble's a ton, or a trouble's an ounce, or a trouble is what you make it. And it isn't the fact that you're hurt that counts, but only how did you take it?*

Joanna's optimistic newsletters were largely responsible for the salaries of the nearly one hundred Haitian nurses and lab technicians, pharmacists, yard workers, cooks, and doctors still on the payroll.

—Keep praying for us, the hospital needs it, she instructed when I leaned down to say goodbye. Her parting words into the microphone were: Don't forget to delete the bad stuff!

She waved jauntily, a wrinkled empress of a dilapidated kingdom.

I knew already that I would fail her. I could not tell the story of the compound without the hurt and heartache, the moments of betrayal and doubt. Even in the Bible that Joanna loved and had built her life around—a book that I, too, found mesmerizing, though half the time, like my father, I wanted to hurl it through a window—the bitter stories had not been left out.

The broken shards were part of the whole: a mosaic composed of all that we feared, hoped for, trusted, sacrificed, loved, and lost. There was beauty, but not in the soaring, redemptive way we imagined when we loftily hinted to our supporters that we were bringing hope to Haiti.

I suspected that, at her best moments, Joanna realized the truth—the truth of all philanthropic enterprises: that she needed Haiti and the hospital more than they needed her. She wanted to die with her boots on, just like her husband. A firefly for Jesus.

Perhaps, after she was gone, a rapprochement would become possible between the missionary hospital and the Convention Baptiste d'Haiti. I wanted to believe that the community that had laid the foundation stones so many years earlier could recruit a team of visionary professionals to reassess the hospital's priorities and restructure the aging institution to reflect the future instead of the past. To take on the burden of responsibility for Haiti's welfare, without recognizing the self-sufficiency and determination of the Haitians themselves, could lead only to grief.

As I stepped outside the hospital gates, children sprinted through twisting alleyways, and women balanced sloshing buckets of water on their heads. Music from a tinny radio floated over into the empty compound. Life was on the other side of the walls.

Cherylene

Gonaïves, 2010

I HADN'T SEEN Cherylene in almost a decade. Having spent so much of my childhood resenting her, I wanted to atone for my apathy, if that was even possible. Having already scouted the area, my father had given up hope. Still, I managed to convince him to at least help me look for her. I wanted to know that she was okay.

In Gonaïves, we climbed down from the back of an open pickup and brushed the dust from our backpacks. The heat pressed in like a damp towel. My father thought that he recognized the old bus station, but most of the streets had changed locations after the floods. The concrete block house where Cherylene's relatives had lived was nowhere to be found.

On a side street, we paused to ask strangers if anyone knew a young woman named Cherylene who had once lived in this neighborhood. She would be in her mid-twenties and would have a pink scar on her chest from a cooking accident. We didn't know her last name.

At first no one remembered her. Then a woman with a raspy voice stood and gestured for us to follow. She led us down an alley to a small unpainted house.

She knocked confidently. A barefoot girl opened the door, perhaps six or seven years old. With her hair in braids and her lower lip trembling, she looked like a more delicate version of the saucy six-year-old I remembered, the girl who had asked to keep my sunglasses.

I knelt down to explain that we were looking for an old friend named Cherylene.

The girl answered shyly that yes, her mother was named Cherylene.

—Does she have a scar on her chest? my father asked.

She nodded yes, then shook her head no. She rocked slowly from one foot to the other as if embarrassed by the attention.

A few minutes later, the girl's mother returned. She smiled but looked confused.

My father shook his head. It was not Ti Marcel.

———

She had survived other calamities: infancy; childhood; the burn that left the skin on her stomach and arms bubbled and pink.

I wanted to believe that Ti Marcel's luck had held. It was not unreasonable to expect that she would have survived adolescence in the slums of Gonaïves, where my father had last seen her, in the crooked house whose walls buzzed with insects in the dry season and whose floor in the rainy season was clammy with mud.

Whenever she could invent an excuse, I imagined, Cherylene would have visited her wealthier relatives in the concrete-block house whose solid walls kept out the rain. Perhaps, if they forgot she was there, she sat on the floor to listen to the radio with the volume turned low. She would have been aware of the injustice. Adolescents are keenly aware of inequity.

But she was nothing if not a fighter. And I hoped that she had emerged into young adulthood with her fighting spirit intact.

She may have watched her aunt die slowly, seen the slow collapse of beauty into despair. But she must have understood, too, the heedless joy of children, their bare feet pounding the dirt in a game of tag, their ragged shirts flapping like sails as they shouted and ran.

I could imagine her, like Olynda as a girl, sorting through piles of rice and beans, her callused hands deftly seeking out the hidden pebbles and the blackened, rotten culls as she sent them flying across the swept dirt.

Did she wish at times that my father had adopted her? That he had challenged her father's parental claims and uprooted her from her homeland? My sisters and I never balanced sloshing buckets of water on our heads to cook the evening meal. We were expected to make our beds, fold clothes, set the table. If we complained, my father was the first to remind us that, indeed, life was not fair: just ask the kids in Haiti.

Adrift in the world, Cherylene must have learned how to fend for herself, to disbelieve in saviors. She never wrote my father a letter, never asked for a handout.

At times—like every girl poised on the edge of womanhood—she must have hated her body, hated the slick pink scar that swirled like a hot flood across her torso, wished instead for the smooth, unblemished skin of the models on the hair-product advertisements. On other days, I want to believe, she would have paraded through her universe like a Taíno chieftess, deigned to snarl at the critics, and ignored the rest. She would have savored a fresh mango when it was in season, sheltered under the overhang of a tin roof to wait out a storm.

I could imagine her at the river, sent to do the washing with the other *ti moun,* the cast-off poor relations, standing to survey her territory with her hands on her hips. Though her nerves may have been worn down to wire shards by the wet heat and the endless slapping of soiled laundry against smooth round river rocks, I wanted to believe that she nevertheless would have dabbled her toes in the water just to feel the delicious softness flutter over her skin.

Hers was a loud laugh, a disquieting laugh, and when it seized her, she covered her mouth with her hands, slapped her palms to her thighs, clapped, roared, fell in a heap in the dust, gasped, wiped her eyes, and then broke out laughing again. She was alive.

Is she still?

Perhaps, like hundreds of other young women, Cherylene moved to Port-au-Prince to find a job. Before the earthquake, perhaps she was able to set up a food stand to sell Chiclet gum and Maggi bouillon cubes from a wooden tray at the edge of a sewer-clogged gutter. Or perhaps she found work at a missionary school for orphans, where she wrung out the laundry or swept the floors.

But it may be that I picture her this way—envying the luxuries of those more fortunate than herself—because it reflects my limited imagination. Perhaps the poverty is mine, not hers.

When I take stock of all that I possess (running water, Internet access, a mortgage, a passport), I cannot conceive of a world in which Cherylene feels herself this fortunate. And yet why should I presume that because I possess more material goods than the daughter of a subsistence farmer and a mother without access to mental health care, I therefore possess a life that is more worth living? I want to believe that she knows her own inestimable worth and pities my ignorance.

Perhaps, like me, she found someone who looked her in the eyes and understood the value of a woman who knew how to fight. Perhaps she let herself be cradled: dropped her defenses, buried her face, and let herself be held while her body shook and sobbed its heartbroken, lovesick anger at the world's deep injustice and defiant beauty.

I want to believe that she cradled children of her own, that she looked down and touched their downy heads as they nursed, her body rippling with pleasure and pain as they gulped her body's very substance transmuted into breast milk. The miracle she never tasted.

The truth of Cherylene's life—what she loved, feared, hated, and hoped for—was a story that only she could tell. I could only guess at it and, like my father and countless others, spend the rest of my life haunted by what I had failed to understand.

With or without intervention, Ayiti would continue to survive—just as it always had—leaving a far deeper imprint on its would-be saviors than any faltering legacy we might leave behind.

No more could I look down from on high, smug with pity. The cloud chariots had dissipated; all of our fates were intertwined. Those of the farmers on the eroded hillsides, the activists and executives cushioned by privilege, the schoolchildren, the lovers, the prisoners. We all belonged to this broken, beloved earth. And the earth's sorrows would leave a mark on all of us.

Work and Rest

Oregon, 2012

I AM STILL working to make peace with my parents, though I think I have made my peace with Haiti. Proud, unbroken, resilient, beautiful, devastated Haiti no longer seems to me a nation that is waiting to be saved.

My father also believes this, and then forgets. He still wants to go down in history as a man who made a difference, in his own country as well as in Haiti. He hikes through old-growth forests to collect yew berries, the red seed of immortality, or along railroad tracks in the rain, stung by yellow jackets and oily with poison oak, to collect snowberry and mahonia for his seed-collection business in Oregon. He laughs when I point out the obvious metaphor: how, in the waning years of his life, he collects seeds to bury in the ground so that new life will emerge. He assures me that he does not feel old.

Like the ant in the parable, he is driven to put away resources against the coming winter. He picks wild plums for jam, grows half an acre of vegetables in a garden that extends further every year, tends the chickens, plants native trees along the creek. He rests only in winter, when the last of the native seeds have been gathered, and then he goes back to Haiti, to walk the eroded hills.

I recognize this same obstinacy in myself and fear it. I must choose deliberately to rest, to make time for my children, to make time for joy—struggling, always, against the guilt that I inherited. Will we ever be free from the burdens our parents carried?

When I finally made it home to my children after reporting on the earthquake, my boys dove into my arms and refused to let go. A canceled flight out of Cap-Haïtien had left me stranded for two extra days in Florida, where I stayed with Olynda and her utterly charming seventeen-year-old son, who kicked his skateboard under the couch and showed me images of his latest clothing design projects.

My two-year-old son, who had stayed up past bedtime to meet me at the airport in his pj's, fell asleep as soon as I curled up next to him in bed, his breathing soft and even.

When I tucked in my eldest, he asked: Mom, why did you have to go?

I rubbed his back and tousled his hair. —To listen to people's stories, I said, trying to keep my voice light.

—But why? he asked. His voice was plaintive; it was as close as he would get to saying that he had missed me.

I paused, suddenly aware that I was filling my father's shoes. —I didn't have to go, I told him. —I chose to. I wanted to be there.

As soon as I said it, all of my own childhood anxieties came flooding back: the fear that my father didn't find me worthy of attention, as compelling as Haiti. I tried again in terms that my four-year-old son would understand.

—You know how you get so excited about stars and planets and solar systems? I asked. He nodded. —When I listen to people's stories, I find it exciting in the same way.

He cocked his head and smiled at me. —No, you're teasing, he insisted.

—It's true! I laughed. —We're different that way: Daddy, me, you, your brother. We each find different things beautiful and interesting, and that's okay. We still love each other.

—Tell me about when I was a baby, he said abruptly, his voice sleepy. And so I did. I told him how I used to carry him around the house in a sling when he was tiny, how I once took him to a three-hour Shakespeare play when he was ten months old (not realizing it would go on so long), and how, afterward, two British ladies complimented me on how wonderful he was.

His eyelids drooped and I ran my fingers across his eyebrows, trying to convince him—to convince myself—that I would never be gone too long, that I would always come home to him, even if only to build block towers and kick a ball around the yard.

I would always carry within me the competing desires to engage with the world and to retreat from it, and I hoped, just as my father once hoped for me, that my children would one day do their small part to make the world more beautiful and more just. But at that moment, my little boy needed to know that he mattered more to me than the stories of strangers. Because he does. We belong to each other. I am his mother; he is my son. Just as I am, in spite of everything, my father's daughter.

Some months later, at the end of four long days at the kitchen table of a Franciscan convent along the Columbia River Gorge—having left my children yet again, this time to write about deforestation and drought in Haiti—I noticed a gap in the rain and pulled on my boots for a walk. There were birds hidden in the Douglas fir trees, and a waterfall thundered endlessly. Within minutes, I felt restored to stillness.

Until, that is, I noticed a green rope of ivy starting to work its way around the trunk of a fir tree, and my father's fierce dislike of invasive species took hold. Ivy has already strangled thousands of acres of Oregon woods. Once it reaches a height of two to three feet, it circles tree trunks and puts out dark berries to tempt the birds, the seeds shat out on other sections of the forest, spreading the blight.

I reached down to uproot a tuft of ivy. A long white feathery root clung to the soil. Dead matted leaves and pine needles fell aside as I yanked harder, pulling up its latticework of roots. It was satisfying work, until I started to think about how each overlooked root fragment would shove out new growth—and these were not my woods; I would not be there to ensure that whatever I'd inadvertently left behind would be uprooted later.

I paused, dirt under my fingernails, palms already aching, and realized that I could spend all morning pulling ivy and never finish the job. What was the point of trying if, in the end, it was a losing battle?

I thought of my father and of the deforestation in Haiti—the numbing downward spiral. I didn't want to admit defeat and walk away, but it felt like a hopeless task. I reached for a tuft of glossy leaves, then realized that they were connected to a massive root as big around as my thumb. I braced myself against a tree trunk and pulled harder, my back straining. Finally, the root ripped loose, and I realized that it had been cut, long before, with pruning shears. Someone had already been here. My mind leaped ahead with immense relief: Others would follow. It was not up to me to complete the work.

As humans, we are capable of leaving enormous desolation in our wake. Few old-growth trees remained after the loggers broke camp in the Columbia River Gorge and even now a handful of fireworks, carelessly tossed, can torch thousands of acres of wilderness in a matter of days.

In Ayiti, after five centuries of plunder, little remains of the rainforest that Columbus once described as immeasurably lush and green. And yet, even if the meager biodiversity that survives represents only a shadow of the earth's former glory, it is still worth protecting. We are more aware than we used to be of our fragility. We, too, are learning the hard way about drought, fires, floods, earthquakes, and hurricanes. If we do not rein in our appetite for consumption, we will lose landscapes and creatures that we can never replace.

As a recovering missionary's daughter, it feels like something of a consolation to recognize that the part I have to play in protecting this beloved earth is laughably small (it is not mine alone to save), but it matters that we care. Love might only be a broken song. But I can still add my voice to that faltering music.

I left the ripped-up ivy dangling from a snowberry bush, for I had other work to return to: a book to write, children to love, students to encourage. I repeated a benediction under my breath: *Let it be enough.*

To Arrive Where We Started and Know the Place for the First Time

Haiti, 2012

FOR SEVERAL YEARS after the earthquake, I returned to Haiti every spring. As a child, I believed that we missionaries had been sent because we had something to give, but Haiti has survived the unspeakable again and again and stood its ground.

Ayiti has learned, through grief, how to endure. And it was in this extraordinary country, which we so naively tried to save, that I first glimpsed what it meant to be fully alive.

If you have come to help me, writes Indigenous Australian artist and activist Lilla Watson, *then you are wasting your time. But if you have come because your liberation is bound up in mine then let us work together.*

My family had moved to Haiti to try to help, but instead, we learned our limitations. Failure can be a wise friend. We felt crushed at times; found it difficult to breathe; and yet the experience carved into each of us an understanding of loss, the weight of compassion. We learned how small we were when measured against the world's great sorrow.

Every time I tracked down another missionary from the compound, I realized that we had all been shaped by those same grinding forces. Ironically, one of the most significant lessons I learned from the missionaries was that it can be a gift to be the outsider, to get it wrong most of the time; to practice humility when I thought that I had the world all figured out. And I have come to believe that if we move toward the things we are afraid of, then we will find them changed—and ourselves changed in the process.

One year I picked up a rental car in Miami and zigzagged across the state of Florida, driving eight hundred miles in three days to interview former missionary kids I had grown up with, now scattered into separate lives. Most admitted that they never talked about Haiti with friends in the States. A few of the adopted children had been taunted as "Fa-tians" (fake Haitians) by Haitian coworkers when it was clear that they couldn't speak Kreyòl. A heaviness that felt like guilt hung over most of us: that we could have so much when others had so little. Only a handful had returned to visit Haiti.

Missionary kids one generation older than me told stories that I had never heard spoken aloud: about Uncle S____, the charismatic pastor whose wife allegedly had been raped by soldiers and could not bear to be touched; the man who laughed and lingered over coffee with the missionary wives; the man who had lured who knows how many girls into his home and violated them, manipulating their innocence into a violent, self-loathing shame from which it took many almost a lifetime to break free.

The indignation that I had felt for years toward the missionary women for their prim, terrified aversion to anything that touched on adolescent sexuality suddenly shifted into grief. They were trying, however imperfectly, to protect us from what they themselves had suffered. Not for the first time, I wished that we had learned, earlier, to speak our fears and sorrows aloud rather than bury them until they festered. Only when shame is spoken aloud can it be stripped of its power.

Ken Heneise, decades after the last greenhouse at the Ag Center had been scrapped for parts, sat with me under an oak tree in northern Florida, at a military school where he taught organic farming to court-assigned juvenile delinquents.

—One of the things I've had to work out is the whole mystique of missionary service, he admitted. —The more you sacrificed, the more you destroyed your family, meant that you were even more respected for what you had done for God. His voice sounded weary. —It proved you were unafraid; you didn't count the cost.

Our eyes followed the honeybees as they dipped and hovered, then disappeared into the dark mouth of the hive. Ken's hair had gone gray in the intervening years, but otherwise he was as I remembered him: lanky, fastidious, affable. After leaving the mission field, he had drifted in and out of various jobs. He hadn't attended church in years, fed up with organized religion and tormented as to why God would seem to answer his prayers but ignore the prayers of a Haitian father for his sick child.

For a few years, burned out and exhausted, he had tried to sever all ties to Haiti. He'd worked as a school bus driver and had built green-certified houses in Florida. He had all but given up on agriculture until he learned of the horticulture job at the military school, where his precisely ordered flower beds and trim greenhouses earned him frequent commendations from the deputy director.

—Your dad and I clashed terribly, Ken admitted. —When you're young, you're so much more certain about things. He kicked at an acorn, nudging it into the subsoil.

I'd visited the Ag Center on a recent trip to Haiti and had found it almost unrecognizable. Ken's carefully grafted orchard of tropical-hardy grapefruits, lemons, and limes had been cleared to make room for a helicopter landing pad for the UN.

—We want to be remembered, but maybe we're not supposed to build institutions that last, he said with a wry smile.

As I stood to go, he told me with a surprised laugh: We're going to celebrate Earth Day at the military base this year for the first time. How about that?

Even with the bitter taste of failure in his mouth, he hadn't lost the missionary impulse.

Like almost everyone from the compound, I'd lost touch with David and Emily Hodges after we left Haiti. I'd heard stories of how David had thundered and roared when the Hodges family had gone to battle with the American Baptist Board of International Ministries, insisting that his father rewrite the constitution of the missionary hospital to turn Hôpital le Bon Samaritain into a private family-run institution, and yet those who knew him well insisted that he was a changed man. David and his family had eventually left the compound to live for a year in a remote rural community in Pennsylvania that was dedicated to peace, before settling in Indiana.

Tiny Emily, whose long dark hair was now streaked with gray, set a plate for me at the table when I drove from Chicago to visit them. —It's good to see you again, she said. Her soft, rough voice was matter-of-fact as she served up a heaping plate of beans and rice with *poul* Kreyòl. She had a farm girl's impatience with wasted words.

David's wild Einstein shock of hair was as unkempt as I remembered. He shook my hand firmly, then sat abruptly at the kitchen table, one long leg folded over the other. He lifted his chin slightly and peered at me as if to gauge my significance. —My training is as a physicist, he intoned. —It's not the long term you have to look at. You have to look at the good you do now, not the good you do over the long term. Nothing is going to survive in the end. In the end, everything is going to become nothing.

He raised an eyebrow and dared me to argue.

He told me that in his father's good years, he had known that the hospital wasn't going to survive indefinitely. —We made my father believe that the mission board was his enemy. I'm not proud of those days, he continued, clearly determined to shoulder the blame. —And I won't even give extenuating circumstances; we should have known better.

David's eyes met mine as he handed down his fierce, unapologetic verdict. —Both sides behaved badly. It was about power, and greed.

After his father died, David had helped to run the hospital along with his mother and siblings. David's sons fell asleep to the chant of submachine gunfire and the beat of U.S. occupation helicopters overhead. They made escape plans and slept in their clothes in case they needed to flee from an attack in the middle of the night.

David's epiphany had taken place in a Limbé jail cell, after he openly challenged a soldier—a childhood friend—who had broken in to hospital property to look for weapons (none were found). The other missionaries were frantic. Barbara tried to bring David dinner, but he was too proud to accept it. Instead, the prisoners shared their meals with him. He spent only one night in prison, but it was enough. He had seen what he needed to see.

After David was released, he took steps to undo the family veto power, eventually restructuring the board of the missionary hospital to include pastors from the Convention Baptiste d'Haiti.

—It was not ours, no matter what we said. We did not have the right to do what we did.

He cleared his throat, sounding very much like his father. —The Haitians need to rule themselves. Toss all the foreigners out. Definitely the UN.

—Even though you would be in Haiti right now to help if you could, I pointed out. Having moved to Haiti as a seven-year-old, he still dreamed in Kreyòl. It wasn't until he was in his late forties that he had moved to the U.S. as a full-time resident. He still felt out of place among his fellow Americans.

David pressed his fingers against his forehead and closed his eyes. —I'm in exile. I remember it every day.

It was four-thirty in the morning before we said good night. A few hours later, I woke to tea and toast in the kitchen with Emily, who wanted to know what good books I had read lately. David was already gone, but Emily and I hugged our mugs of tea and filled the morning with words.

When I met with John Sundquist later that afternoon in Chicago, it had been fifteen years since the American Baptist Board of International Ministries went to battle with Dr. Hodges over who owned the missionary hospital. Sundquist received me graciously, his square face offset by a crown of white hair. Teaspoons and saucers rattled delicately as he fixed me a cup of tea.

The problem, as he had observed it during his tenure as board chair of International Ministries, was that Haiti was too close to the U.S.; the poorest country in the western hemisphere within shouting distance of the richest. Churches in Haiti never matured because every one of them had a pipeline back to the U.S.; dependency was a big issue. He was aware that it was a temptation for missionaries not to point out the strengths of a country when perceived weakness drew heftier donations.

It was not hard to imagine how Hodges and Sundquist, equally admired in their respective fields, had locked horns.

—I had prayed for Bill Hodges since I was younger than you, Sundquist informed me. —We don't want to confess it in public, but we have missionaries, and we have stars. He was a star: the ideal missionary.

He conceded that it was unfortunate, but he'd been forced to act. —I didn't want to remove the king and put resources at risk, but I had to do it. He was a lone ranger. We're not meant to be lone rangers.

Only once did his patrician demeanor crack. He leaned forward with his elbows on his knees and admitted: It is still painful. And it should be. I mean, we blew it. Every piece of this puzzle blew it.

When I said goodbye and stepped outside, seagulls guttered and soared along the edge of Lake Michigan. I took in a long breath of cold air. It seemed that we had all failed. And yet hidden in the wreckage was a reminder that felt somehow reassuring—failure was not the end of the story.

When I asked my sisters if they wanted to return with me to Haiti, Meadow was so hesitant that I didn't even try to talk her into it. Rose, rather sensibly, said no. The first post-earthquake presidential elections in Haiti had prompted a travel warning as, in a stroke of pure lunatic surrealism, both Baby Doc Duvalier and Aristide had returned from exile to take up residence in Port-au-Prince. It was as if Elvis and Tupac had returned from beyond the grave to cohost a reality show on military coups.

My sisters remembered Haiti as a place of uncertainty: rocks hurled at our roof, loud voices over the wall, gunshots, the evacuation. It was a line from Terry Tempest Williams that finally convinced Meadow to join me: *The question that I'm constantly asking myself is, What are we afraid of? I think it's important for us to follow that line of fear, because that is ultimately our line of growth.*

We met at the Cap-Haïtien airport. Meadow had flown in from

Washington, D.C., where she was finishing a science and policy fellowship at the EPA. Steve and Nancy James brought us over the mountains
to Haut-Limbé. We walked arm in arm under the mango trees, past
the yellow concrete seminary house where once we cried ourselves to
sleep at night. Meadow couldn't stop smiling.

—I had forgotten all the things I loved about living here, she admitted, surprised.

—Crazy, isn't it, I said, that this place we were so afraid of could also
be so full of joy?

With six-foot-four Tony Casséus as our guide, we hurtled over
potholed roads and drank Prestige beer with off-duty policemen and
fishermen playing dominoes, then glided over coral reefs in a wooden
fishing boat when the Jeep broke down. We sat facing the waves as the
sun sank into the sea. Tony ordered another round of beers and a plate
of fresh-caught ceviche.

—Haiti is a beautiful country, it is very important that people understand the beauty of Haiti. For a moment, his slurred voice had the
urgent cadence of a Baptist preacher. —People don't understand this.
They only see the negative side of Haiti.

He was painfully aware that, as a third-generation missionary son, he
had been expected, at least by some, to step into his father's role at the
Baptist University. A few still saw him as the black sheep of the family,
but he assured us that he had made his peace with his parents.

I offered him the benediction that an irreverent and holy vicar in
London had given me: *Forgive yourself. Forgive others. Go in peace.*

We clinked glasses.

The missionary mantle, prickly with expectation, was not easily
shaken off, and yet it had been our baptism into sorrow and beauty.

On our last night in Haut-Limbé, Meadow and I cupped in our hands
fledgling parakeets that had fallen out of a nest in a royal palm tree and
were being syringe-fed by Nancy. I sat up late to write, perched on the
end of a twin bed in our shared room. The moon behind the clouds
was so breathtaking that I didn't want to sleep. My pen scratched against

the page as I tried to set down the wind in the leaves, the distant voices through the trees, tinny music from a radio.

Suddenly, Meadow sat bolt upright in bed. Without her glasses, I was only a dim blur in the shadows. —Is that you? she asked, her voice worried, then she leaned back against the pillow, still woozy from half-sleep. —Shouldn't you be writing in the closet for old times' sake?

I had not seen Suzette, the unstoppable ringleader of the Jericho School Circus, since I was nine years old, but she was exactly as I remembered her: a human being fully alive. Her laugh loud, her compassion quick, her insights bracing.

At her home in the mountains, above Port-au-Prince, we sipped Haitian coffee and caught up on stories. After dinner, she brought out the good stuff: homemade *kremas*, raw coconut washed with *klerin*, saved for special occasions.

Willys Geffrard, her husband, was from an old Haitian family, and the two had spent years running development projects across Africa and Haiti. We stayed up until midnight in a passionate conversation with a friend of theirs, a young Haitian economist and business owner. Daniel Jean-Louis explained to me why the missionary habit of hosting volunteer church groups on their properties—without paying hotel taxes—undercut the local economy. Worse yet was when volunteer groups brought their own carpenters and imported supplies; their well-meaning benevolence put local builders and merchants out of work.

He cited a particularly egregious example from after the earthquake: hundreds of jars of donated peanut butter, purchased in the U.S. and shipped to Haiti for the people in the tent cities.

—Peanut butter! he repeated, shaking his head. —We grow our own peanuts here.

Jean-Louis explained that money entered the economy every time a transaction took place: when the peanuts were purchased from the farmers; when the jars of peanut butter were sold. However, when the peanut butter was donated, not only did money fail to enter the local economy, but Haitian farmers could not even sell their produce because the market was flooded.

—No nation has ever pulled itself out of poverty through charity, he insisted.

Suzette raised her eyebrows at me. She would always be my favorite teacher, pushing me to think harder, to ask better questions. Had we stayed up all night, we still wouldn't have run out of stories, but she had an early flight to catch. We drifted onto the porch to watch the stars emerge over the mountains.

As we drove back down the mountains into Port-au-Prince in the dark, Willys felt a tug at the wheel and got out to check the tires but, seeing nothing amiss, kept driving. He drove carefully around the potholes. Schoolchildren congregated under streetlamps, bent over their homework. Flickering kerosene lamps illuminated charcoal *rechos*. Suddenly, without warning, the entire front-left wheel of the vehicle bumped loose and rolled across the road, narrowly missing a line of food vendors seated beside the road.

An overloaded *tap tap* laid on its horn and swerved to avoid an accident. We jumped out of the car and were immediately surrounded.

The missing wheel was already being rolled back across the street by teenagers. Within minutes, they had helped Willys jack up the car and were searching the gutters for the missing lug nuts by the light of their cell phones. One young man was standing in the dark, waving a tree branch to slow the oncoming vehicles.

Suzette and I stood behind the car, taking turns swinging a tiny flashlight, noting the absurdity of our situation. How was it that in a city clogged with earthquake debris—a place too often viewed only with pity or fear—complete strangers had dropped everything to help us without asking anything in return?

Schoolgirls walked past us, singing in the dark.

Li Sanble Ou

Artibonite, 2012

LIKE ME, MY parents kept finding excuses to return to Haiti. They spent a month in a tiny village above Saint-Marc as volunteers with Mercy Corps, helping to build fuel-efficient stoves made of clay and organic material (rotting mangoes worked well as a binding agent when they were in season). The combustion chamber burned off excess carbon monoxide as well as particulate matter, and small sticks could be used instead of charcoal to boil water and cook meals—a strike against deforestation. It was also, for the first time in a long while, a collaboration that suited both of my parents: my mother got to roll clay between her fingers and talk while she cooked; my father had people's attention while he talked about saving the trees. They were thrilled when their YouTube videos about the stoves got hits from refugee camps and eco-lodges around the world (the videos were even more popular with doomsday preppers).

Just before I set out to join them, my father emailed from Haiti to say that he needed me to call a warehouse in the Midwest, order ten to fifteen plastic feed tubs, have them shipped to a farm supply store a forty-five-minute drive from my house, then hand-carry them to Ti Bwa. I tried to imagine myself lugging a four-foot-tall stack of brightly colored plastic buckets through the airport in West Palm Beach, where I would be staying with Olynda for a few nights, then tapped out a terse reply—perhaps he should find a Haitian importer who could procure the tubs and sell them locally for a small profit to make the project sustainable. I was trying to be diplomatic.

When my unsatisfactory reply kicked off a tense round of emails with my father, I confided to my husband: I'm not even sure he likes me.

David shook his head. —I don't think either of you realizes how much you admire each other.

The night before I left, I reminded my two boys to please chew with their mouths closed and not to drop their food on the floor; they told me that the saddest part of their day was that I was leaving for Haiti in the morning.

I threw on my backpack at four-forty-five a.m. David dragged himself out of bed, bleary-eyed and warm from sleep, to put his arms around me. —Don't forget to come home again, he said, and tightened his grip around my shoulders.

A taxi-driver friend was waiting in the driveway. As we raced to the airport in the dark, a thousand frogs hurtled through the rain in the glare of the headlights. In my bag, I'd tucked a hoard of Snickers bars for my mother. Stacked beside me in the backseat, like an ungainly peace offering, were half a dozen plastic feed tubs for my father.

My parents had not yet made it down the mountain from the village of Ti Bwa when I arrived, so the manager at the Mercy Corps office put me through on a cell phone.

After I hung up she asked: Did you tell them that you brought the tubs?

I hadn't.

She laughed. —Because when I asked them if you were going to bring any tubs, your dad said: No, she didn't want to bring them; she's really stubborn, and it's our fault because we made her that way.

It was nice, at least, to be able to laugh about it.

By the time my parents arrived, exhausted and fractious, my mother was on the verge of laryngitis. My father just worked until he collapsed— body sprawled out on the concrete floor, hat over his eyes, sound asleep—and then got up and kept going, no matter how painfully his muscles ached. The other expats in the office were surprised that he didn't like to take time off and relax; no trips to the beach, no downtime. My mother sighed melodramatically. —He's not a normal husband.

They spent the better part of the afternoon arguing over the format of an upcoming class on how to build the stoves. My father was in his stubborn obstructionist mode, determined to poke a hole into every suggestion.

—That's not true, Jon, and you and I both know it! I overheard from the next room. And yet, despite the grumbling and inflammatory statements, the raised voices and the worst-case scenarios, they emerged from the negotiation perfectly cheerful.

—You're my good-luck charm, Jonny, she told him with a winsome smile when he got the water purifier to work.

In Ti Bwa, they shared a single bed in a narrow room off an unused classroom, a box pushed up against the door of the leaking bathroom to keep the resident rat from going through their backpacks while they slept. There was no electricity, but my mother hung a solar lamp out the window to charge each day. The lack of amenities didn't appear to bother them overly much; it was a bit like backpacking—they both knew how to travel light. Even in the States, they did not indulge themselves with undue luxuries, which we three girls had always pined for; we couldn't wait to escape their frugality. In Ti Bwa, they stored shallots and peppers in a cupboard, along with bags of spaghetti and beans, which they brought as gifts to households who invited them over for a meal. By the end of their stay, they knew half the people in the village by name.

—This is my daughter, my mother would explain when she stopped to introduce me. —She is thirty-six years old. She is married. I have grandchildren.

—*Oh! Li sanble ou!* She looks just like you! was the inevitable reply.

At which my father jumped in, right on cue. —She's my daughter, too! What, she doesn't look like me? What are you saying?

One woman agreed that I had my father's nose. Someone else retorted: That's not your daughter, she's too pretty.

—*Oh! Pa fè m sa!* my father declared in mock offense, playing to the crowd. —Don't accuse my wife of that!

My mother was filming a low-budget video to promote the innovations of the local stove-makers, and I followed from courtyard to courtyard to see the progress. My parents' proudest accomplishment was the
clay oven they'd engineered to rest on top of the combustion chamber,
creating a miniature bakery—a valuable side business in a village that
had relied for centuries on three-rock fires.

Remy, a local schoolteacher, had painted the silhouette of a bird in
flight on the side of his stove and had written in elegant script: *Ann bay
yo yon chans pou yo kabab viv.* Let's give the birds a chance to live.

Neighbors told stories of birds that they remembered:

—There was a bird that used to wake me up at four a.m. I always
knew what time it was by the sound of that bird. Now it is gone.

—We cut down the trees where they built their nests.

—The kids caught them all with their little traps; now you never
see them anymore.

My father insisted that the stoves were the key to reforestation,
the beginning of a possible environmental revolution in Ti Bwa. My
mother filmed footage of charming children singing in squeaky, high-
pitched voices a song about the Recho Ti Bwa—although she got
in trouble afterward because she didn't insist that one of the boys go
home and wash the dust off his face; his parents were mortified that he
had been shown to the world without the dignity of a clean-scrubbed
face.

Neighbors crowded around to watch the proceedings. Everyone
whom I hadn't already met asked my name and whether I was *Agwonòm*
Jon's daughter. When a little girl hollered: *Blan! Blan!* I knelt down and
introduced myself. —My name is not *blan,* my name is Apricot. These
are my mom and dad. Do we look alike? She grinned up at me.

On Sunday, I joined my parents for the local Baptist church service,
though I didn't last long. A woman in a starched white dress pointed to a
hand-painted Bible verse on the wall, Lamentations 3:26, and informed
the parents in a strident voice that God wanted *silence* in the church,
and if their children misbehaved, then they should beat them. I elbowed
my mother. She looked sheepish. Was it the fault of the missionaries, I

wondered, that churches were so often legalistic and conservative? Or was legalism a universal human impulse—a cheap bid for power? My father furrowed his eyebrows in disappointment when I slipped out of the pew before the sermon had even started, but my mother smiled and whispered: *Enjoy yourself.*

I grabbed a broom and dusted off a corner of the porch behind the room where we slept, slipped off my sandals, and bent forward in a sun salutation. Tinder-dry hills spread out red and brown against the sky, the bare courtyards edged by cactus. Within minutes, half a dozen girls had joined the yoga practice. We swept out our arms together in warrior pose, our wide-planted feet powdery with dust.

Just a few miles away as the crow flies, in another village nestled against a dry mountain, I had sat down under a *zanmann* tree a few days earlier with two of the founding members of an *òganizasyon peyizan,* a peasant cooperative, that had grown, over its twenty-five year existence, to 2,225 members.

—We wanted this to be a place where people would want to live, Ronick St. George explained. —We didn't want everyone with an education to leave.

Members paid small monthly dues and logged hours in the communal gardens, and the proceeds went to fund educational initiatives. Concerned by the high infant mortality rate in the area, a member of the cooperative had been sent to take a course on hygiene. Latrines, vaccinations for children, and attention to protein and diet had all been initiatives funded by the cooperative.

—We have no more children with *cheve wouj,* Célestin Léopold told me proudly. No more children whose red-tinged hair was a sign of protein-deficient *kwashiorkor.*

Occasionally over the years, the cooperative had partnered with NGOs to subsidize projects that otherwise would have proved unaffordable for the community, but even the long-term success of these projects was, arguably, due to the fact that the *òganizasyon peyizan* remained active long after the NGOs had moved on. Ninety-eight percent of the households in the village had recently agreed to pay two hundred gourdes each for buried cement cisterns attached to new tin roofs, allowing rainwater to be harvested and stored for later use; a German not-for-profit organization had covered the remaining cost of the water catchment systems.

—We wanted to make it so that the *peyizan* didn't feel that the people in the city could look down on them. We wanted to make it so people didn't want to live anywhere else, Ronick explained.

He and Célestin cited examples of children who had left the village for secondary school but had returned to share what they'd learned. And the organization was not religious, they insisted: Vodouisants, Baptists, Adventists, Catholics all worked together.

Zanmann leaves rustled overhead as we spoke, the hidden *too-whoo* of pigeons in its branches. Hand-cut boards leaned against a wall. Flies buzzed. A pig squealed in the underbrush, followed by the scolding timbre of a woman's voice. Painted across the doorway of a house, a hand-lettered Bible verse announced: *Tout est posible à celui qui croit.* All things are possible for those who believe.

The members of the cooperative did not assume that their work was finished; they wanted to see the road improved and to find a more reliable water source, and they hoped to convince people to plant more trees—when the last hurricane hit, entire gardens had washed away, scouring deep ravines into the sides of the mountain. They did not mention, however, a television for every home or a motorcycle for every family.

To a well-heeled philanthropist, the village might have appeared deceptively impoverished. Chickens scratched in the dirt, and I saw broken glass and a pair of underwear stuck in the crotch of a tree, and tattered plastic bags and candy wrappers in the dust. But when asked to gauge their success on a scale of one to ten, Célestin Léopold smiled and said that he would give it a seven. I thought of Bessel van der Kolk, the Dutch psychiatrist who has explained that trauma is compounded when people are prevented from being agents in their own recovery.

The *òganizasyon peyizan* had not escaped the attention of potential donors. A Mercy Corps officer was quick to point out to me that a dime invested in a community that was self-organized was equal to a dollar spent in less organized communities: less corruption, less likelihood of failure.

—We don't want to be the cane that supports a sick body. That's not functional. But if people are already walking on their own and they get to a ravine, we help to build a bridge so that they can get across.

It sounded so persuasive, and yet while I was there, the NGO, under pressure from a million-dollar donor, decided that it did not have time to schedule yet another preliminary meeting to discuss the terms of the work agreement with the elected leaders of the peasant cooperative— some of whom lived so far up the mountains that it required a full day's walk to reach the meeting place.

Impatient with the slow pace of negotiations, the NGO had issued an ultimatum: either accept the terms or lose the project. The leaders of the cooperative had walked out in protest.

It remained to be seen whether the *òganizasyon peyizan* would be able to withstand the NGO's rushed timeline and maintain their autonomy. I hoped they could pull it off, but I left with a sinking feeling in my gut. Communities perceived as being in need of outside assistance can quickly become pawns in the hands of would-be altruists. How much have we already destroyed in our earnest desire to help?

A tattered poster in faded blue calligraphy was pasted to a door in the village—*L'Eternel est Grand*: God Is Great—beneath which had been scrawled: *Don't steak your Nose in my buissness.*

Piti pa Piti, Zwazo fè Nich

Camp Coq, 2012

Even in the age of cell phones, the coverage was spotty and my father seemed reluctant to set up a visit ahead of time, so, as usual, we showed up at Zo's house unannounced. My mother wanted to get video footage of Zo's gardens to show the farmers back in Ti Bwa, but my father felt trapped by long-range plans; he preferred to wait and see how things developed.

We knocked at the open doorway and called out: *Onè*. We could hear a mortar and pestle being set down in the kitchen. As soon as Madame Zo saw my mother, the two gray-haired women laughed and reached for each other's hands. Madame Zo leaned in close to kiss us on each cheek. She smelled of pepper and cinnamon.

Zo could not come to meet us, she apologized, because he had been having heart trouble, but she led us down the long hallway to his room, the doorways billowing with lace curtains. He was curled up under a thin sheet in the dark, his body cramped with illness. His voice was weak, but he lifted up his head and smiled as we entered.

—*Frè* Zo. My brother, my father greeted him, his voice suddenly constricted.

—Oh! *Frè* Jon!

My father held out his hand, and Zo grasped it. He propped his head on his elbow so that he could receive his visitors with more dignity, but my father said: Please, you can put your head down. *Ou mèt kouche, monchè.*

After we left Haiti in 1991, Zo had harvested and sold truckloads of grasses and hundreds of pounds of seeds to soil conservation projects across the country. A son and daughter who had emigrated sent funds to build their parents an elegant concrete-block house. Even with the unfinished second story and the latrine in the yard, it bore little resemblance to the humble mud-and-wattle house where Zo had hosted our going-away party. By working-class standards, he had become a wealthy man.

—I came to find the house of Zo, and instead, I find a hotel, my father teased.

—That's a compliment. Zo grinned. —*Ou fè m viv.* You give me life.

—It is God who gives us life, my father countered, but Zo's extravagant compliments seemed to be his own private joke.

Zo leaned his head back against his pillow. —God needs me to plant trees, he said. —After that I can die. They're like children to me. It is because of trees that I am here: *avèk bwa m viv.*

—I know that about you. My father laughed gruffly. They call you Bwa Zo, did you know that? The tree man.

—I planted many, many trees, Zo murmured with a tired smile. —Cocoa, grapefruit, avocado.

—And pineapple? my father asked.

—I have lots, Zo assured him.

Zo smiled again, a wide exhausted grin. —I'm glad to see you, he told my father. I've been wanting to see you.

They exchanged news of old friends. Edner, the *agwonòm* whose salary had been paid with blueberry u-pick money from Oregon, had lost his oldest son in the earthquake, and his wife had folded in on herself with grief. The two men shared a long moment of silence. But their voices grew strong again when they talked about trees.

—When you see the ravines, you will enter into my dream, Zo promised. He'd planted trees even on rented land, and had built stone terraces to catch the soil that washed down from the mountains. He had paid the masons out of his own pocket.

My father shook his head, worried that the trees on the rented land would be cut down by the landowners after the lease expired, as had been the case with four hundred full-grown cinnamon trees later harvested for charcoal.

—It's not so important to me who owns the land, Zo explained. It needed to be reforested. Now I can go and walk under the trees where the birds sing. It's like paradise for me. Now I don't fear the rain.

When we left Zo's house, promising to return the next day to visit his gardens, my father, out of his friend's hearing, expressed exasperation at Zo's strategy. —It's not repeatable, my father complained.

Although they shared a similar vision, my father worried that Zo was too generous, too foolhardy. What he hadn't told Zo was that, behind his back, people sometimes called him a *moun fou*. I pointed out that Zo's grandiose gesture felt extraordinary in an economy where the margins were so thin. The only people with the luxury to think about an entire ecosystem were NGOs and missionaries—who, historically at least, had done such a consistent job of bungling the effort that little evidence could be found now of their labor. Zo's vision was more stubborn and all the more astonishing because he had invested so much of his own profit to create it.

Still irritated, my father pointed out that Zo once sold a piece of land to pay off his sister's debt, and the man who bought the land had cut down the trees for a profit equal to what he'd paid for the land itself. —At least, my father muttered, the trees had been a species that coppiced readily.

—So, Zo's efforts were not completely in vain, I pointed out. Even if the trees had been cut down, the roots would push up new growth that could be harvested again and again. —So who can say who wins in the long run? I argued. —The trees, maybe. The man who stuffed his pockets with profit. Maybe Zo.

My father scowled, unconvinced. —But Zo can't do it all himself. If he doesn't take the time to persuade younger farmers to follow his example, then all of this work will just disappear when he dies.

I thought of Ken Heneise's observation, following the collapse of the Ag Center—that what we create rarely outlives us. I thought of Joanna's devotion to the hospital. The trees that my father had guarded so carefully on Morne Bois Pin had all been cut down, and the springs that had bubbled up on the peninsula were now dry. But the hidden aquifers remained, waiting beneath the surface for a time when they might be refilled with rainwater trickling down through new branches. Restoring the earth was not the work of one lifetime.

T. S. Eliot's lines from *The Four Quartets* came to mind: *There is only the fight to recover what has been lost / And found and lost again and again.*

What did any of our lives amount to in the end? A tangled melody. A broken song.

The next morning, at Zo's insistence, we met his son, Franz, for the promised tour, so my father could see what had been accomplished since his last visit. We found a place to park by the edge of the Limbé River just as it started to rain. My father predicted that the storm would blow over in a few minutes, so we waited in the car until it passed.

Franz had worked in the past as a mechanic and a driver and he asked hopefully if my father knew of any NGOs or missionaries who were hiring. My father did not. He did, however, use the opportunity provided by the rainstorm to lecture Franz about continuing his father's work. It appeared irrelevant that vehicles, not trees, were Franz's passion. My father insisted that if no one took care of the trees that Zo had planted, then it would be like the Haitian proverb: *Sa a se yon travi ki lavi men, siye a tè.* It's like washing your hands and then drying them in the dirt.

Franz smiled awkwardly. —Shall we get out of the car? he suggested. —The rain has stopped.

Poor Franz. It was no small task to bear the brunt of my father's disappointment.

We slipped off our shoes to wade across the Limbé River to Zo's gardens and climbed out under a canopy of mahogany trees. A crooked path wound through orchards of avocado and *sitron* and thick plantations of *banann*. High above the valley floor, on land so steep that my mother and I had to hold hands to clamber over the ridged mounds of manioc and yams, we found wild, untrimmed hedges of Leucaena that my father had helped plant. The *ramp vivan* towered over terraces of vetivè and elephant grass.

From the ridge, the deep bowl of the valley was edged with green. Everywhere we looked, we could see isolated swaths of forest. A hawk wheeled overhead.

—Who replanted those hillsides? I asked, pointing to other mountains thick with trees.

It was the same answer each time: Zo.

As we hiked down, my father pointed out, pleased, that the *bwa blan* trees were everywhere now; the birds must have been planting the seeds.

The rich smell of cedar drifted over the path as we approached the river, and my father veered us off course to see if a tree that he remembered Zo planting twenty years earlier was still alive. And there it was, so wide that neither Mom nor I could reach around it, and we had to link arms, staring up into the leafy branches. Our hands smelled sweet when we uncircled them.

When we reached the ravines, the terraces were everything that Zo had promised and more. Falling water burbled over stacked stones. Thickets of green dazzled with wildflowers. Behind the carefully built rock ledges, low depressions had been engineered to catch what washed down from neighboring gardens—trapped topsoil that had been prevented from draining into the rivers and burying the coral reefs offshore. Birds warbled overhead.

In wealthier nations, where landowners and wilderness clubs could afford the luxury of benevolence, such measures might be considered less extraordinary, but in Haiti, for one man to rent tracts of deforested land and rebuild them into wildlife habitat was a defiant act of beauty, an investment in a future he might not live to see. Zo had signed his name in green.

In My End Is My Beginning

Ayiti, 2016

M Y SONS WERE eight and ten when David and I took them to Haiti for the first time. —I didn't know it would be so beautiful! they exclaimed as the plane made its descent into Cap-Haïtien.

Their voices sounded almost too eager, as if anticipating what I'd hoped they would say.

They were dismayed, however, by the piles of discarded plastic bottles that lined the harbor (an environmental crisis accelerated by the cholera epidemic—yet another unanticipated legacy of those who thought they had come to help; in this case, UN peacekeepers). Immediately, both boys wanted to get to work inventing a solar-powered trash-collection vehicle. The missionary impulse, already at play.

It was hot and muggy when we waded across the Limbé River to visit Zo, now fully recovered and back to work in his gardens. The boys could follow very little of the long conversation in Kreyòl about trees, but they tried to nod politely and express the requisite admiration for each new species that Zo pointed out. Still, I confessed to Zo's son, Franz—out of Zo's hearing—that I remembered how hard I had found it as a kid to listen to my father talk on and on about trees.

—You and your father have changed places, Franz said with a wry smile. I laughed. It was too obvious.

Zo was gracious, as always, with our unplanned interruption to his work. When we found him, he had a brace of sugarcane stalks over one shoulder and he paused and broke open the soil with his machete to kneel and cover the roots before leading us through his riverfront garden—land that had been so badly eroded by storms when he purchased it that it was considered unfit to grow food. He'd planted water-loving trees to stabilize the bank, then filled in the soil with twenty different species of vegetables, vines, and tubers; each reliant on the other to flourish.

But he wanted most to show me the red coconut palms, descended from ones that my father had given to him at our going-away party twenty-five years earlier.

It was a story that my father had cited for years as a failure: the virus-resistant, imported palm trees had ended up with torn roots and leaves during the disorganized giveaway. And yet, I realized, Zo had planted and replanted the descendants of those same red coconuts all over Camp Coq. They were still bearing fruit decades later.

It isn't always ours to know what impact we will have. What good—or what harm—we leave in our wake isn't always immediately apparent.

I'd wanted the boys to see the places and people I remembered from childhood, and was relieved when Mueller Jean-Jacques graciously agreed to drive us around the north of Haiti in Steve and Nancy's borrowed pickup. As a six-year-old at the Ag Center, I had always been delighted when I ran into Mueller, then a skinny twenty-year-old mechanic with a big grin. He was just as teasing and welcoming with my boys as he had been with me. My eight-year-old, loving the attention, leaned his arms across the front seat to practice a few words in this new language.

Mueller was patient with our fumbling Kreyòl, and with the endless potholes, stopping to wave market women safely across the highway, and offering rides to strangers.

He took us to see what was left of the Ag Center, and to the compound in Limbé. The sidewalk in front of Jericho School was even more cracked than in years past. The boys were impressed by how high the roof of the school was. I was amazed that so small a scrap of beauty—a few tree trunks, a patch of sky—could have given me so much room to breathe.

The Guahaba Museum, across the highway, had received several thousand visitors over the previous year, although it was painful to see the Doctor's carefully lettered signs pocked with termite holes. The boys were proud to sign their names in the guest book and had no hesitation whatsoever when it came to writing where they were from: Oregon. (Even though one of them had been born in London.) I envied their confidence.

My sons' favorite memories from their week in Haiti are the same ones that I would have picked at eight and ten: doing flips into the Mont Joli pool; their first taste of Coca-Cola; the bright red ixora flowers, which they strung into necklaces and fed to Nancy James's Hispaniolan parakeets; playing soccer with a new friend, no common language required. We hiked to the Citadel, where they perched astride cannons and pretended to take out the French army, and we spent one glorious day at the beach. They had never imagined that water could be so warm.

A Haitian university student named Elio Dortilus, just back from a scholarship semester abroad in the U.S., led us to the top of a mountain that overlooked the Limbé Valley where kids flew kites at dusk. Elio held a coin up to his eye, blocking the view, to show us how if we focus only on the problems in front of us, we lose our perspective.

—There is so much more to Haiti than problems, he told the boys. They didn't need convincing.

Laurie and Casso were a month away from retirement when we had dinner with them around the old dining room table. It had been almost seventy years since Ivah and Harold had moved to Haut-Limbé to start the seminary; the years of the missionaries were ending. The incoming president of the Baptist university was a Haitian man who had studied in Belgium and would be bringing his family with him from New Jersey. He told us that his twelve-year-old son was reluctant about the move, even though he spoke Kreyòl fluently. But they were doing God's work, he assured us; his son would adjust.

Crowded around the small television in Laurie and Casso's living room, we cheered on the America's Cup soccer tournament with a dozen university students and professors (the U.S. lost badly) and made it back to our cottage during a break in the rain. The lightning was spectacular through the trees.

—I think that's more lightning than I've seen in my entire life! my eight-year-old told me, amazed, as David and I tucked him under the mosquito netting.

—No more talking, I reminded him as he rolled over and threw his arm around his brother.

—I was just telling him that he was the best brother I could have, he confided sleepily.

Rain pounded on the tin roof, and lightning flashed through the screens. Thunder boomed overhead. The storm was as powerful and exhilarating as the ones I remembered from my own childhood.

—I'm so HAPPY, I said to David, laughing, as I leaned back on my heels to listen. My sweaty, exhausted husband smiled. This beloved place that at times had been so hard to love and yet still, after all these years, felt like coming home.

Joanna's final trip to Haiti, although no one realized it at the time, was in the spring of 2015. Representatives from the town of Limbé had wished to honor her husband's legacy by renaming the street that ran in front of the hospital as Route Dr. William Hodges. She was ninety-two years old. By the following summer, her cancer had returned. She spent her final days at a hospice center in Florida. Even after she could no longer remember the names of her children and grandchildren when they came to see her, she still, in her best moments, could speak a little Kreyòl with the Haitian staff. Olynda gently massaged her mother's shoulders and fed her tiny bites of brownie and sips of coffee when the nurses weren't looking. Told that her face still looked as young and smooth as a *demwazèl*'s, Joanna replied: *Oh se vre?* Do you think it's true?

She asked to be cremated so that her ashes could be placed next to her husband in Haiti.

In the beginning, Hôpital le Bon Samaritain, like the *zanmann* tree that Joanna planted from seed and fought to protect, was thin and spindly, tossed by rainstorms, threatened by goats. But as the tree put down roots and reached for the sunlight, it towered above the Limbé River.

The branches spread a canopy over the dusty courtyard, important with visiting surgical teams and medical students from Europe and North America; Haitian nurses bustled through the corridors to set bones and IVs; technicians bent over slides in the lab.

The tree provided shelter—children were born in its shade, orphans were settled into new homes, lives were saved—but over the years, vines twisted up its broad trunk. Pharmaceuticals, pilfered from the missionary hospital, provided the seed money for newer, smaller pharmacies that sprang up along the town's crowded streets. Nurses and lab technicians, trained at the hospital, took their skills to scrappy upstart clinics that competed for clientele. The tree, some said, had contracted a virus.

Eventually, as all living things must, it would collapse and decompose. Branches would fall and be carried to other projects.

This was, in a sense, a fulfillment of the missionary vision: *Unless a kernel of wheat falls to the ground and dies, it remains alone; but if it dies, it bears much fruit.*

The tangle of latticework vines would hold the shape of that loss for a time. The outline of the tree, as if in photographic negative, would be visible against the sky; but as the nutrients seeped back into the earth, its final purpose would be revealed: to nourish the life of significant soil.

A Note to Readers

AMONG THE INNUMERABLE books and documents to which I owe thanks are: *The Travels of Marco Polo*; *The Taínos: Rise and Decline of the People Who Greeted Columbus* by Irving Rouse; Robert Fuson's translation of *The Log of Christopher Columbus*, which includes a generous nod to the archeological research of Dr. Hodges in Appendix E; *A Short Account of the Destruction of the Indies* by Bartolomé de las Casas; Maya Deren's seminal work on Vodou, *Divine Horsemen: The Living Gods of Haiti*; Jean-Bertrand Aristide's *In the Parish of the Poor: Writings from Haiti*; *The Magic Orange Tree*, a collection of Haitian folk tales transcribed by Diane Wolkstein; *West Indian Folk-tales* retold by Philip Sherlock, which includes a version of the Carib origin myth that ends with the planting of trees; *A Child's Christmas in Wales* by Dylan Thomas, to whom I owe a debt of gratitude for the line "I said some words to the close and holy darkness, and then I slept."

It is worth noting that when my family moved to Haiti, in 1982, Kreyòl Ayisyen (Haitian Creole) was not yet recognized as an official language, although it is a language of resistance that predates the Haitian Revolution. Predominantly French in vocabulary but African in syntax, Kreyòl was created when slave owners forbade their captives from speaking in their mother tongues. Yet even after Haiti won its freedom in 1804, French remained the language of power; as of 2017, most maps retain colonial-era French place names, illustrating the irreducible complexity of Haiti's history. It was not until 1991, the year my family left Haiti, that Kreyòl was finally recognized as one of Haiti's two official languages by President Jean-Bertrand Aristide in an attempt to level the playing field between those who had traditionally held power and those who struggled to make their voices heard. The Akademi Kreyòl

Ayisyen was founded in 2014 to promote the language as an integral part of Haiti's culture, in recognition of Kreyòl's inherent power, music, and subtlety, and to standardize the grammar and spelling. For clarity, I have corrected quotations from missionary journals, letters, and newsletters to reflect these standards. In every other respect, however, I have endeavored to remain faithful to my original sources.

I am deeply grateful to the newsletters of Dr. Bill and Joanna Hodges, Steve and Nancy James, Alta Hodges, Dorothy Lincoln, Milos and Christa Dolesji, Sue Mionske Tyrrel, Cornelia Scheulke, Suzette Goss Geffrard, Laurel and Jules Casséus, Ivah and Harold Heneise, Ron and Susan Smith, Maralu Whitt, Jeremy Bagge, Logan Cook, Mark and Sandy Jo Thompson, Wayne and Katherine Niles, and my parents. *By the Light of my Kerosene Lamp* and *Pioneers of Light* by Ivah Heneise provided invaluable insights into the early years of the American Baptists in the Limbé Valley. It should be noted, however, that the cassette tapes, letters, newsletters, and journals quoted throughout this memoir reflect the observations—and, at times, misperceptions—of missionary expatriates trying to make sense of an adopted country; books by Haitian authors tell a very different story.

I cannot recommend highly enough the work of Edwidge Danticat (*Brother, I'm Dying* is particularly beautiful); *Masters of the Dew* by Jacques Roumain; *Love, Anger, Madness: A Haitian Trilogy* by Marie Vieux-Chauvet; *Ayiti* by Roxane Gay; and in response to the 2010 earthquake: *The World Is Moving Around Me* by Dany Laferrière and *God Loves Haiti* by Dimitry Elias Léger. Laurent Dubois offers an excellent introduction in *Haiti: The Aftershocks of History*.

Acknowledgments

I HEREBY RAISE my glass:

To the generous, extravagant spirit of Rona Jaffe and to Beth Mc-Cabe for the implausible gift of time and space to do nothing but write.

To Oregon Literary Arts, for your energetic support of an entire community of writers: conversations around the long table; Writers in the Schools; Oregon Book Awards; a literary fellowship. Thank you.

To my agent, Jin Auh, fiercely insightful and generous of spirit, for trusting my curiosity.

To Kate Johnson, kindred spirit and kindest of advocates. Thank you for missing your train stop.

To my editors and the extraordinary team at Simon & Schuster. To Leah Miller, who believed in this book even before it was finished. To Millicent Bennett for nudging me gently toward the slow, painful art of self-compassion. To Emily Graff, for incisive critiques and for pushing this final draft toward excellence. To the expertise of Elisa Rivlin, Emily Beth Thomas, Sam O'Hara, and Jackie Seow, to Carly Loman for the beautiful interior book design, Thomas Colligan for gorgeous cover art, and Sarah Wright for her impressive patience and careful eye.

To Ira Glass, Julie Snyder, and Sarah Koenig at *This American Life* for loaning me a microphone and for your masterful storytelling.

To Cécile Accilien, to whom I will never be able to adequately express my thanks for fifteen years of inexhaustible encouragement, for questions that invite nuance and complexity, for patience with my naive assumptions and misspelled Kreyòl. *Mèsi anpil, zanmi mwen.*

To mentors who sharpened my thinking and coaxed me into believing in myself: Alice Ann Eberman, Dr. Steve Cook, Bart Tarman, Dave Tomlinson, Michael McGregor, Debra Gwartney. Thank you.

To students whom I will never forget in Tennessee, Ireland and London, Bandung, Portland, and Gresham: I carry with me always your courage.

To patient readers who have given invaluable feedback on the many, many drafts of this manuscript: my family (particularly my father, who gave me copious notes on each draft), Kathleen Holt, Dan Deweese, Mary Rechner, Jamie Passaro, Kristin Kaye, Maude Hines, Heather Morton, Tyler Merkel, Kate McCullum Hall, Jacqueline Alnes, Marilyn Nichols, Kathy Cafazzo, Abigail Chipley, Laura Gibson, Steph Gehring, and Tom George (to whom I owe particular thanks for his insightful analysis of a fifteen-year-old narrator).

To friends who have shared kitchen tables and given me quiet spaces to disappear and write: Tristan Robinson and Mari McBurney, cosponsors of the Tanglewood writing retreat; Jennifer Creswell and Ian Doescher; Linda and Doug Sugano; Dina and Jason Guppy; and Heather Thomas, whose roots go deep. Thanks especially to Sister Marcia and the nuns at Bridal Veil for sharing your waterfall.

To grandparents, honorary grandparents, great grandparents, sisters, aunts, uncles, cousins, and great aunts (Myrna!) who cheered from the sidelines, shared stories, and distracted small boys. And to Grandma Lois, who saved a lifetime's worth of family letters in Roman Meal bread bags. Without you this project would have been immeasurably more difficult.

To friends too numerous to count for your laughter, insights, and encouragement: long may you live. Here's to lifting a glass in person next time we're together. To the beloved community of St. Luke's West Holloway; to Emily Cafazzo, Ryan Domingo, and Larch Provisions for transcendent meals; Hilarie Lesveaux, Liesel Swanson, Mallory Spanjer, and Kendal Hocking for transcription help and for giving my children wondrous summers while I holed up in the studio to write; Elise Astleford, *anam cara,* and Joe, for baking cookies; Evonne Tang, curator of stillness, for your kind welcome (always) and endless cups of tea.

To writers whose exquisite sentences made it seem worth the agony: Annie Dillard, Brian Doyle, Nikky Finney, Ben Fountain, Alexandra Fuller, Nadine Gordimer, Mary Karr, Maxine Hong Kingston, Colum

McCann, Michael Ondaatje, Zadie Smith. And to the music that carried me: Neko Case, Laura Gibson, Isan, Lhasa, Leyla McCalla, Emeline Michel, Ozomatli, Thao.

To Ayiti Cheri: *Fòk mwen te manke w pou mwen te kapab apresye w.*

To friends from Haiti and beyond who shared stories. I only wish that I could have included them all. Your trust is a tremendous gift, and if I have portrayed a scene differently from how you remember it, I ask your forbearance. I have spent long years trying to tell one story in many voices, but my voice is the filter through which all other perspectives are revealed, so I alone can claim responsibility for whatever flaws you may find. My goal was empathy, and if I have fallen short in this, I ask your forgiveness. Thank you for trusting me with your stories.

To all who shared food and lodging on research trips over the years: Olynda Durinvil Hodges-McLymont, Joanna Hodges, HBS, Clark and Pat Moore, Steve and Nancy James, Laurie and Jules Casséus, UNCH, David and Emily Hodges, John and Susan Vendeland, Suzette and Willys Geffrard, Drew Kutschenreuter, Jennifer McCormack, the Mercy Corps office in Saint-Marc, Zo Alexandre, Mesha Williams, Ken and Debbie Heneise, Reuben Smith, Lorraine Taggart.

To Tamara and Tony: We will always remember you.

To the inimitable Suzette, guardian of my first published work, sold for twenty-five cents to my favorite teacher. Your magic words have kept me humming since I was seven years old.

To my father and mother, without whose breathtaking courage and vulnerability this book would not have been possible. Thank you for your blessing. And to my sisters: I will be forever grateful that no matter where we touched down, we always had each other, and that the hard memories are interspersed with so much good.

To my two boys, who make me laugh (often), who ask delightful questions and remind me to stop and play. Thank you for your splendid creativity and for trying to convince me that you love me more than I love you (not that it's actually possible).

And to David. Beloved adversary, companion in this life, most loyal of friends. Thank you for holding on to me.

About the Author

© TYLER MERKEL

Apricot Irving is currently based in Oregon, but has lived in Haiti, Indonesia, and the United Kingdom. Her missionary parents moved to Haiti when she was six years old; she left at the age of fifteen. She returned to Haiti in the spring of 2010 to cover the earthquake for the radio program *This American Life*. She is the recipient of a Rona Jaffe Foundation Writers' Award and an Oregon Literary Fellowship. Her renowned oral history project, BoiseVoices.com, is a collaboration between youth and elders to record the stories of a neighborhood in the midst of gentrification. *The Gospel of Trees* is her first book.

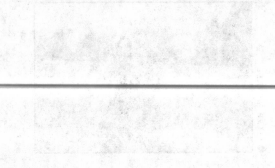